# START & RUN A COFFEE BAR

Tom Matzen
Marybeth Harrison

**Self-Counsel Press**
*(a division of)*
International Self-Counsel Press Ltd.
USA     Canada

*Self-Counsel Press acknowledges the financial support of the Government of Canada through the Book Publishing Industry Development Program (BPIDP) for our publishing activities.*

*Printed in Canada*

*First edition: 1997; Reprinted: 1998; 1999*

*Second edition: 2001; Reprinted: 2002; 2003; 2004; 2006*

*Third edition: 2007*

**Library and Archives Canada Cataloguing in Publication**

Matzen, Thomas, 1963–
    Start & run a coffee bar / Thomas Matzen, Marybeth Harrison. — 3rd ed.

(Self-counsel business series)
Accompanied by CD-ROM.
ISBN 978-1-55180-771-3

    1. Coffeehouses—Management.  2. New business enterprises—Management.
I. Harrison, Marybeth, 1965–  II. Title.  III. Series.

TX911.3.M27M37 2007          647.95          C2007-902926-4

 **ANCIENT FOREST FRIENDLY**  Self-Counsel Press is committed to protecting the environment and to the responsible use of natural resources. We are acting on this commitment by working with suppliers and printers to phase out our use of paper produced from ancient forests. This book is one step toward that goal. It is printed on 100 percent ancient-forest-free paper (100 percent post-consumer recycled), processed chlorine- and acid-free.

**Self-Counsel Press**
*(a division of)*
International Self-Counsel Press Ltd.

| 1704 North State Street | 1481 Charlotte Road |
|---|---|
| Bellingham, WA 98225 | North Vancouver, BC V7J 1H1 |
| USA | Canada |

This book is dedicated to the hardworking men, women, and children who harvest coffee by hand, bean by bean, so that we may enjoy this tasteful brew.

MUCHAS GRACIAS, AMIGOS.

# CONTENTS

# CHECKLISTS

# SAMPLES

# TABLES

# PREFACE

It's a funny thing about life; if you refuse to accept
anything but the best, you very often get it.

— SOMERSET MAUGHAM

Hello, fellow coffee lover. Congratulations on taking a major step toward success in the coffee industry!

This book will give you a comprehensive overview of what you can expect in owning and operating your own coffee business. If you are already in the industry, this book will help you build your existing sales and increase your profit.

The secrets revealed to you in this book are based on our many years of coffee bar ownership and consulting. We personally have opened some 47 coffee bars, more than half of them roaster/retailers. We are honored that our book is the best-selling coffee bar start-up guide on the planet, with more than fifty thousand copies sold.

We especially love the feedback we receive on all the hands-on techniques we provide in this book. They have been tested and proven to produce real-world results (if applied within our guidelines, of course). You will have the opportunity to commit on paper to using the techniques we describe: at the end of every chapter you will find a "commitment box" for you to sign to hold yourself accountable for a great performance level.

**Note:** Prices, commissions, fees, and other costs mentioned in the text or shown in samples in this book probably do not reflect real costs where you live. Inflation and other factors, including geography, can cause the costs you might encounter to be much higher or even much lower than those we show. The dollar amounts shown are simply intended as representative examples.

# INTRODUCTION

# THE COFFEE BAR BUSINESS — WHAT'S IN IT FOR YOU

Coffee is the world's most popular beverage with only water being consumed in larger quantities!

— McCOY AND WALKER

The coffee business is an exciting industry, far-reaching in its economic impact and rich in history.

Coffee is indigenous to Ethiopia and was most likely discovered as a food before it became a drink. The most popular legend of how coffee was discovered involves an Abyssinian goat herder named Kaldi. Kaldi awoke one night to find his goats dancing around a tree speckled with red cherries. When he tasted one of the cherries, he too started dancing with his goats.

As interesting as this story may be, it is more likely that coffee was used as a food supplement by wandering Ethiopian tribesmen. The tribesmen are said to have squashed the coffee cherries and carried them on long journeys, eating them for nourishment as needed.

Later, the coffee cherries were soaked in water, possibly to make wine, but some historians say it was not until AD 1000, when the Arabs discovered how to boil water, that coffee was served hot.

Coffee was also believed to have medicinal properties. Avicenna, an Islamic physician and philosopher of the 11th century, said of coffee: "It fortifies the members, it cleans the skin and dries up the humidities that are under it, and gives an excellent smell to all the body."

## 1. MARKET SIZE

Coffee has a projected annual sales volume of over $55 billion in 2006, according to the National Coffee Association (NCA), making it the second largest commodity in the world next to oil. And according to the

International Coffee Organization (ICO), 400 billion cups of coffee are consumed each year.

Coffee is grown in over 60 countries around the world and is the principal commercial crop of over a dozen countries, half of which earn 25 percent to 50 percent of their foreign exchange revenues from coffee exports. More than 14 billion pounds of coffee beans are grown per year, providing more than 20 million jobs to coffee growers alone.

Overall coffee sales in North America are expected to grow modestly (approximately 3 percent annually) over the next several years. Coffee sales in the US in 2005 were estimated to be approximately 11 billion dollars in the retail sector, according to Specialty Coffee Association of America (SCAA) data. Consumption figures for Americans have 54 percent of the population drinking coffee daily, and some 18 percent of Americans drinking *gourmet* coffee beverages daily (NCA).

Canadians drink over 14 billion cups of coffee a year, making it Canada's favorite hot beverage. And it's not just in North America — many countries around the world love their coffee. Scandinavians, Germans, and the Japanese join Canadians and Americans as the most crazed in terms of consumption per capita. And recent trends show many South and Central American citizens consuming more and more. For example, Brazil went from 8 million bags of coffee consumption to 14 million in the last several years alone. (One "bag" refers to an equivalent of 60 kg of coffee.)

The US handles about a quarter of global coffee imports (2.45 billion pounds). Canada imports nearly 400 million pounds.

The US specialty coffee industry is responsible for only approximately 17 percent of the total US green coffee imports mentioned above but its sales represent approximately 40 percent of the $17.9 billion US coffee market.

"Specialty coffee" includes all espresso-based beverages, such as cappuccinos, lattes, and mochas. The United States contains the largest specialty coffee market in the world, and in this market, specialty coffee is the only segment of the coffee industry that has shown consistent and notable growth. According to the ICO, most potential specialty coffee markets are far from saturated. Specialty coffee sales continue to expand by 5 percent to 10 percent per year according to most estimates.

## 2. THE COFFEE BAR MARKET

### 2.1 Why all the interest in cappuccino bars?

Specialty coffee houses have low start-up barriers and high margins. In addition, space requirements are low and the business is not excessively labor intensive. Finally, expertise levels are not as high as those required for other businesses such as restaurants.

In terms of profitability, a cup of coffee that retails for $1.45 costs about nine cents — a food cost of less than ten percent. This is a very favorable statistic especially when compared to the food cost of a food establishment franchise. For example, McDonald's runs a typical food cost of 30 to 35 percent.

While these are the types of figures that appeal to potential coffee bar owners, it should also be noted that there are costs in addition to just the coffee itself. There is the cost of cream, milk, and sugar, and if the coffee is takeout, there are the additional costs of cup, lid, and stir sticks, and perhaps cream and sugar packets. In the end, however, the profit margins are still very favorable. For example, 65 shots of espresso can be extracted from one pound of coffee. For a cappuccino that retails for $2.00, this results in a $1.60 profit margin (with a total cost of 40 cents per cup, which takes into account the milk, etc.).

## 2.2 The future

If we look to coffee-crazed Europe — in places like Italy — and also consider the success of Starbucks in North America, the growth potential for the coffee industry here appears to be tremendous.

# 3. MARKET TRENDS

Coffee consumption in the United States is steady or growing slowly in most markets. In Canada it is growing by $2.5 million a year and is expected to continue to increase in the long term. Part of the reason for the increase is the trend away from alcohol and toward perceived healthier choices. Cappuccino bars also offer a social alternative to the often loud, dimly lit, smoky atmosphere of a nightclub.

Worldwide, coffee consumption is actually declining slightly. However, areas within the industry such as the market for gourmet coffees continue to rise.

## 3.1 The gourmet coffee trend

In the late 1970s, for example, only 10 percent of coffee on the North American market was "gourmet" (i.e., arabica coffees) while 90 percent was made up of the inferior quality robusta coffees. By the end of the 1980s, however, this number had shifted to 20 percent arabica and 80 percent robusta, and some results such as those of research firm FIND/SVP have indicated that the market has shifted again by as much as an additional 20 percent for the arabicas. This translates into a total market volume of more than seven billion dollars per year in North America for gourmet coffee alone!

The trend toward quality is also noted by the famous futurist Faith Popcorn who indicates that consumers are becoming increasingly demanding of higher quality products.

Coffee bars are also consistent with a number of other trends she discusses in her best-selling book *The Popcorn Report*:

(a) **Cocooning.** People are spending more time entertaining at home and serving gourmet coffees.

(b) **Small indulgences.** This trend describes the movement away from spending large sums of money on expensive new cars and toward spending on smaller quality items such as gourmet coffees.

(c) **Fantasy adventure.** People are looking for a fantasy adventure in their lives; gourmet coffee tastes from around the world help provide the coffee drinker with a sense of the exotic.

(d) **Egonomics.** People want unique items. Custom roasting coffee allows for just that.

(e) **The vigilante consumer.** People are becoming aware of socially and environmentally responsible practices including organic coffees. One needs only look at the success of the

Body Shop, with 1,400 locations worldwide, to see how profitable these socially conscious practices can be.

## 3.2 The roaster/retailer trend

Roaster/retailers are the wave of the future. They typically combine a cappuccino bar with an in-store coffee roasting operation. It is our belief that coffee bars without in-store roasting will fall prey to those that do, because customers will continue to demand better and fresher quality coffee that only a roaster/retailer can provide. Being able to significantly capture the wholesale market and to produce freshly roasted coffee on demand make on-site roasting a must.

According to the SCAA, the most fundamental change in the coffee industry will be the continued increase of these "micro-roasters." In 1969, there were approximately 20 micro-roasters in the US. By 1979 the number had doubled, and in 1989 there were 385 micro-roasters in operation. Since 1990, the number of micro-roasters opening annually has increased by increments of 100. This growth rate is projected to continue.

The SCAA believes that retail roasters will have a major influence on shaping consumer opinion. Because of their daily face-to-face encounters with the consumer, retail roasters will be the first to discover which products will create the greatest demand. These roasters will be able to adjust their product lines rapidly to meet changing consumer desires. Because the retail roaster will need to differentiate their products from those in the supermarkets (including competitors within the specialty coffee industry), they will need to achieve higher levels of quality and innovation, offer distinctive "estate"

coffees, and raise the standards of freshness through better handling and packaging. The success of the micro-roaster will reverse a 50-year trend of consolidation in the coffee roasting industry. Smaller roasting firms will take advantage of the expanding niche markets.

## 3.3 International flavors

Over the past few years, coffees and teas that originated in Asian countries have become very popular. For example, bubble tea originated in Taiwan in the 1980s and has quickly spread around the world. Bubble tea shops are numerous in areas with a large population of Asian residents, and bubble tea is starting to appear on the menus of some traditional coffee shops as well.

Flavors of traditional Asian teas have also been adapted to mimic coffee drinks. India's chai tea, a blend of black tea, spices such as cinnamon and star anise, and milk, and matcha, the green tea traditionally served in Japan's elaborate tea ceremony, are the latest flavor trends. It is no longer unusual to be able to order "chai lattes" and "matcha frappuccinos."

Read food and travel media to find out new trends in coffee and tea, and profile your customers to predict if they will demand the latest beverages and flavors.

## 3.4 The organic coffee trend

Another area of the coffee industry that is growing is the market for organic and sustainably farmed coffees.

Coffee is the most chemically treated food crop in the world and the third most heavily sprayed agricultural crop next to cotton and tobacco. While to date there is little evidence that the harmful substances actually end up in our cup, there are other factors to consider.

The first factor is the environmental effect in the area that the coffee is grown. For example, artificial fertilizers and chemical pesticides that are used end up in the soil systems and waterways of the areas the coffee is grown. This in turn affects the food chain and biodiversity. The second factor is the dramatic effect on the people who work with these chemicals. Some reports suggest that the life expectancy of a crop sprayer is half that of another person living in the same country. A third factor is the impact on the overall ecosystem. For example, migratory birds are heavily dependent on shade trees, which are not destroyed in sustainable coffee-farming practices.

### 3.4a What is organic coffee?

Organic coffee typically means that the coffee has been produced without the use of synthetic fertilizers, pesticides, insecticides, or other harmful chemicals. These substances threaten the long-term sustainability of our soil, ecosystem, and groundwater supplies, as well as the economic viability of the farm sector. In many instances the chemicals used on coffee are banned from crops in North America, but are freely used in developing nations.

### 3.4b What does it mean to be "certified organic"?

In order for coffee to be certified and sold as organic in the United States, it must be produced in accordance with US standards for organic production and certified by an agency accredited by the US Department of Agriculture. US requirements for organic coffee production include the following:

- It must have been grown on land without synthetic pesticides or other prohibited substances for three years.
- There must be a sufficient buffer between the organic coffee and the nearest conventional crop.
- The farmer must have a sustainable crop rotation plan to prevent erosion, the depletion of soil nutrients, and control for pests.

Certified organic coffees guarantee chemical-free growing conditions and are therefore the best way to know that the beans you buy are pure.

### 3.4c What is the growth potential for organic coffee?

Organic food consumption is growing rapidly. In 2005, organic specialty coffee sales in the US have been estimated to be at $89 million, according to the Organic Trade Association. Today at least 56 percent of US specialty coffee firms sell certified organic coffee (SCAA). Sales growth has exceeded 20 percent per year for the last several years and shows no signs of slowing down. According to the World Bank, global organic coffee production now exceeds 42,000 metric tons per year. More and more consumers are now choosing healthy food options. The market for multigrain breads, freshly squeezed juices, products without trans fats, etc. has grown rapidly along with the market for organic foods.

Certification will be important to a large majority of the industry over the next several years; this is particularly true for organic coffees. As more firms support third-party certification, they will help promote accuracy in labeling and further educate the marketplace with consistent and common terminology.

### 3.4d Quality and consistency of supply

Specialty coffee surveys indicate that coffee quality and consistency of supply are the two most important attributes in the specialty coffee trade. Producers who seek to be competitive must consider how well they can fulfill these two expectations in the future. Approximately half of the respondents expect an increase in sustainable coffee business over the next two years led by organic coffee (58 percent). Very few (less than 2 percent) expect to experience decreases in any category.

## 3.5 Fair Trade coffee

Similar to organic coffee, Fair Trade coffee is grown in an environmentally friendly manner. The difference between the two types of certifications is Fair Trade coffee is grown and sold with a focus to protect the health and livelihood of coffee farmers and workers. Much of the world's coffee is exported from some of the world's poorest nations, such as Ethiopia, Vietnam, Colombia, and Indonesia. The following are the basic criteria for certification:

- Fair prices paid to the farmer or the co-op

- Fair labor practices for coffee workers, including protecting their right to unionize

- Environmentally friendly growing practices, such as shade-grown plants and limiting chemical fertilizers and pesticides

Fair Trade Certified™ coffee is currently the fastest growing segment of the US specialty coffee market, according to Transfair USA, an organization that monitors and certifies coffee growers and importers around the world. (Go to www.transfairusa.org, and in Canada, www.transfair.ca.) Several major coffee, fast food, and retail store chains are now selling Fair Trade coffee, and hundreds of colleges and universities across North America are also offering Fair Trade coffee on campus.

Coffee drinkers are becoming more conscious of the true ethical and ecological cost of their daily cup. It makes sense to offer your customers a guilt-free cup.

## 3.6 Sustainability, a Trend That's Here to Stay

A sustainable business philosophy involves adopting the idea that a business is responsible for the products and services it provides from inception to end use. In our industry for example, this means an inclusive vision from how coffee is grown and processed (inception) to what happens to the grinds in the home brewing basket (end use).

One key sustainability issue to consider is shade grown coffee, which is grown under a natural canopy of unaltered or minimally altered native vegetation. It is the traditional method of growing coffee and is used by small farms producing modest coffee crops. Further to this is the practice of growing "bird friendly" coffee, a term which the Smithsonian Migratory Bird Center has trademarked to describe shade grown coffee that adheres to specific growing criteria, including shade produced by no fewer than ten species of trees, encouraging diversity of both trees and birds, and a minimum 40 percent shade coverage.

Business leaders are beginning to understand that operating in a sustainably conscious manner means good business. It's clear that protecting our environment and our planet is and must be an economic imperative.

### 3.6a Rationale for sustainable business philosophy

Not only is the planet demanding that we clean up our act, but today's consumers are demanding that companies be environmental responsible and offer environmentally friendly products.

Stanford University completed a detailed customer satisfaction survey in which they found that 66 percent of customers are willing to pay more for a company's products and services if they believe that the company is environmentally and socially responsible.

### 3.6b Measuring sustainability

While measuring sustainability is not an easy task, one international organization called the Coalition for Environmentally Responsible Economies ("Ceres"), made up of various business, government, legal,

church, and environmental organizations, has developed a code of conduct called the Ceres principles. They are as follows:

1. Protection of the biosphere
2. Sustainable use of natural resources
3. Reduction and disposal of wastes
4. Energy conservation
5. Risk reduction
6. Safe products and services
7. Environmental restoration
8. Informing the public
9. Management commitment
10. Audits and reports

Details of these principles are available by going to www.ceres.org.

When building your coffee bar, also explore the feasibility of building a LEED Certified site (Leadership in Environmental and Energy Design) and using the US Green Building Council standards (see www.usgbc.org/leed/ for details). Join business associations that actively promote sustainable practices such as Business for Social Responsibility (www.bsr.org) and Canadian Business for Social Responsibility (www.cbsr.bc.ca).

# PART 1
## GETTING STARTED

# 1
# PREPARING A BUSINESS PLAN

A business plan is a road map of where you want to go in your business, the various routes you will take to get there, the stages along the way, and most importantly, where you will be when you have arrived at your destination.

— DOUGLAS GRAY & DIANA GRAY

## 1. WHY PREPARE A BUSINESS PLAN?

Many entrepreneurs — whether experienced veterans or first timers — often miss the vital step of preparing a business plan when preparing to start a business. As a result, many fail in their efforts to achieve wealth and fame through their business. It is critical that you take time to prepare a business plan so you are clear on where you want to go with your coffee business and are better prepared to deal with the challenges that inevitably will arise along the way.

Why is preparing a business plan for your coffee business so important?

(a) Preparing a business plan will help crystallize your reasons for getting into the coffee business and your goals for the business. If you do not have a strong sense of "why?" and "what?" you will be without focus, direction, and satisfaction in your efforts.

(b) Preparing a business plan will help crystallize your concept. A clear, concise, well-thought-out concept will form the foundation for every decision you make: everything from choosing which color to paint the walls of your coffee bar to what kind of biscotti to serve with a cup of coffee.

(c) Preparing a business plan will help crystallize your vision of the opportunities and the limitations of the market you are in. Where is the most potential in the coffee industry? Who will your competitors be? How will you compete against them?

(d) Preparing a business plan will help crystallize your vision of exactly who you will be serving. If you are not clear on who your customers are, you will not be able to meet their needs and your business will not succeed. The knowledge you acquire about your target market will be invaluable to you in your concept and marketing efforts.

(e) Preparing a business plan will help determine what products you will offer your customers. Once you know the demographic and psychographic characteristics of your target market, you are in an excellent position to decide what products will appeal to it.

(f) Preparing a business plan will help determine what services you will offer to your customers: Home delivery service? 24-hour ordering service? Wholesale service?

(g) Preparing a business plan will force you to look at the dollars involved, from initial setup through your first few years in business. Budgeting and financial planning will be vital to your success.

(h) Preparing a business plan will force you to look at the risks involved in owning your own business. Eighty percent of businesses fail in the first five years. This is usually because of lack of planning and preparation, lack of capitalization, and a lack of management and marketing skills.

(i) Preparing a business plan will help you outline the exact steps required to get your business up and running smoothly and profitably.

(j) Finally, preparing a business plan will hopefully inspire and motivate you to take action! Knowing what you want to do isn't very useful unless you actually do it.

## 2. YOUR VISION OF YOUR BUSINESS

Take out a pen and a piece of paper, or sit yourself down in front of your computer as you read through the rest of Part I. Write down your thoughts and answers to the questions we raise. Taking action now will give you a good head start on your business plan and will help you formulate what exactly it is that you want to do and how you are going to do it. Take action now.

Your vision of your business lays the foundation for your business. Your vision is what will give you a sense of direction and give your life a sense of purpose as you build your business.

What is your vision for —

(a) **Your day-to-day activities?** What will you do on a daily basis? Do you see yourself serving customers? Do you see yourself networking with other business owners in your local area? Do you see yourself being a positive force in your community?

(b) **Your lifestyle?** Are you early to bed, early to rise? Do you see yourself working six days a week? Do you want annual holidays?

(c) **Your time?** How do you want to spend your time? Think of leisure, family, work, fitness, and private time for yourself.

(d) **Your future?** Do you plan to own your coffee bar long term or sell it down the road? What do you see yourself doing a year from now, five years from now, ten years from now?

While you may not address each of these issues specifically in your business plan (e.g., your banker may not be interested in what time you plan on getting up each morning), being clear on these issues now will help guide you as you build your business.

If your goal is to run the coffee bar as an absentee owner, hiring a good manager will be vital to the success of your business. If you plan to work the coffee bar yourself, hiring staff will be a higher priority. If you are a late riser, plan on hiring and training staff who can open the coffee bar. If you have high family priorities, keep in mind that you may need to spend a considerable amount of time in and on your business, especially in the early stages. And if you have a clear vision for your future, it will help you get where you want to go, whether that is lying on a beach in Hawaii or running a multiple location franchise.

Once you know where you want to be, you'll need to start clarifying the vision you have for your coffee business. You will need to decide whether you want to start out with a franchise, buy an existing business, or start from scratch. Below we have listed some of the pros and cons of each.

# 3. HOW SHOULD I START OUT?

## 3.1 Should I buy a franchise?

A franchise can offer you many benefits, including name recognition and clout in negotiating better pricing. Many franchises also offer assistance in obtaining financing, site selection, coffee bar design, training, and marketing. A good franchise will save

you money, give you a proven system, and increase your odds of making money.

However, one disadvantage is that the assistance provided by most franchises costs you in the form of an initial franchise fee as well as monthly royalties. You may also be restricted in terms of product lines and menu items and may be required to get written approval for use of names and logos in any advertising you do. You may be given a very small territory, which limits your ability to expand.

Franchises don't always deliver what they promise. Many franchisors mark up the products they sell to you, thereby defeating one of the major purposes behind franchising — that is, the chance for franchisees to purchase supplies that were bought in bulk at a lower price than an independent store would pay.

As well, if the franchise gets a bad name or bad publicity, you are often stuck along for the ride.

## 3.2 Should I buy an existing business?

Buying an existing business can save you the time, effort, and expertise necessary to find a good site, plan and build the coffee bar, and then develop a client base. If the business you are considering purchasing is profitable, you may find you can start earning a profit immediately.

Keep in mind, though, that you will end up paying for someone else's time, effort, and expertise through the purchase price of the business. This is where you must weigh the trade-off. Ultimately, you will need to decide which option will net you the best return.

Make sure you thoroughly research any business that you are interested in buying. Find out about the marketing systems being implemented. Spend a lot of time in the coffee bar — watch traffic patterns, count customers, look for what is being done well. Look for areas you would improve and estimate how that would influence sales.

In determining areas you would improve, it may help to think of yourself as a customer in the business. What would you look for? A better atmosphere? Better service? Better products? Better marketing? And if these things were improved, would it make you want to come back and bring friends? How much more money would you spend if these improvements were made? Keep in mind that even a 25 percent increase in the average amount a customer spends can result in thousands of extra dollars per year in pure profit.

When considering whether to buy an existing business, remember that it is difficult to change customers' perception of a business once that perception is ingrained. If an existing business has developed a bad reputation in the community, you may be fighting an uphill battle trying to win customers back.

## 3.3 Should I start my business from scratch?

Starting a business from scratch has its advantages and disadvantages. One advantage is that you have more flexibility than you would if you bought a franchise or bought an existing business. You won't be locked into the location, lease, and contracts that are already in place. It will also be easier for you to incorporate your own coffee bar design, and introduce your own menu.

On the other hand, starting from scratch means you don't get the benefits or support a franchise can offer, or those that come with a successful, established business.

One of the most important factors in any business is a marketable location. If the location of an existing business isn't suitable, or the franchisor is not able to find you a good site, you'll end up paying the price for a poor location. Finding a good location and beginning from scratch can sometimes be the best option.

Do as much research as you can to explore these three alternatives. A good business consultant will also be able to help you determine the best option for your situation.

## 4. CUSTOMER PROFILES: FINDING YOUR TARGET MARKET

In the past, the coffee market was flooded with inferior, blending-type coffees packaged in an instant coffee can. As a result, coffee drinkers didn't have much to compare their morning cup of coffee to. Today, however, thanks in part to large-scale marketing campaigns (like those featuring Juan Valdez and Colombian coffee), coffee lovers have become much more sophisticated. As consumers become better educated about the coffee choices they have, they gravitate toward better taste, flavor, and aroma.

The major consumers of gourmet coffee are adults with high levels of formal education, although sophisticated teens are now getting in on the cappuccino craze. The more post-secondary education a person has, the more likely he or she is to consume gourmet coffee. Seventy percent of bean buyers are women.

Surprisingly, there is no correlation between income and gourmet coffee drinking habits. This is an important point because many businesspeople believe that gourmet coffee is a drink of the "yuppies" and, as a result, structure their concepts and their marketing campaigns in such a way as to miss out on an entire segment of the market. Small indulgences cross all income streams.

Knowing your customer profile will help you better meet your customers' needs. For example, if your typical customer visits after dinner for a latte and slice of cheesecake, you will want to ensure that you have a wide selection of appealing desserts. If you are near a high school and your typical customers consist of students visiting after school, you will want to ensure that you have smaller, lower-priced snack items that help fill that post-learning need for calories!

But how do you determine your customer profile? You already know who the typical coffee customer is. The next step is to fine-tune this knowledge through the research you do in the area you plan to open up shop.

Is your location near an office tower? If so, your customers will probably be mid-life professionals looking for a jump start to their day and a grab-and-go breakfast. Is the coffee bar in a residential area? You will probably see more parents with children stopping in during the day to purchase beans for home use. Are you near a fitness facility? Your customer profile will be partly made up of health-conscious, possibly weight-conscious people looking for an after-workout caffeine boost or a low-fat carbohydrate replacement.

Make sure you spend the time *now* getting to know who your customers are going to be, and incorporate this information into your business plan (whether you plan to present your business plan to a private investor or financial institution or not). The more detailed your customer profile, the more successful you will be. Let's look at an example.

Assume you are near a college in an environmentally conscious community. You know that your customer profile will be made up partly of young students who will want to relax and also spend time studying in your coffee bar. Based on your general knowledge of post-secondary curriculums, you realize that because of the diverse schedules of the students, you will likely have a constant flow throughout the day. You may also discover that a young, tech-savvy customer will visit more often and stay longer if you offer wireless Internet (Wi-Fi) access.

Armed with this information, you will be able to make decisions about your coffee bar's atmosphere and design elements. Given that your community cares about the environment, you may want to display a line of informative posters about current environmental topics. You are in a better position to make decisions about everything in your coffee bar, from the staff uniform to your product lines. And, of course, because you know who your target market is, you can create and implement effective, sales-building marketing campaigns.

# 5. WHAT TYPE OF COFFEE BAR IS BEST?

Keeping in mind your knowledge of the typical coffee drinker, you now need to determine which coffee bar concept will best meet your target market's needs. The following is a brief description of the main types of coffee bars and the strengths and weaknesses of each (and have a look at Table 1). While a focus will be one of the keys to your success, it is possible to successfully combine two or three concepts, if they are done properly and if your marketing strategies take each into account.

## 5.1 Cafés

Cafés are the European model of coffee bars. They typically focus on liquid coffees (not bean sales) and often serve both lunch and dinner items. Sometimes they are licensed and, in fact, could be considered restaurants. As such, they are a concept outside the scope of this book.

## 5.2 Coffee bars

Coffee bars are typically high-traffic locations that focus on liquid coffees. Product lines often include gourmet and specialty coffees, and baked goods. These operations can be very profitable with low risk if done well.

## 5.3 Coffeehouses

A flashback to the Haight-Ashbury district of San Francisco, coffeehouses typically have dim lighting, comfy sofas, and poetry nights. They attract a younger crowd and focus on long visits and lots of conversation over steaming hot cups of java.

## TABLE 1
## TYPES OF COFFEE BARS

| Type of operation | Typical size (sq. ft.) | Rent (cost/sq. ft.) | Fun level | Ease of staffing | Set-up budgets | Profitability | Overall opportunity |
|---|---|---|---|---|---|---|---|
| Café | 1,000–1,500 | medium–high | low–medium | difficult | $75,000–195,000 | low | high risk, just like restaurants |
| Coffee bar | 400–1,200 | medium–high | high | not difficult | $45,000–125,000 | high | low risk, vulnerable to competition |
| Coffeehouse | 1,200–2,200 | low | medium–high | not difficult | $95,000–275,000 | low–high | rent and marketing determines risk |
| Retail coffee shop | 700–1,200 | medium–high | medium–high | moderately difficult | $55,000–125,000 | medium | location, location, location |
| Drive thru | 250–2,200 | low–high | low–high | not difficult to moderately difficult | $55,000–300,000 | medium | varies tremendously depending on site |
| Cart | 85–125 | very high | low–medium | difficult | $15,000–30,000 | low–high | good cash flow, no equity |
| Roaster/retailer | 600–2,200 | low–high | medium–high | not difficult to moderately difficult | $95,000–225,000 | high | very strong, long-term |
| Teahouse | 1,200–2,000 | low | medium–high | not difficult | $85,000–245,000 | low–medium | rent and marketing determines risk |

## 5.4 Retail coffee shops

Retail coffee shops typically focus on bean, tea, and giftware sales. They may or may not offer liquid coffee sales and are often found in mall locations or gift districts.

## 5.5 Drive thrus

Drive thrus can work well on the right site. The most successful locations are those with high volume on the going-to-work side of the street. Drive thrus focus primarily on liquid coffees and baked goods.

## 5.6 Carts

These "mini-stores" focus almost solely on liquid coffees. They can work well in high-traffic areas, but are challenged by difficulties in building customer loyalty. Because they are mobile, there is little, if any, equity creation as the business grows (unlike the types of coffee bars listed above).

## 5.7 Teahouses

There is a recent fad for teahouses as an offshoot of the coffee business. Do keep in mind that while tea is a popular drink, it typically represents only less than 10 percent of the total gourmet beverage market. This means you will need to be five times better than the norm to do even 20 percent of what a coffee bar will do.

## 5.8 Roaster/retailers

As the name suggests, roaster/retailing contains two key elements:

(a) On-site roasting of green coffee beans

(b) Retailing of coffee and coffee products

We believe that roaster/retailers are the wave of the future. They offer you a number of advantages that spell out strong bottom-line profit.

### 5.8a Lower food cost = Profit

Roasters typically mark up green coffee $2 to $4 per pound. The money you save by roasting your own coffee directly converts to lower food cost in your operation.

### 5.8b Savings = Profit

If your coffee business goes through 100 pounds of roasted coffee per week, you are spending at least an extra $200 per week, or $10,000 per year, because of the mark-up from roasters. Think of how many trips to Hawaii you could take with that money.

### 5.8c Meeting customer needs for freshness = Profit

Today's consumer wants the best. You'll be left behind by your competition if you don't give customers the freshness they are demanding. Coffee loses about half of its flavor within the first 14 days after it is roasted. It is tough to meet customer freshness demands if you're not doing your own roasting.

### 5.8d Competitive edge = Profit

In-store roasting gives you a unique element that gives you a huge edge over your competitors. How could you compete if the coffee bar down the street offered its customers beans to take home still hot out of the roaster?

### 5.8e An additional revenue stream = Profit

In-store roasting means you are adding an additional profit center to your coffee bar: wholesale. Because you aren't paying someone else to roast your coffee for you and you are paying only $3 or $4 per pound (including shipping, handling, brokerage, and exchange rates), you can afford to offer discounts competitive with other coffee roasters to wholesale customers.

You can supply wholesale coffee from your business to:

- Bars serving coffee
- Businesses serving coffee
- Cafés and restaurants
- Car repair shops serving coffee
- Coffee bars
- Coffee shops
- Corner stores
- Gas stations serving coffee
- Hairdressers serving coffee
- Hotels and motels
- Offices
- Supermarkets

### 5.8f Long-term appeal = Profit down the road

While it is our opinion that in-store roasting will be with us well into the foreseeable future, if we had to predict the next "hot" trend after in-store roasting, we would say "in-home" roasting. Should this trend develop in the years to come, roaster/retailers will be well protected because people will still need to buy the green beans. If you have been successful at building a solid roasted-bean business, it is simply a matter of transforming your roasted-bean customers into green-bean customers. (We design all our coffee bars to take this into account so that this conversion, should it ever be necessary in future, will be simple and inexpensive.)

Contrary to what many roast masters of the world may tell you, today's technology makes roasting beans easy. Many roasters, such as the one produced by Universal Coffee, require as few as five simple steps: checking the roaster temperature (done by the touch of a button), weighing your beans, setting an automatic timer, comparing roasted samples to a color chart to determine roasted level once the timer rings, and then allowing the beans to cool in a cooling bin.

The real art of roasting is in determining which bean is better at which roast and in blending different beans together to produce a roast with the results you want. See Chapter 9 for more on roasting.

For the remainder of the book, we will refer to all coffee bar concepts as a "coffee bar" for simplicity's sake.

# 6. CHOOSING YOUR PRODUCTS AND SERVICES

What products will appeal to your customers? Will you offer beans for home use? Food and baked goods? Gourmet teas? Coffee-related gift items? Brewing equipment? Below are some of the basic products and services most successful coffee bars offer.

## 6.1 Products

### 6.1a Gourmet coffees

Gourmet coffees are the liquid coffees you will serve on a daily basis. We recommend featuring the following "daily roasts":

- A signature medium-roast house blend
- A dark roast
- At least one flavored coffee
- Decaffeinated coffee (if the demand is high)

### 6.1b Flavored coffees

Flavored coffees represent up to 40 percent of the liquid coffee market. By offering at least one flavor a day, you are satisfying the needs of a large percentage of a market you might otherwise not capture. Flavored bean sales are also a great suggestive sell to flavored-coffee lovers.

### 6.1c Specialty coffees

Specialty coffees include the espresso-based drinks such as cappuccinos, lattes, and mochas.

### 6.1d Other coffee products

Other coffee products may include items such as coffee-flavored chocolate bars or espresso-flavored ice cream. A great favorite among North American customers is chocolate-covered espresso beans.

### 6.1e Baked goods

Baked goods include muffins, scones, cakes, biscotti, cookies, and squares. The key here is to provide a wide enough range of baked goods to appeal to your traffic flow while still maintaining a clear focus on your product line.

### 6.1f Coffee-related gift items

Gift items include mugs, coffee plungers, other coffee makers, and espresso equipment.

### 6.1g Lunches and other foods

These products include quiches, soups, and sandwiches.

### 6.1h Whole bean coffee — retail and wholesale

Plan for a huge focus on retail and wholesale bean business. Your bean sales volume can quickly grow to a steady, long-term revenue stream made up of a loyal clientele (especially if you are doing in-store roasting). We recommend setting a first-stage goal of being able to pay your rent from wholesale bean volume alone.

### 6.1i Gourmet teas

There are a number of beautifully packaged, high-grade teas that can be a nice complement to your coffee selection. Loose teas are very popular among tea lovers because they are typically made from higher grade tea leaves. The challenge with loose teas, however, is containment. If you are going to sell loose teas, it is a good idea to carry a line of tea balls (infusers) or, alternatively, sell loose tea in gauze tea bags. Gauze tea bags expand when steeped in hot water (unlike paper tea bags), allowing the tea leaves to reach their full flavor. The best sources of tea we have found are Tazo and Royal Gardens Tea, the latter available from Thanksgiving Coffees in California. See the Appendix for contact information.

There are a lot of companies that sell supplies for specialty teas such as chai, matcha, and white tea, along with the ingredients and equipment for bubble tea. Look online for sources or ask your current coffee and tea supplier.

### 6.1j Juices

Freshly squeezed juices and health blends can be a great addition to your product line and offer your customers a cool, healthy alternative to coffee.

## 6.2 Services

What services will appeal to your customers?

### 6.2a Custom roasting service

We recommend you make custom roasting the heart of your business. Because you will be roasting in small quantities (assuming you decide on a roaster/retailing concept), you will be able to offer not only fresh roasted coffee beans but also custom roasted beans. Custom roasting means blending and roasting to the individual tastes of a customer. A customer may order, for example, a blend of Guatemalan and Peruvian beans roasted to a medium-dark roast.

Custom roasting also means you can develop signature blends for your wholesale accounts. A large restaurant or hotel may want to market the coffee you provide them as their own blend. A hotel in Vancouver for example, may want to call one of its variations the "Vancouver Hotel Breakfast Blend" and promote the coffee in its hotel rooms and on its restaurant menus. With a small batch roaster you will be able to provide this marketing opportunity to wholesale accounts.

A custom roasting service will be a key selling feature for all the bean business you do.

### 6.2b Free home delivery service

A free home delivery service can be a great way to launch your whole bean coffee business. You can easily plan drop-off routes along your way to and from the coffee bar in early morning or evening. Five stops a day, five days a week can translate into an additional $15,000 in revenue per year (based on a $12 per pound purchase price).

### 6.2c 24-hour telephone ordering service

This is a service that is simple to implement; it requires only that you purchase and hook up an answering machine. When you are unable to take a call, customers are able to place their orders on the machine, 24 hours a day. (For a sample message, see Chapter 16.) With this service, you can encourage your customers to call ahead to place their order, making your roasting efforts that much more efficient.

### 6.2d Wholesale coffee services

As we indicated above, wholesale coffee volume can quickly grow to cover major expenses such as your rent and labor costs. A wholesale coffee service involves giving discounts off your retail price for larger coffee orders and possibly working in conjunction with a finance company to provide brewing equipment to your large accounts. Typically, you would offer a 30 percent discount off retail price for orders of five pounds or more.

### 6.2e Office coffee services

Coffee is supplied to thousands of offices across North America on a daily basis.

# 7. RISK ASSESSMENT

Eighty percent of all businesses fail in their first five years. To ensure that you don't become just another statistic, you need to examine all the risks associated with your venture.

Spend a few minutes now to brainstorm on anything and everything that could go wrong in your business. Ask yourself how you will overcome these challenges should you encounter them. To help you get started, we've included several sets of questions for you to answer.

(a) Should you own your own business?
- Are you prepared to put in the time and effort necessary to build your business?
- Are you prepared for the sacrifices you will need to be successful?
- Are you prepared to learn the skills you will need?
- Are you prepared to implement the strategies successful businesses use?
- Building a wholesale business involves knocking on doors and selling your service — are you comfortable with this?

(b) Are you familiar with the market you are choosing to get into?
- What are the current trends?
- What are the trends of the future?

- How will these influence you and your concept?
- Are you well positioned to meet these trends?

(c) Is your concept suitable?
- How strong is your concept?
- How focused is it?
- How vulnerable is it to competition?

(d) Are you offering the right products?
- Will your products appeal to your specific target market?
- Is your product line focused or are you trying to sell all things to all people?

(e) Are you offering the right services?
- Will your services appeal to your target market?

(f) Are you financially set?
- Do you have enough start-up capital to fund your concept properly? (We discuss this in detail in Chapter 2.)
- Have you considered how negative cash flow will affect you?

As you continue through this book, you will see that there are many other potential risks. They include —
- Poor site
- Too high rent
- Poorly designed coffee bar
- Unaccounted-for cost overruns during construction
- Poor staff hiring and training practices
- Poor business, product, staff, facilities, and financial management practices

- Inferior quality products
- Poor customer service
- Failure to market the business
- Lack of funds to market the business
- Poor marketing strategies
- Lack of willingness on the business owner's part to build wholesale business

## 8. THE BUSINESS PLAN

Once you have addressed each of these issues, you must prepare the actual business plan. There are a number of resources available to you at this stage. Your community's chamber of commerce or government business information center can provide you with sample business plans. There are also many books available at libraries or local bookstores on preparing a business plan. We have included a sample business plan outline that should help you get started organizing the information we've discussed so far (see Sample 1).

If you are using your business plan to obtain financing from a financial institution or private investor, you will want to ensure that it is clearly presented, well organized, and professional looking. Make sure there are no grammatical or spelling errors. It is also well worth including graphs, photographs, and artist renderings, if possible. You may also want to spend the extra dollars and buy a presentation folder or binder that will help convey your professional image.

You will need to put particular emphasis on your financial figures. We recommend preparing four sets of profit and loss projections, called pro formas, that look at worst, best, break-even, and most realistic case scenarios. Pro formas are discussed in more detail in Chapter 4.

If you are looking for private financing, be sure to include projected return on investment figures for your potential investors.

If you will be using your business plan for internal use only, you may wish to keep the plan on your computer or in a file, and refer to it as needed to help keep you on track. It doesn't need to be as presentable as it would be for a banker or investor, but you still want it well organized and complete.

---

# COMMITMENT BOX

I, _____ , commit to completing a business plan for my coffee business.

_____          _____
(your signature)                              (today's date)

## SAMPLE 1
# BUSINESS PLAN OUTLINE

### CONTENTS

EXECUTIVE SUMMARY

THE COFFEE MARKET
Market size
Market trends
Customer profiles

THE CONCEPT
Name
Mission statement
Principles of operation
Products and services
Pricing strategy
Distribution strategy
(for wholesale)

COMPETITIVE ANALYSIS

MANAGEMENT PLAN
Board of advisors
Corporate structure
Operating management

OPERATIONS PLAN
Location
Site selection criteria analysis
Site plan

MARKETING PLAN
Sales objectives
Marketing objectives
Marketing strategies

FINANCIAL INFORMATION
Start-up budget
Five-year financial projections
Return on investment analysis

RISK ASSESSMENT

TIMELINE

REFERENCES

APPENDIXES [*not all these items will be applicable, necessary, or available*]
List of products and services
Product or service literature, brochures, etc.
Price list
Detailed management biographies
Market research (e.g., traffic counts, interviews with people in the local area, etc.)
Completed site selection criteria sheets
Lease documentation
Annual marketing calendar
Sample marketing pieces

# 2
# SETTING UP YOUR BUSINESS

All things are difficult before they are easy.

— JOHN NORLEY

## 1. CHOOSING A NAME

Creating a strong name for your coffee business is important because it is what will draw your customers in and what they will remember about you. It will be the base of all your outside store signage; it will be displayed on your business cards, letterhead, and checks you send out to your suppliers; it may even be on your take-out cups, ceramic mugs, and napkins. So make it a great name.

The name you choose for your business should fit three major criteria:

(a) **Unique.** The name must be different — a stand-out-from-the-crowd type of name that will catch the attention of your target market.

(b) **Fitting.** Naming your business "Joe's Fish House" when you're selling coffee obviously isn't a good idea. The name you choose must be consistent with your concept and the image you are creating.

(c) **Easy to remember.** Imagine one of your customers proudly serving up a pot of your wonderful coffee to all his or her friends at a social gathering. One of the friends asks, "Where did you get this wonderful coffee?" And there is a resounding silence. OOPS! — the customer can't remember the name. Keep it simple. Three words maximum.

## 1.1 Your coffee bar's UCP

UCP stands for Unique Client Proposition. The purpose of a UCP is to convey to your customers the benefits of what you have to offer. While your business name may be

16

unique, fitting, and memorable, it is usually quite difficult to motivate your customers to come to you just because of your business's name. A UCP is designed to give your customer the major reason to come to you over your competition.

For example, the tag line "Fresh hot pizza in 30 minutes or less" created a fortune for Domino's because it clearly conveyed to potential customers what Domino's had to offer over the rest of the competition. Note that Domino's didn't say "great pizza" or "mom's special sauce" — it didn't describe what it was offering. Instead, it chose to focus on what it could deliver (pardon the pun); it described the benefit to its customers. When choosing a UCP, remember that people care about what's in it for them. Convey to your customers what they get by using your products and services.

Study all the competition in your area and make a list of your competitors' UCPS, but do not necessarily use them as a guide. Most coffee bar owners do not have a powerful UCP.

Keep in mind that you want to be different and unique. If you're not the first in a category, you should create your own category to be number one in (e.g., roaster-retailing or free home deliveries).

While marketing slogans can be your UCP, they aren't always the same thing. A UCP is a fundamental positioning statement that tells the customer why he or she should consider you over all other options. It sets a long-term standard for the business. A marketing slogan, on the other hand, is something used to catch attention and build interest through advertising, and, therefore, it will change frequently.

You may have a different UCP for each target audience. For example, at Entrepreneur Coach Inc. our UCP for the overall operation is "To build and nurture fun-loving, money-making entrepreneurs," while the UCP we use for our full franchise development program is "Zero to one million a month in five years or less ... guaranteed!"

One final point. Once you have developed your UCP, test it on your target market (don't test it out on your mother or father if they don't fit your customer profile). Spend an afternoon talking with your potential customers; stop them as they walk by your potential site or interview them in the lunchroom of the local college.

When conducting your interviews, don't ask questions such as, "Which one [UCP] do you like better?" or "Do you like this?" These types of questions are too vague and give you little information about your UCP and target market. Most people you ask won't understand that a UCP should be designed with the benefits to the customer in mind, not the features of the business, and their feedback won't be of much help to you. If you end up falling into the descriptive trap, you'll end up with an ineffective UCP that does little to help you establish market share.

Instead, ask this key question: "What does this sentence make you think of?" This is an open-ended question that encourages people to give their true opinion. If people say, "Oh, this makes me think of taking a package of freshly roasted coffee home to share with my friends," you are on the right track.

Many UCPS in the coffee business are boring, so have fun and be creative.

## 1.2 Designing and trademarking your coffee bar's logo

A logo is a visual representation of your name and identity, often accompanied by symbols, drawings, or other graphics. Designing logos is a special skill. We recommend that you hire a graphic artist to work with you to create the image you want. Local art schools can be a source of quality, inexpensive labor.

You may want to consider registering your design and logo if you plan to expand your concept nationally or internationally. Federal registration can cost up to $5,000. You will need to register your trademark separately in the United States, Canada, and the European Union if you wish to be protected in these areas. Registering in the United States does not protect you from trademark infringement in Canada, for example. All three registrations can be done for $10,000 to $20,000, depending on the complexity of your registration.

To begin the process, contact a trademark registration agent, and request a search for potential conflicts with other designs. The agent will describe the process from there. (Here in Vancouver we use a great firm called Accupro Trademark Services. Call (604) 661-9292.)

Always use a superscript ™ as evidence of your trademark, whether or not you register your trademark. Later, when your business name or logo is registered, that mark will switch to a ®.

## 2. YOUR BUSINESS STRUCTURE

One of your most important decisions will be choosing how to organize your business. There are basically three forms of legal structure: proprietorship, partnership, and limited company. You should seek competent legal and accounting advice before deciding on your business structure, as there could be distinct advantages or disadvantages to each depending on your situation.

Many entrepreneurs start out as a sole proprietor, as that is the easiest way to start a business.

Setting up a partnership means you can share the work, but there is a danger that conflict will occur when two or more people share decision making but have individual dreams and goals. It is common for such arrangements to have problems and dissolve.

Forming a corporation is a third option. The corporation can be owned by just one person (similar to a proprietorship) or two or more people (similar to a partnership).

This section discusses the factors that you and your professional advisers should examine when making a decision about your business structure.

## 2.1 Sole proprietorship

A sole proprietorship is a business owned and operated by one person. It is operated either in the businessperson's personal name, or with a trade name. To establish a sole proprietorship, you need only obtain whatever local licenses you require and open your business. It is the simplest form of business structure and operation. We recommend that you operate as a sole proprietorship until your taxable income builds significantly. In most North American jurisdictions, the tax advantages are better for sole proprietorships, but always check with a tax professional in your area.

### 2.1a Advantages

(a) **Ease of formation.** There is less formality and few legal restrictions associated with establishing a sole proprietorship. You can start almost immediately. There are no complex forms to complete and no documentation is required between you and any other party. In most jurisdictions, all that is legally necessary to operate as a sole proprietorship is to register the business and obtain the proper licenses. Licenses can be required by various levels of government.

(b) **Cost.** Registering the business and obtaining licenses involves minimal costs. There are no partnership or corporate agreements required by you because you are the sole owner. Legal fees are reduced accordingly.

(c) **Lack of complexity.** A sole proprietorship is straightforward. Unlike other forms of business, there is little government control and, accordingly, fewer reports are required to be filed with government agencies and departments. The owner and the business are taxed as one. Business losses can be offset against other income.

(d) **Decision-making process.** Decisions are made exclusively by the sole owner, who has complete authority and freedom to move. The owner does not have to obtain approval from partners or shareholders or a board of directors.

(e) **Sole ownership of profits.** The proprietor does not have to share the profits with anyone. The profits generated by the business belong to one person. The sole owner decides how and when the money will come out of the business.

(f) **Ease of terminating/sale of business.** Apart from legal responsibilities to employees, creditors, and perhaps clients, you can sell the business or close it down at your will. It is also relatively easy to roll a sole proprietorship into a corporation later, if you wish to.

(g) **Flexibility.** You are able to respond quickly to business needs with day-to-day management decisions governed only by various laws and common sense.

### 2.1b Disadvantages

(a) **Unlimited liability.** The sole owner's personal assets, such as house, property, car, and investments, are liable to be seized if necessary to pay for outstanding debts or liabilities. As mentioned earlier, the proprietor and the business are deemed to be one and the same in law.

(b) **Less financing capacity.** It is more difficult for a proprietor to borrow money than for a partnership with various partners or a corporation with a number of major shareholders. A lender looking for security and evidence of outside resources can turn to other people connected with the business rather than to just the one person in a proprietorship. A partnership or corporation can give an investor some form of equity position, which is not available in a proprietorship.

(c) **Unstable duration of business.** The business might be crippled or terminated upon the illness or death of the owner. If there is no one to take over the business, it may have to be sold or liquidated. Such an unplanned action may result in a loss.

(d) **Sole decision making.** In a partnership or a corporation, there is generally shared decision making or at least input. In a proprietorship, just one person is involved. If that person lacks business ability or experience, poor decision making can cause the business to suffer.

(e) **Taxation.** At a certain level of profit there are tax disadvantages for the sole proprietor.

(f) **Customer perception.** Some customers and creditors may have the negative perception that your business is short term if you do not incorporate.

## 2.2 Partnership

A partnership is usually defined as an association of two or more persons to carry on a business with a view to making a profit. The partnership is created by a contract, either verbal or written, between the individual parties.

The partnership agreement, sometimes called articles of partnership, is absolutely necessary in this kind of business structure. The agreement normally outlines the contribution of each partner in the business, whether financial, material, or managerial. In general, it defines the roles of the partners in the business relationship. There are many different roles for partners, as listed in section **2.2c**.

If you are considering a partnership relationship, you should see your lawyer and accountant after considering the advantages and disadvantages described.

### 2.2a Advantages

(a) **Ease of formation.** Legal formalities and expenses in forming a partnership are few compared to incorporating.

(b) **Pride of ownership and direct rewards.** Pride of ownership generates personal motivation and identification with the business. Profits could be increased if more people have a vested interest in seeing the business do well.

(c) **Availability of more capital.** A partnership can pool the funds of a number of people compared to a sole owner who has only his or her own resources to draw upon, unless loans are obtained.

(d) **Combination of expertise and talent.** Two or more partners, by combining their energies and talents, can often be successful where one person alone would fail. This is particularly true if the business demands a variety of talents such as technical knowledge, sales ability, and financial skills. It is important that working partners bring complementary skills to the business, thereby reducing the workload of each partner.

(e) **Flexibility.** A partnership may be more flexible in the decision-making process than a corporation, but less so than a sole proprietorship.

(f) **Relative freedom from government control and special taxation.** Compared to a corporation, a partnership is relatively free of restrictions and bureaucratic red tape.

## 2.2b Disadvantages

(a) **Unlimited liability.** The major disadvantage of a partnership is the unlimited liability. This unlimited liability is much more serious than in a proprietorship because all the partners are individually and collectively liable for all the debts and liabilities of the partnership. Each partner's personal assets are liable to be seized, if necessary, to pay for outstanding business debts.

(b) **Unstable duration of business.** Any change in the partnership automatically ends the legal entity. Changes could include the death of a partner or the admission or withdrawal of a partner. In each case, if the business is to continue a new partnership agreement must be written.

(c) **Management of difficulties.** As mentioned, when more than one owner assumes responsibility for business management, there is a possibility that differences of style, priorities, philosophy, and other factors will arise. If these differences become serious disputes and are unresolved, the partnership may need to be terminated, with all the financial and personal trauma involved. It is difficult for future partners to foresee whether or not personalities and methods of operating will clash.

(d) **Relative difficulty in obtaining large sums of capital.** This is particularly true of long-term financing when compared to a corporation.

(e) **Partnership agreement problems.** The larger a partnership becomes, the more complex the written agreement has to be to protect the rights and identify the responsibilities of each partner. This can result in additional administration and legal costs.

(f) **Difficulty of disposing of partnership interest.** To withdraw capital from the business requires approval from all other partners. This takes time and involves legal and administrative expenses.

## 2.2c Kinds of partners

An **ostensible partner** is active in the business and known as a partner.

An **active partner** may or may not be ostensible as well.

A **dormant partner** is inactive and not known to be a partner.

A **secret partner** is active but not known as a partner.

A **silent partner** is inactive and not known as a partner.

A **nominal partner** (partner by estoppel) is not a true partner in any sense, not being a party to the partnership agreement. A nominal partner, however, presents himself or herself as a partner, or permits others to represent him or her as a partner. A nominal partner, therefore, is liable to third parties as if he or she were a partner.

A **sub-partner** is a person who is not a member of the partnership but contracts with one of the partners to represent that partner by participating in the firm's business and profits.

A **limited** or **special partner** risks only his or her agreed investment in the business, assuming that statutory formalities have been complied with. As long as he or she does not participate in the management and control of the enterprise or in the conduct of its business, the limited partner is generally not subject to the same liabilities as the general partner.

## 2.3 Corporation

A corporation is a legal entity, with or without share capital, which can be established by one or more individuals or other legal entities. It exists separate and distinct from these individuals or other legal entities. A corporation has all the rights and responsibilities of a person with the exception of those rights that can be exercised only by a natural person.

### 2.3a Advantages

(a) **Limited liability of shareholders.** Shareholders' personal assets are separate from the business and cannot be seized to pay outstanding business debts incurred by the corporation. There are exceptions, but these relate primarily to issues of fraud.

(b) **Flexibility for tax planning.** Various tax advantages are available to corporations that are not available to partnerships or proprietorships. Tax planning must be undertaken with the help of a professional accountant.

(c) **Corporate management flexibility.** The owner or owners can be active in the management of the business to any desired degree. Agents, officers, and directors with specified authority can be appointed to manage the business. Employees can be given stock options to share in the ownership, which can increase their interest and give them an incentive to make the business work.

(d) **Financing more readily available**. Investors find it more attractive to invest in a corporation with its limited liability than to invest in a business whose unlimited liability could involve them to an extent greater than the amount of the investment. Long-term financing from lending institutions is more readily available, since lenders may use both corporate assets and personal guarantees as security.

(e) **Continual existence of corporation.** A corporation continues to exist and operate regardless of the changes in the shareholders. The death of a shareholder does not end the corporation. Continual existence is also an effective device for building and retaining goodwill.

(f) **Ownership is readily transfer-able.** It is a relatively simple procedure to transfer ownership by share transfer unless there are corporate restrictions to the contrary.

(g) **Draws on expertise and skills of more than one individual.** As in a partnership, more partners or shareholders contribute diverse talents. However, a corporation is not required to have more than one shareholder.

## 2.3b Disadvantages

(a) **Extensive government regulations.** There are more regulations affecting a corporation than a sole proprietorship or partnership. Corporations must report to all levels of government.

(b) **Activities limited by the charter and bylaws.** Depending on the jurisdiction, charters can be very broad or can severely restrict a company's activities.

(c) **Manipulation.** Minority shareholders are potentially in a position to be exploited by the decisions of the majority of the company.

(d) **Expense.** It is more expensive to establish and operate a corporation due to the additional documents and forms that are required. As well, operating losses stay in the corporation.

## 2.3c Corporate purposes

Some jurisdictions require that the articles of incorporation include a statement of the purposes of the corporation. When you provide a list of the purposes of the corporation,

make sure that you define them expansively. Don't restrict the activity of your corporation. A general clause should be included that allows the corporation to expand into any business activity permitted by law. A competent lawyer can help you prepare this document so that you maximize your corporate options.

## 2.3d Shareholders' agreement

A shareholders' agreement involves the same concepts of protection as a partnership agreement. Many of the provisions outlined in the partnership agreement are also included in the shareholders' agreement. There are additional provisions frequently covered in the shareholders' agreement, including:

(a) A restriction on the transfer of shares

(b) A buy-sell provision setting out the formula for buying and selling shares in the company

(c) A provision on personal guarantees of corporate obligations

(d) A provision on payback by the corporation of shareholders' loans

(e) A provision giving shareholders the entitlement to sit as a director or nominate a director as their representative. This protects minority shareholders from lack of managerial information and provides them with a directorship vote or veto on corporate decisions. If you intend to be a majority shareholder, you may not wish to volunteer this provision.

Many shareholders believe that corporate bylaws set out the recipe for resolving problems within the corporation and between the shareholders, directors, and officers in some magical way. In fact, the bylaws generally cover formulas for resolving disputes in a few circumstances only. It is the shareholders' agreement that expands the protections to resolve fairly any disputes between shareholders.

If you intend to incorporate and have one or more additional shareholders in your corporation, you should get your lawyer's advice on a shareholders' agreement to protect your interests.

## 2.4 S corporation (United States)

If you live in the United States, you may wish to consider the advantages of structuring your business as an S corporation (also known as sub-chapter or sub-S). This structure permits a small business corporation to treat its net income as though it were a partnership. One objective is to overcome the double-tax feature of taxing corporate income and shareholder dividends. Another purpose is to give the shareholders the benefit of offsetting business losses incurred by the corporation against their income.

Only closely held corporations, that is those with 35 or fewer shareholders, may make the S election. All shareholders must consent to the S election, and only one class of outstanding stock is allowed. A specific portion of the corporation's income must be derived from active business rather than passive investments. No limit is placed on the size of the corporation's income and assets.

If you make an S election now, at some future point you may wish to revert to a full corporation for tax advantage reasons. This is permitted, but the corporation may not be able to reelect the S vehicle for several years once the S election is reversed. This is to prevent small corporations from changing frequently to maximize tax advantages. Since S forms of incorporation are not recognized in all states, you should obtain further information from your professional advisers.

## 2.5 Limited liability corporation (United States)

A limited liability corporation (LLC) is a form of doing business that combines the limited liability for loans and lawsuits of a corporation with the "pass-through" tax benefits of a partnership. Pass-through taxation means that the business is taxed only once — at the member/shareholder level — rather than at both the member/shareholder and LLC/corporate level.

S corporations are also eligible for pass-through taxation, so why form an LLC instead of an S corporation? Because certain limitations are placed on S corporations that do not affect LLCs.

For instance, an S corporation must not have more than 75 shareholders, and the shareholders must be individuals, estates, or certain types of trusts. Corporations, partnerships, LLCs, and nonresidents may not be shareholders in an S corporation. All these entities, however, can be members in an LLC.

Another limitation placed on S corporations is that they may have only one class of stock. As a result, the financing options are limited. S corporations are not good tax shelters because deductions for losses are limited to the shareholder's basis in the corporate stock.

LLCs have an advantage over S corporations when it comes to foreign investors.

Because an S corporation cannot have non-resident shareholders, it is unable to have much interaction in the fast-growing international business market. Also, LLCs, unlike S corporations, are not subject to additional partnership tax status qualification requirements. LLCs must simply meet partnership tax requirements. LLCs need not elect partnership tax status and then be continually vigilant in order to retain such status as S corporations must.

For more information refer to the Self-Counsel book *Limited Liability Company: How to Form and Operate Your Own.*

# 3. START-UP COSTS

Now that you've got your name and your structure, you'll need money. Start-up costs for coffee bars can range anywhere from $95,000 to $395,000 for a typical 1,500 sq. ft. (140 sq. m) site. Start-up costs are obviously dependent on a wide range of factors, including —

(a) leaseholds required,

(b) tenant improvement dollars (if any),

(c) equipment, and/or

(d) initial marketing budgets.

These factors are all discussed in the following chapters. We have included a typical start-up budget (see Sample 2) here and you may want to use it as a guide for comparison purposes as you do your shopping around. (We have also included a blank spreadsheet on the CD-ROM that you can use.) Make sure to adjust your start-up budget to meet the requirements of the site once you have secured one. In Chapter 4 we discuss in detail how to choose a site for your coffee bar and tell you how to determine what the ongoing operational costs for your site will be.

Keep your start-up costs separate from your operating costs. This is particularly important during the first month you are open. For example, a phone hookup is a start-up cost. The cost of having that phone operating that month and the charge for any long-distance calls you make in the regular course of operating your business are operating costs. Keep a separate file for all your start-up receipts. (See Chapter 15 for a discussion of operating costs.)

The cash required for your venture can come from a variety of sources: your personal savings, relatives and friends, banks, private investors, and, sometimes, the government. Most business funding is a combination of the above. Review each option discussed below and think about which ones will work for your business.

But before you think about borrowing money, from whatever source, keep in mind the risks involved. Understand the damage that irresponsible borrowing can have on a business. Unnecessary debt cripples a business, eliminates options, and weakens its ability to survive. You may not be able to escape it entirely as your coffee bar grows and prospers, but if you must borrow, *borrow only what you need and only when you need it*. By following this simple rule, you ensure two things: a stronger business and a calm state of mind.

## 3.1 Personal savings

If you have enough personal resources to run your business until it yields a profit, go for it. You will have no anxious lenders to account to, no financial responsibilities

# START-UP BUDGET

## LEASEHOLDS

|  |  |
|---|---|
| Plumbing | $5,000 |
| Electrical | 5,100 |
| Counters | 12,000 |
| Stools and chairs | 1,000 |
| Floor | 5,000 |
| Menu boards | 1,200 |
| Faux finishing | 3,600 |
| Paint | 400 |
| Shelving | 250 |
| Bean display | 800 |
| Rubber kickguard | 200 |
| Phone installation — two lines | 300 |
| Alarm | 400 |
| Permits, licenses, and plans | 1,400 |
| Venting of fan | 800 |
| Artwork | 350 |
| Construction — misc. | 4,000 |
| **Subtotal** | **$41,800** |

## EQUIPMENT

|  |  |
|---|---|
| U/C fridge | $500 |
| In-line fan | 400 |
| Cups/mugs | 1,000 |
| Roaster | 14,000 |
| Thermoses and baskets | 400 |
| Cap machine and two grinders | 7,600 |
| Bag grinders (2) | 3,000 |
| Batch grinder | 1,200 |
| Convection oven | 2,500 |
| Brewing system (thermal carafe) | 2,000 |
| Juicer | 500 |
| Computer system | 5,000 |
| Hot water | 500 |
| Two-door cooler | 2,500 |
| One-door cooler | 1,000 |
| Misc. small wares | 850 |
| Stereo | 400 |
| Microwave oven | 200 |
| Electronic scale | 750 |
| Dishwasher | 3,600 |
| Display showcase | 3,900 |
| Freezer | 650 |
| Answering machine | 150 |
| Triple sink | 800 |
| Blender | 100 |
| Broom/mop | 100 |
| Patio furniture | 500 |
| Vacuum | 100 |
| Fax | 500 |
| **Subtotal** | **$54,700** |

## MISCELLANEOUS

|  |  |
|---|---|
| Inventory | $2,500 |
| Green bean inventory | 4,200 |
| Packaging | 1,100 |
| Insurance deposit | 100 |
| Float | 300 |
| Marketing start-up | 2,000 |
| Rent deposit estimate | 3,000 |
| Office supplies | 100 |
| Staff ad | 150 |
| Music CDs | 50 |
| Coffee Kids membership | 400 |
| Uniforms | 200 |
| Sign deposits | 500 |
| **Subtotal** | **$14,600** |

| | |
|---|---|
| **SUBTOTAL** | **$111,100** |
| *Add: Working capital* | *$10,000* |
| **TOTAL** | **$121,100** |

other than to yourself and your business — and no bank interest to pay. There is no better, or less stressful, way to start a new enterprise than debt free.

## 3.2 Relatives and friends

Money from relatives and friends usually takes the form of a loan. The money is lent on trust and accepted with good intentions. If the business is successful and the money is repaid promptly, both parties remain happy and satisfied. If not, the borrowed money can become a long-lasting contentious issue. There is always a danger in mixing money with a personal relationship, well-meaning as both parties might be, and it is wise to consider carefully before asking for such a loan. If money from relatives and friends is an option open to you, give the possible consequences serious thought. Is your business worth the risk of a friend or family member's money?

If you do start your enterprise using money from friends and relatives, it will no doubt be your intention to pay it back through the profits of the business. Before agreeing to the loan, think about a backup payment plan should your business be unable to repay the debt.

The terms and conditions of the loan should be fair and negotiated in a business-like manner. Be scrupulous in honoring the trust that is inherent in such a loan. Prepare a proper promissory note that outlines all the terms and conditions. (Promissory note forms can be purchased at most stationery stores.) Most important, be as certain as you can of your ability to pay it back on time and in full.

## 3.3 Commercial loans

Banks are the most common source of start-up funding. Take the time to develop a business plan and package the loan request in a complete and professional manner. If your business idea is sound, and you do your homework, you should not have a difficult time.

## 3.4 Personal financing

Often, taking out a personal loan is the most direct route to cash for your business. Simply borrow the funds you need under your own name. While you need to have sufficient collateral to cover the loan, you do not need to advise the banker on all details of your business venture.

Later, as your business and your ability to pay off debt increase, switch to commercial borrowing. This type of loan is generally term financing: money received in a lump sum with a specified pay-back period that includes payment on the amount borrowed plus interest.

Taking out a personal loan is sometimes the easiest method for many, particularly when the amount needed for start-up is small. There is no requirement for a business plan and in some instances the cost of the money can be less. As long as you have the collateral and can satisfy the bank of your ability to pay, you should have not have any difficulty.

If you plan on this type of borrowing, remember that the money is for your business, so incorporate the principal and interest payments into your business records as a loan from you. You borrow from the bank and your business borrows from you.

## 3.5 Credit cards

Many businesses start by using the unused line of credit available on their credit cards. Some credit cards have lines of up to $10,000 available. This is often overlooked as a source of business cash, but can be a quick alternative to bank financing if the loan amount is small. However, use caution if you use credit card financing to start your business: this kind of money is expensive.

## 3.6 Private investors

A private investor can be hard to find, and money obtained in this way generally comes with conditions. The investor may want control of the company, for example, or, if the money takes the form of a loan, an extremely high interest rate. While such conditions can be fair depending on the degree of risk, often the strings attached to this kind of financing are so stringent as to limit your ability to control your operation effectively.

Should you find an investor you haven't been personally referred to (e.g., if you find an investor through the newspaper), check him or her out carefully. Ask a lot of questions. Don't let your good sense evaporate because a stranger is willing to put cash on the table.

A good source for finding private investors is your accountant. People with money to invest in small, start-up ventures often rely on their accountants to guide them. They will ask the accountant to keep an eye out for promising business investments.

If your accountant happens to be the potential investor's accountant, a good relationship can result. Expect such investors to be cautious and to attach conditions to the loan. Their approach to lending money or taking an equity position in a small business is similar to that of a bank. They require complete and accurate information on the business seeking funds.

## 3.7 Government

The governments of both the United States and Canada provide financial assistance to small business.

In the United States, the funding is administered through the Small Business Administration (SBA) which helps small businesses both educationally and financially. You can call the local SBA office at 1-800-U-ASK-SBA. Since the SBA is a government agency, its policies are liable to change, so make sure your information is current before you apply for funds.

In Canada, money for small business comes through a variety of government departments, both federal and provincial. The best source for information is the small business development department of your provincial government. It can advise you on what is available and what information is required to apply.

Most government lending is done as "last resort" lending. It often takes the form of loan guarantees rather than direct loans. Government is not, nor should it be, in the business of competing with banks, trust companies, or other commercial lending institutions. You will probably be required to prove that you were unable to obtain money from other sources before approaching government sources for money. You will probably also need to have some of your own money invested in the business. Make sure you prepare proper documentation on your business before approaching any government lending department for funds.

Many government programs give loans to, or guarantee loans for, incorporated businesses only. Small proprietorships are often ineligible for certain types of government funding.

## 4. LICENSING

Always remember to have the appropriate business license, health permits, and other local registration. City or municipal government agencies usually require you to have a business license. Check with your city hall business development officer for a complete list of all appropriate registration needed. Be sure to do this before you open — it's a lot easier then.

State and provincial organizations usually require business name registration. Contact your local business development officers for details.

---

# COMMITMENT BOX

I, _____ , commit to taking time to plan my business structure.

_____     _____
*(your signature)*         *(today's date)*

---

# 3
# INSURANCE

Take calculated risks. That is quite different from being rash.

— GEORGE S. PATTON

In the previous chapters we've mentioned the risks of starting up a coffee bar. Don't let risks stop you setting up a coffee bar, but do be aware of the problems you might face.

Proper risk management means planning for potential problems and attempting to insure against them. You should be familiar with the various types of insurance available, the method of obtaining the insurance, the best way to reduce premiums, and the pitfalls to avoid.

## 1. OBTAINING INSURANCE

Insurance companies market their services chiefly through the methods discussed below.

### 1.1 Agencies

These are the small, individualized operations that place home, car, or other common types of insurance with several insurance companies to which they are contracted. In some cases, to earn their commission, small agencies are under an obligation to place a certain volume of insurance with each company they deal with. Therefore, it is possible that you might be sold a policy that does not suit your needs and is not necessarily priced competitively.

### 1.2 Insurance brokers

Insurance brokers claim to have complete independence from any insurance company and more flexibility than the common agencies. In comparison with agencies in general, brokers from the larger companies are more knowledgeable about and flexible in the types of coverage and policies they offer, and they specialize in certain areas. Also, a broker should have no vested interest in placing insurance with any particular company and will therefore attempt to get you the best price and the best coverage to meet your needs. You should make specific inquiries to satisfy yourself.

As in all matters of obtaining professional advice or assistance, you should have a minimum of three competitive quotes and an opportunity to evaluate the relative strengths and weaknesses of each. If the brokers are using the same insurance base for the best coverage and premiums, then all three brokers should recommend to you, in theory, the same insurance companies for the different forms of coverage you are requesting.

## 1.3 Clubs and associations

Ask your local Better Business Bureau and chamber of commerce about their group rates for insurance. These two organizations frequently have various types of insurance coverage available at a reduced group rate.

# 2. PLANNING YOUR INSURANCE PROGRAM

It is important to consider all criteria to determine the best type of insurance for you and your business. Your major goal should be adequate coverage, avoiding both over- and under-insurance. To achieve this, periodically review your situation and keep your agent informed of any changes in your business that could potentially affect your coverage.

The following principles will help you plan an insurance program:

(a) Identify the risk to which your business is exposed.

(b) Cover your largest risk first.

(c) Determine the magnitude of loss the business can bear without financial difficulty, and use your premium dollar where the protection need is greatest.

(d) Decide what kind of protection will work best for each risk:

- Absorbing risks

- Minimizing risks

- Insuring against risks with commercial insurance

(e) Insure the correct risk.

(f) Use every means possible to reduce costs of insurance:

- Negotiate for lower premiums if loss experience is low

- Use deductibles where applicable

- Shop around for comparable rates and analyze insurance terms and provisions offered by different insurance companies

(g) Risk exposure changes, so a periodic review will save you from insuring matters that are no longer exposed to the same degree of risk. Conversely, you may need to increase limits of liability. Review can help avoid overlaps and gaps in coverage, and thereby keep your risk and premiums lower.

(h) If you are pleased with a particular broker who can handle your various forms of insurance, it is preferable to be selective and have just one broker company. An advantage of the larger broker firms is that they have a pool of insurance professionals, expert in various areas, that you can call on as resource people.

(i) Attempt to keep your losses down in every way. Although your business may have adequate coverage, losses could be uninsurable, exempt from coverage, or have a large deductible. Problems with insurance coverage could seriously affect the survival of your business.

# 3. TYPES OF BUSINESS AND PERSONAL INSURANCE

The types of insurance you might need will vary according to the structure and concept of your coffee bar. The following overview of insurance policies is provided to make you aware of what exists and of what might be appropriate for your business. These types of insurance are not necessarily recommended; only you can decide what to buy after an objective assessment of your needs and comparative research in a competitive insurance market.

## 3.1 General liability

A general liability policy covers negligence causing injury to clients, employees, and the general public. The policy is normally written up as a comprehensive liability policy which will encompass such things as:

(a) Money you must legally pay because of bodily injury or damage to the property of others.

(b) All emergency, medical, and surgical expenses incurred by an accident.

(c) Expenses for investigation, your defense, settlements, and a trial.

## 3.2 Products or completed operations liability

This policy offers protection against a lawsuit by a customer or client who used your product or service and, as a result, sustained bodily injury or property damage from it.

## 3.3 Errors and omissions liability

This coverage protects you and other professionals against litigation arising from losses incurred by your clients as a result of an error or omission in your advice to them.

## 3.4 Malpractice liability

This insurance protects you from claims arising from any losses incurred by your clients as a result of negligence or failure on your part to exercise an acceptable degree of professional skill.

## 3.5 Automobile liability

This coverage includes other people's property, other automobiles, persons in other vehicles, and persons in the insured automobile.

If you are using your car for business, exclusively or occasionally, it is important that you have your premium cover business use. It is possible that your current motor vehicle insurance policy has a premium based on personal use only. Problems could occur if you are in an accident and it is discovered that your car, insured for personal use only, was in fact used for business.

## 3.6 Fire and theft liability

It is important to make sure that you have satisfactory coverage for fire and theft.

## 3.7 Business interruption insurance

The indirect loss from a fire or theft can be greater than the direct loss. If your business premises or files are destroyed, you can lose revenue, but certain expenses must still be met. Such a situation could put a severe strain on working capital and seriously affect the survival of your business.

Business interruption insurance is designed to cover the period between the time of the loss and the return to normal operating conditions. The insurance policy could also include the costs of temporarily renting other premises.

## 3.8 Personal disability insurance

You could be disabled for a short or long period of time. This insurance pays you a certain monthly amount if you are permanently disabled, or a portion of that amount if you are partially disabled but capable of generating some income.

## 3.9 Key person insurance

The death of a key person could seriously affect the earning power of your business. For example, if you have an associate, partner, or consultant who is critical to a particularly large project or your business as a whole, life insurance should be considered.

The death of a key person may result in decreased confidence on that part of your existing or potential clients, leading to a loss of future contracts, competitive position, and revenue, and to the expense of finding and/or training a replacement. The amount and type of insurance you should carry will depend on many factors, as designing an evaluation formula for a key person is difficult.

Proceeds of the key person policy are not subject to income tax generally, but premiums are not a deductible business expense.

## 3.10 Shareholder's or partner's insurance

If it is your intention to have a partner in your coffee bar or a shareholder in your corporation, you may wish to consider shareholder's or partner's insurance. Usually this type of insurance is part of a buy-sell agreement that allows for a deceased shareholder's or partner's interest to be purchased by the surviving partners or shareholders of the corporation.

In summary, the procedure is that each partner shareholder applies for a life insurance policy on the life of the other. The applicant is the beneficiary and pays the premiums on his or her partner's life insurance policy. When a partner dies, the funds from the insurance are received tax free by the beneficiary (the partner). These funds are then used to purchase the deceased partner's share of the business. The surviving partner retains control of the business, and the heirs of the deceased get cash for their interest.

In the absence of a buy-sell agreement funded by life insurance, the death of a partner could cause the immediate dissolution of the partnership in law. Unless there is an explicit agreement to the contrary, the surviving partner's duty is to liquidate the business, collect all outstanding accounts, pay off all debts, and account as trustee to the personal representative of the deceased partner for the value of the deceased's interest in the business.

With a corporation, in the absence of a buy-sell agreement, the deceased shareholder's interest would be considered an asset and would go to the beneficiary outlined in the deceased shareholder's will, if a will existed. Naturally, the introduction of a new shareholder who owns an interest in the company, especially a majority interest, could have a very traumatic effect on the shareholders and the company's continued operation.

## 3.11 Business loan insurance

Often your lender will be able to provide you with insurance coverage for the outstanding amount of your loan and will then incorporate the premium payments into the loan. If you die, the outstanding balance of the loan is paid off.

## 3.12 Term life insurance

This insures a person for a specific period of time. The most common period is five years. If the insured dies within the term of the policy, the insurance company pays the full face amount to the heirs. The cost of premiums is based on life expectancy for the person's age during the five-year period. Term life does not have a cash or loan value.

Because term life insurance can be written for various time periods, and because the premiums are generally inexpensive, it is valuable to the businessperson. Term policies are often used to provide collateral security for loans to the firm or for personal obligations.

It is wise to have term insurance for at least the amount of personal and business financial obligations for which you have a direct or contingent liability. This area is frequently overlooked.

## 3.13 Medical insurance

It is important to take out sufficient medical coverage for your needs. If you are doing any business assignments outside the country, you should have extended coverage that pays for medical bills that may be incurred by injury or illness in a foreign country.

## 3.14 Group insurance

You may be eligible for group insurance rates if you have four or more employees. The policies of insurance companies vary, but medical and dental plans are available for small groups.

## 3.15 Workers' compensation insurance

If you have a number of employees, ensure that you are covered by workers' compensation insurance. With this coverage, the insurer pays all costs for any injury to the employee. The insurer also covers the employees for all benefits and compensations required by the appropriate laws.

If you have failed to pay your employer's portion of the insurance coverage, or have failed to meet your responsibilities adequately to your employees in terms of safety, it is possible that you as the employer could be held liable for any injury to the employee as determined by the common law as well as under workers' compensation laws. Employee coverage and the extent of the employer's liability vary considerably.

## COMMITMENT BOX

I, _____ , commit to
obtaining adequate insurance for my new business.


_____          _____
(your signature)                   (today's date)

# 4

# SECURING A SITE
# FOR YOUR COFFEE BAR

There are two things to aim at in life: first, to get
what you want; and, after that, to enjoy it.

— LOGAN PEARSALL SMITH

Finding a great site involves many factors, some of which are quantifiable, while others come from experience and an intuition about a site's suitability. Often you won't find a great site, you will create one. Because the best sites are usually either already occupied or haven't even been built yet, you won't find a big "for lease" sign sitting in the window. Finding a great site requires that you do a lot of planning and digging to come up with that big diamond.

## 1. WHERE ARE THE BEST LOCATIONS?

The "best" location for you will depend on your vision, your concept, and your customer profile. It is our belief that any site can be made to work with enough time,

energy, and marketing money, but obviously you will want to find a site that keeps your efforts minimized and your profits maximized. In this section we examine the pros and cons of different sites to help you decide where you want your coffee bar to be.

## 1.1 Downtown versus the suburbs

Generally, downtown sites are more vulnerable to competition than suburban sites, primarily because significant retail coffee bean volume can be generated only in suburban sites where most people do their grocery shopping. While wholesale volume can be generated from any site, the high rents for downtown locations can make these sites cost-prohibitive even for wholesalers.

In a downtown location, you may get a lot of traffic in the morning as people go to work, and much of your business may be "to go." You may be able to secure some loyal customers who *do* think to stop in to pick up beans for the weekend, but they are not the norm.

In the suburbs, on the other hand, people are often out specifically to grocery shop and run errands such as picking up coffee for the coming week. The majority of shopping is still done by women (although this is changing), so don't forget that women are your primary bean-buying target market.

We have also found that people generally have more time to relax in the suburbs, away from work, and can afford to take the time to sit and enjoy a latte or cappuccino.

## 1.2 Regional shopping malls

Regional shopping malls are enclosed shopping areas made up of many different stores. Regional centers have multiple anchor tenants (large stores like Sears or Wal-Mart) and usually at least 100 other retail tenants.

Malls are not good locations for coffee bars. We learned this the hard way over three years of owning our own store in a major mall. Malls have grown to be so expensive in both rent and operating costs that you will likely regret any decision to locate in one. Rent is typically high if you are in a good mall because there is a lot of walk-by traffic. Beware of cheap mall rents — they are cheap for a reason.

However, the high rent you pay for walk-by traffic does not necessarily translate into more sales. This is due to a number of reasons.

(a) Most people go to malls to do retail shopping rather than grocery shopping, and coffee beans are most often purchased in conjunction with the weekly grocery trip.

(b) While some people will pop in to grab a cup of coffee while they do their shopping, many will not. Shopping is often done in the late morning or afternoon, after the typical coffee-drinking times of the day.

(c) Unless you can offer a seating area (which you must pay extra rent for), you will miss out on the part of the shopping crowd that wants to take a break from shopping by sitting and enjoying a cup of coffee.

(d) It is difficult to build up a loyal evening crowd at a mall. Most people will not go to a mall for a latte and a piece of cheesecake.

You also end up with higher labor and overhead costs in a mall. Malls are often open long hours and as many as 364 days each year, which affects your labor costs. On the other hand, mall hours are highly restrictive — unless you have outside access — and can cut off large portions of a coffee drinker's purchasing time (i.e., early morning), which affects your sales.

Common area maintenance costs (described in section **3.3**) are typically very high because malls are expensive to maintain — just think of all those plants and the waterfall in the center court that need constant attention, as well as garbage removal and property taxes.

Finally, you will have to pay into the mall's media funds for advertising and promotion. While this is good in that these marketing efforts are designed to bring traffic to the mall, they usually involve blanket, rather than targeted, advertising, so most of your coffee bar's marketing dollar is wasted. You will have little, if any, say in how the money is spent.

On the other hand, a site with both outside and inside access may work well, especially if the project has a major grocery anchor, such as a Safeway. You can probably count on staff in other mall stores becoming your customers. And bad weather has a positive impact on traffic in a regional shopping mall.

## 1.3 Strip malls

Strip malls involve a number of storefronts lined in a "strip." They are usually not enclosed and feature drive in/drive out shopping for a variety of products and services. They are very common in suburban areas and can work very well if the tenants are strong.

Strip malls are often underrated. You can get excellent value for your rent dollars. If there is a major grocery anchor, strip malls can work really well because people typically come to the mall to run errands and do their grocery shopping. Picking up coffee can easily become one of the many things that they do during their trip.

Being in a strip mall also allows you to draw on the other tenants' staff as customers. This customer base tends to be loyal (if you have good products and service) with consistent purchasing patterns you can rely on.

The disadvantages to locating in a strip mall are that there is not a lot of walk-by

traffic and it can be weather-vulnerable. (This is not always the case, however, and you should check the site out in cold and rainy weather or ask some of the tenants what happens to traffic on such days.) As well, parking can be a problem if the strip is busy, turning potential customers away.

## 1.4 Public markets

Public markets are great locations for coffee bars. If you're fortunate enough to live in an area that has a busy public market without a coffee roaster, go for it. You'll love the potential there to sell coffee beans. Make sure that the market is doing well. You will want to talk to other tenants and examine traffic flow patterns on a daily, weekly, and seasonal basis.

Most tenants in a public market focus on freshness, a focus consistent with in-store roasted coffee. There are many food-focused and errand-related businesses in a market so this is a great opportunity to sell people coffee as they stop in to grab their groceries. Because markets usually offer both inside and outside entertainment opportunities, they are not usually weather-vulnerable. And as with regional and strip malls, the staff of other tenants in the market can provide you with a regular, loyal customer base.

Because markets are usually managed by smaller marketing groups than, for example, a regional shopping mall, markets often allow you to take a more active role in the market's advertising and promotional decisions. Some public markets set up tenant committees for this purpose, although you may find that you still do not have as much say as you would like in how your group marketing dollars are spent. Other tenants can also offer excellent opportunities for cross-promoting (see Chapter 16).

There are, of course, drawbacks to locating in a public market. Typically, markets (especially the good ones) command high rent and have high operating costs. It may also be difficult to have outside access, so your hours of operation will be restricted and coffee drinkers' traffic flow patterns disrupted.

Some public markets can be rather isolated and you will need to take into consideration customer access by car, bus, or rapid transit.

## 1.5 Street sites

There are certain pros to setting up your coffee bar in a street-accessible site. For instance, you can set your own hours (you're not obligated to follow mall hours), and you can cross-promote with other businesses on the street. You are likely to find a higher level of acceptance for this type of promotion among street stores than in malls.

As well, depending on your site, you may be able to have a front patio area — always a good draw for customers. Generally, street sites have lower rents and lower operating costs than other types of sites, since the cost to build a street site is less than that to build a mall, and the landlord* does not need to charge as high a rent to cover his or her investment.

However, there are some disadvantages to a street site. Although there may be a lot of drive-by traffic, there is less walk-by traffic, which is easier to draw in to your coffee bar.

A street site is also weather-vulnerable; while coffee consumption increases in bad weather, many street sites' walk-by traffic drops. Another disadvantage to a street location is that there are no group marketing funds, although a local business association may be involved in marketing a particular street or retail area. Contact your local chamber of commerce or ask tenants in other stores if they have any information about this possibility.

## 1.6 Office towers

Office tower locations are usually on the ground or main level of the tower. If you do a good job, you can build a loyal customer base from the people working in that tower. If there is outside access, you can also draw from walk-by traffic. Since traffic flow is predictable, costs such as labor and food can be more easily controlled.

Office tower locations also allow you to capitalize on staff-meeting catering services of coffee and baked goods, office coffee services, or gourmet coffee gift basket business. Gift baskets do particularly well in office tower sites because they are popular gifts not only from bosses to staff and vice versa but from company to company. Gift baskets are consistent with the trend toward gourmet and small indulgences. While baskets can also sell well in other locations, especially malls, an office tower location gives a coffee bar owner the opportunity to capitalize on this specific corporate market.

Sometimes, however, office tower businesses are limited to the building staff (e.g., if you have no outside access) and are dependent on the success of the building (i.e., how full the building is).

The hours of business of an office tower site may be either an advantage or disadvantage, depending on what you want. For instance, hours are usually Monday to

---

*The word "landlord" in this book should be read to include both men and women.

Friday, with early morning starts and early evening closes (e.g., 5 a.m. to 6 p.m.). These hours limit sales times.

Depending on how restrictive the use clause in your lease is (this is the clause that says what products you can sell at your site), it may be difficult to get customer visits past the busy early morning coffee rush.

As well, the size and electrical and plumbing capacities of the location may be limited. Some office towers may be conducive only to a small kiosk, for example.

## 2. MAPPING IT OUT

Once you have decided on the type of location that best fits your concept and appeals to your target market, you will want to start researching other businesses in the area where you plan to do business. The idea is to map out businesses that have a similar target market to yours, so that your job of drawing customers to your coffee bar is easier. Many marketing strategies, including those we discuss later in the book, rely heavily on relationships you build with your neighbors, so make sure the sites you are considering have plenty of businesses around that will help you in your sales building efforts rather than hinder you.

Map out your location using a wall map of your city and the yellow pages. Buy a package of small colored dot stickers to stick on your map. Sticker your map as follows:

- Find all major grocery stores (such as Safeway) in the Yellow Pages, and sticker their locations with red dots.
- Use yellow dots to indicate all major video stores, such as Blockbuster.
- Use green dots to indicate all major parent draws, such as Toys 'R' Us.

- Use blue dots to indicate all major female client draws, such as weight-loss or fitness centers.

If you think of other businesses that might have a positive impact on your coffee bar traffic, assign them a color code and sticker them as well. Once you have completed this task, you will be able to pick out major clusters of dots and will have a good visual representation of which areas make sense to begin the site selection process.

In each area, look for a large, well-established business. By placing your coffee bar near such a business, you will be able to benefit from the traffic this store brings to the area. Major chains have invested a considerable amount of time, expertise, and capital in choosing their sites, and you can rely on them to a large extent when choosing a good location for your coffee bar. However, these chains do make mistakes, so don't rely exclusively on them.

## 3. THE SITE SELECTION CRITERIA CHECKLIST

A site-selection criteria checklist allows you to compare the rankings of several sites in a given area. It's a powerful way to take the emotion out of site selection and measure the site objectively.

The idea is to score at least 20 potential sites in an area that earned a large dot cluster in the mapping exercise you did, compare the total scores of each of the 20 sites, and then select the top four or five. These four or five sites are the sites you will begin preliminary lease negotiations on.

Why score 20 potential sites? There are two reasons. First, most people neglect to do enough research in looking for the best site; as a result, their businesses either fail to perform to expected standards or simply fail. Second, because the best sites are usually occupied, finding 20 sites will force you to do more research. And more research ultimately means finding a better site.

Checklist 1 is a site selection criteria checklist for you to use when you are viewing possible sites. (This checklist, along with all the other checklists in the book, can also be found on the accompanying CD-ROM.) Because the checklist is a relative ranking system, you do not need to be an expert to use it. As long as your rankings of each item are consistent, it should work very well for you.

You will see that there is room on the checklist for you to enter your target numbers and goals so you can rank the specific site against the ideal. A score of three out of five means the goal or target is met, five out of five means you have greatly exceeded your goal, and one out of five means you have fallen short of your goal.

## 3.1 Size

One of the first considerations of any site is size. Size will be partly dependent on your concept and the target market you are catering to. Keep in mind that you will need enough space for washrooms and storage areas. Whether or not you follow our recommended concept of a roaster/retailer, you should have about 1,000 to 1,500 sq. ft.

## 3.2 Monthly rent

Rent is dependent on a number of factors, including location of the site and traffic flow. Usually, the higher the rent, the higher the traffic flow. For example, if your rent is $1,000 per month, but you are in a low

traffic flow area with only 60 customers a day (average customer check of $3.50), you would realize sales of only $6,300 per month and your rent would be 15.8 percent of your sales. Your profit, assuming a 25 percent food cost, would be $3,725 per month.

On the other hand, you might be paying $10,000 per month for a high traffic location and getting 600 customers each day for sales of $63,000 per month (again assuming an average customer check of $3.50). Your rent is still 15.8 percent of your sales, but your profit has skyrocketed to $37,250 per month (with a 25 percent food cost).

You will need to decide if a location has a good balance of these factors for you, your concept, and your target market, and whether the rent is reasonable given your projected sales. Generally, we target $20/sq. ft. or less.

## 3.3 Common area maintenance (CAM)

Common area maintenance (CAM) fees cover the costs associated with the maintenance of the building site. CAM may include security services, garbage removal, and window cleaning. Make sure to check your lease for specifics on this. Other considerations include water costs and property taxes. All projects require the tenant to pay for operating costs and a surcharge for management: the landlord does not pay these costs. Target $8/sq. ft. or less per month.

## 3.4 Restrooms

Most city health codes require that your coffee bar have at least one restroom; it's a good idea to have one that is accessible for people in wheelchairs. Depending on your

# CHECKLIST 1
## SITE SELECTION CRITERIA

*A score of three out of five means the goal or target is met, five out of five means you have greatly exceeded your goal, and one out of five means you have fallen short of your goal. On the back of this sheet, draw a general area map of the specific site relative to major roads.*

| Criteria | Target | Actual | Notes | Score |
|---|---|---|---|---|
| Size | _____ sq. ft. | _____ sq. ft | | |
| Monthly rent | $_____/sq. ft. | $_____/sq. ft. | | |
| Monthly common area maintenance (CAM) costs (include property taxes and water, but not electricity) | $_____/sq. ft. | $_____/sq. ft. | | |
| Restrooms (at least one handicapped) | | | | |
| Tenant Improvement Allowance | $_____/sq. ft. | $_____/sq. ft. | | |
| Term | _____ years | _____ years | | |
| Free rent | _____ months minimum and CAM | _____ months minimum and CAM | | |
| Ease of access and parking | | | | |
| Signage | | | | |
| Street visibility | | | | |
| Proximity to coffee competitors (the closer the better) | | | | |
| Closeness to target location (if there is one) | | | | |
| Potential for expansion | | | | |
| Ventilation for roaster (needs roof accessibility) | | | | |
| Storefront (width) | | | | |
| Heating/ventilation/ air conditioning units | Minimum air flow of _____ cubic feet per minute | Air flow of _____ cubic feet per minute | | |
| Proper zoning | | | | |
| Electrical | 200-amp service minimum | | | |
| Neighbors (list all relevant neighbors on back side of list; up to ten points for strong neighbors) | | | | |
| Extra relevant factor (list here): | | | | |
| | | | **Total score for this site:** | |

Completed by:

_____

Date:

_____

Action:

_____ Required soon

_____ Required at your convenience

| Ranking: |
|---|
| _____ of _____ |

city's requirements and the number of seats you want, a second restroom may be required. If you plan on having more than 20 seats, plan to have two restrooms for customer convenience and appeal, whether it is the law or not.

## 3.5 Tenant improvement allowances (TIs)

Tenant improvement allowances (TIS), also referred to as tenant allowances, is the term used to describe monies that a landlord provides to a tenant to improve the site. While TIS are certainly desirable, the most popular sites may not include them. If the site is popular and a landlord has many people bidding on a site, he or she will be less likely to offer TIS. Generally, target at least $20/sq. ft.

Keep in mind that if a landlord offers you money to build or improve your site, it does not necessarily mean that will be the best site for you in the long run. Getting $20,000 up front but losing your entire $250,000 investment does not make good business sense. Having said that, good negotiations usually result in the landlord helping out somehow.

## 3.6 Term

"Term" refers to the term of your lease and can be particularly important if you are planning to sell your business later. Generally, your business will be worth more the more time you have left on your lease, since a buyer will want to be guaranteed of some time to obtain a return on his or her investment. Most leases contain an option to renew, but this does not always ensure that the lease will be renewed and will not convince a buyer to put up a lot of money for a business whose lease is soon up for renewal. As well, renewals almost always mean increased rent rates. Aim for a term of ten years; seven is acceptable.

## 3.7 Free rent

Most landlords will allow a free rent period while you construct your site. At minimum, 30 days' free rent and CAM should be negotiated on a site. Three months' free rent is ideal. Always ask for more free rent than you hope to get. The more desirable the site, the less flexible landlords will be in offering free rent, especially if they think they can get other tenants willing to pay rent right away.

## 3.8 Ease of access

Make sure that the site has easy customer access. Obviously you don't want your customers to have to go through an obstacle course to get to your coffee bar! Unless you will rely completely on walk-by traffic, ensure there is ample parking — most importantly for your customers, but also for you and your staff. If you plan to draw morning commuters or if you plan to have a drive-thru window, remember to locate on the busiest going-to-work side of the street. Draw a map on the back of your checklist showing the site in relation to major roads.

## 3.9 Signage

Check city bylaws for signage restrictions. The research you do now will be important for your negotiations with landlords and will prevent surprises after you open (for example, being told, "You can't put that here," after you've spent $5,000 on a sign for your coffee bar). Check out the signage possibilities of the site, including building sides, awnings, and sign pylons. If you have not done this before, talk to a respected sign company that has put up signs in that area. (Look for a company name on other signs in the area.)

## 3.10 Street visibility

Street visibility is measured by the volume of traffic on the street and the overall visibility of your coffee bar. Make sure the site is visible to your target market, whether drive-by or walk-by. This factor becomes less important, however, with the more emphasis you put on wholesale business. If you plan to get the majority of your income wholesaling, and liquid coffee is a secondary factor, visibility will be less important to you. Many cities have traffic count books that you can access for free or for a small charge. This will allow you to find out vehicle and/or pedestrian traffic numbers for that location. Call your city hall to find out if it provides this information.

## 3.11 Proximity to coffee competitors

Investigate coffee competitors in your area. What are their concepts and how do they compare to yours? Who are their target markets and how do those compare to yours? How are your competitors marketing their business and how do their strategies compare with yours? If you have a strong concept, you may want to be near coffee competitors, since groups of similar businesses are able to "feed off" each other and are stronger together than separately. Food fairs are a good example of this, as are the McDonald's, A&W, Wendy's, and other burger places of the world that are almost always found in a row on a busy street.

## 3.12 Closeness to target location

You may want to be near a particular area for an arbitrary reason, for example, wanting to be within five minutes of your home or wanting to be near the chamber of commerce in your area. If you do not have a target location, score this section a zero each time.

## 3.13 Potential for expansion

Ensure that there is a potential for future expansion. This is important because if you have underestimated the amount of space you require, whether for storage or to accommodate a growing customer base, there is an option available to you other than the very expensive process of relocating.

## 3.14 Ventilation for roaster

If you choose to roast beans, you must ensure that you can properly ventilate the roaster. This means you need easy access to the roof. If you use the hot air roaster, all you will need is a 5- to 9-inch hole for what's called a "Class A" vent. We recommend that you contact a ventilation expert. We have seen some poorly ventilated roasters that have filled the coffee bars with smelly smoke, driving customers away because of the strong smell that roasting produces. For this reason, as well as from an environmental standpoint, we highly recommend that you purchase an afterburner, a gas-burning appliance that takes the exhaust from a roaster and "supercooks" it to make it virtually pollutant-free, eliminating almost all smoke particles and odor. If you use an afterburner, you can be less cautious about where you vent the smoke (e.g., the side versus the roof of the building). Before buying an afterburner, check the manufacturer's customer references.

## 3.15 Storefront

Your storefront is important for visibility. The wider your storefront is and the more glass you have, the better. Corner units can also have some tremendous advantages. Keep in mind that you can usually replace a brick wall with windows quite easily and without huge expense.

## 3.16 Heating, ventilation, and air conditioning units (HVAC)

Check the air flow requirements for the heating, ventilation, and air conditioning units (HVAC). Also, a roaster may require a "make-up" air system that essentially brings in air to replace what you blow up your stack. It is important to know in advance if this may be needed — check with the manufacturer.

Ask the landlord whether the site you are looking at has heating and air conditioning units. If it does not have facilities equal to those of the other potential sites you've looked at, you can reasonably expect the landlord to provide them. For example, if most sites have air conditioning, and the one you're interested in doesn't, it is reasonable to ask the landlord to install air conditioning when you are negotiating the lease.

## 3.17 Zoning

Confirm with your city's zoning department that your type of use is allowed in that area. Many restaurant uses require special zoning permits, a certain thickness of Sheetrock walls, and parking spaces. Check with the city as soon as a site makes your short list.

## 3.18 Electrical

Your electrical needs will be based on the total electrical requirements of all the equipment you plan to use in your coffee bar. You will probably need an electrical system capable of handling at least 200 amps. As you put together your equipment list (see Chapter 6), you will want advice from someone with knowledge in electrical wiring. Ask your local electrician or the leasing agent to help you determine what is available at your site. If you need additional electrical power, you will need to hire an electrician.

## 3.19 Neighbors

List all relevant neighbors — any neighbors whose business has a similar target market as yours (e.g., dry cleaners and physiotherapists) — on the back side of your checklist. Use the city analysis map you made when evaluating this section. Remember, *great* neighbors include the ones we mentioned above: large grocery, toy, and video store chains, as well as businesses targeting women.

The guiding question is, "Can this particular tenant's customers visit that business and my coffee bar easily in the same trip?" Score your neighbors on a scale of one to ten (ten is the highest).

## 3.20 Extras

"Extras" are extra relevant factors — extra bonuses. They might include items such as being next door to a recreation center, across the street from a library, in front of a busy bus stop, next to a busy rapid transit station, near a school, or across from a movie theater.

Do not rescore neighbors that you have already listed, but do score large tenants near but not at the same site. Again, score businesses on a scale of one to ten.

## 3.21 A final word

Don't make a decision because you like the spot. Add up the score of each site evaluation to determine which is the best location. The worst mistake you can make in site selection is getting emotionally attached to any site. This becomes increasingly important in negotiations with landlords. In order to strengthen your negotiating position, you need to be able to walk away from the site. Save the emotion for when you have finally signed the lease that you want.

# 4. EVALUATING THE COMPETITION

## 4.1 Direct competitors

Direct competitors are other coffee bars, coffeehouses, and coffee roasters within your target area that will be competing for the same "coffee dollar." To evaluate the impact these competitors will have on your business, create a reference list of competitors in your local market, like the one below.

Then create a profile of the major competitive advantages each of these operations has. For example:

- Consistently high quality products
- Friendly, efficient, and knowledge-able service
- Clean, friendly environment
- Environmentally and socially responsible bean-buying practices and general corporate philosophies
- Proven successful marketing strategies
- Strong support of a franchise system
- On-site roasting
- Great location

Once you have gathered all the information you can about your competitors, your next step will be to analyze the data. First, look at your competitors' strengths. (For example, are they deeply committed to the environment? Do they have an excellent line of cheesecakes?) What do you like about their concepts and how can you incorporate what you like into your concept?

Are there strengths that you cannot incorporate into your concept, such as location, that you will be directly competing with? If so, what strategies will you use to compete?

Next, look at their weaknesses (e.g., no in-store roasting). What opportunities do you see? What can you do that will be better than your competition?

| Location | Phone | Source of beans | Roasted locally? |
|----------|-------|-----------------|------------------|
| Fred's Café | 555-3123 | ABC Roaster | No |
| Donna's Coffee | 555-8445 | DEF Roaster | Yes |
| Melville's | 555-0161 | GHI Roaster | No |
| Village Market | 555-2030 | JKL Roaster | No |

Your job in analyzing is to sift through the information you have gathered. Throw out what you don't like, consider adding what you do. Do be careful, however, about copying too many elements of a competitor's concept. Look for ways you can be original and do it better.

## 4.2 Indirect competitors

Indirect competitors are any other operations competing for the food and beverage dollar. This includes cafés, donut shops, bagel shops, and cookie shops. As you compile this list, keep in mind that many on this list may be potential wholesale coffee accounts.

Analyze the information you gather by asking yourself the same questions you asked about the direct competition, above.

## 5. EVALUATING THE FINANCIAL VIABILITY OF THE SITE: THE PRO FORMA

To determine what your ongoing operational costs for the site will be, you will need to do a pro forma. A pro forma projects what your profits or losses will be for your business in both the short and long term. It is made up of two parts: income and expenses. Expenses are further broken down into fixed and variable. Sample 3 shows a basic pro forma.

We recommend doing four basic pro formas to reflect pessimistic, projected, optimistic, and break-even sales figures. This gives you the opportunity to examine four different scenarios and analyze how fluctuations in sales influence your bottom line. What kind of sales do you need to break even? To make a profit? What if you don't make those sales? Make sure you

develop an action plan for the pessimistic scenario, especially if you plan to approach a bank or investor for financing. They will want to know how you will cover any cash shortages and what you will do if your projections are wrong.

The easiest way to create a pro forma is to set up a computer spreadsheet on a program such as Excel. (One is available on the CD-ROM accompanying this book.) This will allow you to plug in different numbers for different locations as you go through the site selection process.

A location will greatly influence the pro forma, and we recommend that pro formas be adjusted for every site you consider before you make a final decision. You will want to include variables such as site size, rent, days and hours of operation, and labor costs.

## 5.1 Sales projections

Gross sales figures will be the most difficult to predict, as a location's volume of sales will vary depending on several factors. Generally, coffee bars achieve a sales per square foot total of twice the retail sales average. This means that if a shopping project is performing at $250/sq. ft., a well-run coffee bar in a similar location should perform at $500/sq. ft. Wholesale bean volume can add an additional 10 percent to 30 percent. These figures should be used as a general guideline only. Sales will depend greatly on the site, your product quality and customer service, and most importantly, the strength of your marketing efforts.

What can you do to ensure that your sales projections are as accurate as possible? If you do not have a consulting company or site selection expert to assist you, it takes plenty of old-fashioned research on your

# SAMPLE 3
# PRO FORMA — PROJECTED

## Pro Forma — Projected

| | | | | |
|---|---|---|---|---|
| Square feet | 1,200 | Rent/sq. foot | $19.00 |
| Sales per square foot | $250.00 | CAM/sq. foot | $6.00 |
| Annual sales | $364,500.00 | Product cost | 31.25% |
| Hours open/week | 108 | Promotions | 3.00% |
| Total hourly wage | $12.00 | Advertising | 4.00% |
| Sales per person hour | $27.55 | Inflation | 10.00% |
| Wholesale sales | 25.00% | | |

**YEAR ONE**

| | August | September | October | November | December |
|---|---|---|---|---|---|
| **INCOME** | | | | | |
| Sales — retail | $24,900.13 | $27,450.90 | $24,192.40 | $25,837.50 | $26,266.30 |
| Sales — wholesale roasting | $6,225.00 | $6,862.50 | $6,045.00 | $6,457.50 | $6,352.50 |
| **Total sales** | **$31,125.13** | **$34,313.40** | **$30,237.40** | **$32,295.00** | **$32,618.80** |
| Percent of year | 8.52% | 9.39% | 8.28% | 8.84% | 8.93% |
| Average retail $/day | $803.23 | $915.03 | $780.40 | $861.25 | $847.30 |
| Average # of lbs wholesale/week | 277.90 | 306.36 | 269.87 | 288.28 | 281.35 |
| | | | | | |
| **LESS VARIABLE COSTS** | | | | | |
| Cost of goods | $9,726.59 | $10,722.68 | $9,445.34 | $10,089.87 | $9,925.81 |
| Advertising | 1,245.00 | 1,372.50 | 1,209.00 | 1,291.50 | 1,270.50 |
| Promo | 933.75 | 1,029.38 | 906.75 | 968.63 | 952.88 |
| **LESS FIXED EXPENSES** | | | | | |
| Rent and CAM | $2,500.00 | $2,500.00 | $2,500.00 | $2,500.00 | $2,500.00 |
| Salaries and wages | 5,184.00 | 5,184.00 | 5,184.00 | 5,184.00 | 5,184.00 |
| Management | 2,000.00 | 2,000.00 | 2,000.00 | 2,000.00 | 2,000.00 |
| Legal/audit fees | 25.00 | 25.00 | 25.00 | 25.00 | 25.00 |
| Utilities | 300.00 | 300.00 | 300.00 | 300.00 | 300.00 |
| Telephone | 150.00 | 150.00 | 150.00 | 150.00 | 150.00 |
| Repair and maintenance | 200.00 | 200.00 | 200.00 | 200.00 | 200.00 |
| Licenses and insurance | 125.00 | 125.00 | 125.00 | 125.00 | 125.00 |
| Bank charges | 35.00 | 35.00 | 35.00 | 35.00 | 35.00 |
| Office expenses | 25.00 | 25.00 | 25.00 | 25.00 | 25.00 |
| Accounting fees | 25.00 | 25.00 | 25.00 | 25.00 | 25.00 |
| Security system | 35.00 | 35.00 | 35.00 | 35.00 | 35.00 |
| Cost of money | 900.00 | 900.00 | 900.00 | 900.00 | 900.00 |
| Other operation expenses | 250.00 | 250.00 | 250.00 | 250.00 | 250.00 |
| **TOTAL CASH OUT** | **$23,659.34** | **$24,878.56** | **$23,315.09** | **$24,104.00** | **$23,903.19** |
| | | | | | |
| **NET PROFIT** | **$7,465.79** | **$9,434.84** | **$6,922.31** | **$8,191.00** | **$8,715.61** |
| | | | | | |
| Opening cash balance | $5,000.00 | $12,465.79 | $21,900.63 | $28,822.94 | $37,013.94 |
| Total cash in | $31,125.13 | $34,313.40 | $30,237.40 | $32,295.00 | $32,618.80 |
| **Total cash** | **$36,125.13** | **$46,779.19** | **$52,138.03** | **$61,117.94** | **$69,632.74** |
| Total cash out | $23,659.34 | $24,878.56 | $23,315.09 | $24,104.00 | $23,903.19 |
| **Closing cash balance** | **$12,465.79** | **$21,900.63** | **$28,822.94** | **$37,013.94** | **$45,729.55** |

| January | February | March | April | May | June | July | Total 1st yr |
|---|---|---|---|---|---|---|---|
| $22,289.93 | $20,340.04 | $21,300.10 | $23,715.00 | $26,054.88 | $26,977.50 | $23,160.10 | $292,484.78 |
| $5,572.50 | $5,085.00 | $5,325.00 | $5,928.75 | $6,513.75 | $6,742.50 | $5,790.00 | $72,900.00 |
| $27,862.43 | $25,425.04 | $26,625.10 | $29,643.75 | $32,568.63 | 33,720.00 | $28,950.10 | $365,384.78 |
| 7.63% | 6.96% | 7.29% | 8.11% | 8.91% | 9.23% | 7.92% | |
| $719.03 | $726.43 | $687.10 | $790.50 | $840.48 | $899.25 | $747.10 | |
| 248.77 | 227.01 | 237.72 | 264.68 | 290.79 | 301.00 | 258.48 | |
| | | | | | | | |
| $8,707.05 | $7,945.33 | $8,320.33 | $9,263.70 | $10,177.76 | $10,535.18 | $9,046.90 | $113,906.54 |
| 1,114.50 | 1,017.00 | 1,065.00 | 1,185.75 | 1,302.75 | 1,348.50 | 1,158.00 | 14,580.00 |
| 835.88 | 762.75 | 798.75 | 889.31 | 977.07 | 1,011.38 | 868.50 | 10,935.03 |
| | | | | | | | |
| $2,500.00 | $2,500.00 | $2,500.00 | $2,500.00 | $2,500.00 | $2,500.00 | $2,500.00 | $30,000.00 |
| 5,184.00 | 5,184.00 | 5,184.00 | 5,184.00 | 5,184.00 | 5,184.00 | 5,184.00 | 62,208.00 |
| 2,000.00 | 2,000.00 | 1,500.00 | 1,500.00 | 1,500.00 | 1,500.00 | 1,500.00 | 21,500.00 |
| 25.00 | 25.00 | 25.00 | 25.00 | 25.00 | 25.00 | 25.00 | 300.00 |
| 300.00 | 300.00 | 300.00 | 300.00 | 300.00 | 300.00 | 300.00 | 3,600.00 |
| 150.00 | 150.00 | 150.00 | 150.00 | 150.00 | 150.00 | 150.00 | 1,800.00 |
| 200.00 | 200.00 | 200.00 | 200.00 | 200.00 | 200.00 | 200.00 | 2,400.00 |
| 125.00 | 125.00 | 125.00 | 125.00 | 125.00 | 125.00 | 125.00 | 1,500.00 |
| 35.00 | 35.00 | 35.00 | 35.00 | 35.00 | 35.00 | 35.00 | 420.00 |
| 25.00 | 25.00 | 25.00 | 25.00 | 25.00 | 25.00 | 25.00 | 300.00 |
| 25.00 | 25.00 | 25.00 | 25.00 | 25.00 | 25.00 | 25.00 | 300.00 |
| 35.00 | 35.00 | 35.00 | 35.00 | 35.00 | 35.00 | 35.00 | 420.00 |
| 900.00 | 900.00 | 900.00 | 900.00 | 900.00 | 900.00 | 900.00 | 10,800.00 |
| 250.00 | 250.00 | 250.00 | 250.00 | 250.00 | 250.00 | 250.00 | 3,000.00 |
| $22,411.43 | $21,479.08 | $21,438.08 | $22,592.76 | $23,711.58 | $24,149.06 | $22,327.40 | $277,969.57 |
| | | | | | | | |
| $5,451.00 | $3,945.96 | $5,187.02 | $7,050.99 | $8,857.05 | $9,570.94 | $6,622.70 | $87,415.21 |
| | | | | | | | |
| $45,729.55 | $51,180.55 | $55,126.51 | $60,313.53 | $67,364.52 | $76,221.57 | $85,792.51 | |
| 27,862.43 | 25,425.04 | 26,625.10 | 29,643.75 | 32,568.63 | 33,720.00 | 28,950.10 | |
| $73,591.98 | $76,605.59 | $81,751.61 | $89,957.28 | $99,933.15 | $109,941.57 | $114,742.61 | |
| 22,411.43 | 21,479.08 | 21,438.08 | 22,592.76 | 23,711.58 | 24,149.06 | 22,327.40 | |
| $51,180.55 | $55,126.51 | $60,313.53 | $67,364.52 | $76,221.57 | $85,792.51 | $92,415.21 | |

| YEAR TWO Aug–Oct | Nov–Jan | Feb–April | May–July | YEAR THREE Aug–July | YEAR FOUR Aug–July | YEAR FIVE Aug–July |
|---|---|---|---|---|---|---|
| $78,177.00 | $82,533.00 | $85,206.00 | $74,844.00 | $441,045.00 | $485,149.50 | $533,644.45 |
| $19,544.25 | $20,633.25 | $21,301.50 | $18,711.00 | $110,261.25 | $121,287.38 | $133,416.11 |
| **$97,721.25** | **$103,166.25** | **$106,507.50** | **$93,555.00** | **$551,306.25** | **$606,436.88** | **$667,060.56** |
| | | | | | | |
| $849.75 | $897.10 | $936.33 | $822.46 | $1,208.34 | $1,329.18 | $1,462.09 |
| 872.51 | 921.13 | 950.96 | 835.31 | 4,922.38 | 5,414.61 | 5,956.08 |
| | | | | | | |
| $30,537.89 | $32,239.45 | $33,283.59 | $29,235.94 | $172,283.20 | $189,511.52 | $208,462.68 |
| 3,908.85 | 4,126.65 | 4,260.30 | 3,742.20 | 22,052.25 | 24,257.48 | 26,683.22 |
| 2,931.64 | 3,094.99 | 3,195.23 | 2,806.65 | 16,539.19 | 18,193.11 | 20,012.42 |
| | | | | | | |
| $7,680.00 | $7,680.00 | $7,680.00 | $7,680.00 | $31,512.00 | $32,383.20 | $32,383.20 |
| 17,107.20 | 17,107.20 | 17,107.20 | 17,107.20 | 70,139.52 | 77,153.47 | 84,868.82 |
| 6,000.00 | 6,000.00 | 6,000.00 | 6,000.00 | 24,000.00 | 24,000.00 | 24,000.00 |
| 82.50 | 82.50 | 82.50 | 82.50 | 338.25 | 372.08 | 409.28 |
| 990.00 | 990.00 | 990.00 | 990.00 | 4,059.00 | 4,464.90 | 4,911.39 |
| 495.00 | 495.00 | 495.00 | 495.00 | 2,029.50 | 2,232.45 | 2,455.70 |
| 660.00 | 660.00 | 660.00 | 660.00 | 2,706.00 | 2,976.60 | 3,274.26 |
| 412.50 | 412.50 | 412.50 | 412.50 | 1,691.25 | 1,860.38 | 2,046.41 |
| 115.50 | 115.50 | 115.50 | 115.50 | 473.55 | 520.91 | 573.00 |
| 82.50 | 82.50 | 82.50 | 82.50 | 338.25 | 372.08 | 409.28 |
| 82.50 | 82.50 | 82.50 | 82.50 | 338.25 | 372.08 | 409.28 |
| 105.00 | 105.00 | 105.00 | 105.00 | 420.00 | 420.00 | 420.00 |
| 2,700.00 | 2,700.00 | 2,700.00 | 2,700.00 | 10,800.00 | 10,800.00 | 10,800.00 |
| 825.00 | 825.00 | 825.00 | 825.00 | 3,382.50 | 3,720.75 | 4,092.83 |
| **$74,716.08** | **$76,798.79** | **$78,076.82** | **$73,122.49** | **$363,102.71** | **$393,611.01** | **$426,211.77** |
| | | | | | | |
| **$23,005.17** | **$26,367.46** | **$28,430.68** | **$20,432.51** | **$188,203.54** | **$212,825.87** | **$240,848.79** |
| | | | | | | |
| $54,249.86 | $77,255.03 | $103,622.49 | $132,053.17 | $152,485.68 | $340,689.22 | $553,515.09 |
| $97,721.25 | $103,166.25 | $106,507.50 | $93,555.00 | $551,306.25 | $606,436.88 | $667,060.56 |
| **$151,971.11** | **$180,421.28** | **$210,129.99** | **$225,608.17** | **$703,791.93** | **$947,126.10** | **$1,220,575.65** |
| $74,716.08 | $76,798.79 | $78,076.82 | $73,122.49 | $363,102.71 | $393,611.01 | $426,211.77 |
| **$77,255.03** | **$103,622.49** | **$132,053.17** | **$152,485.68** | **$340,689.22** | **$553,515.09** | **$794,363.88** |

part. You will want to start off by spending lots of time in your competitors' shops around town. Count customers. Examine traffic flow patterns. Watch the purchases that are being made. Estimate average checks (the amount of money the average customer spends). Compare pricing strategies. Spend some time in the library researching newspaper and magazine articles on coffee bars — they often mention gross sales figures. You can often get a pretty good idea of the sales a competitor is doing in a particular spot.

You will also need to research the specific sites you are considering:

- Do drive-by and walk-by traffic counts.

- Evaluate drive-by and walk-by traffic patterns and flows during a day and over a week.

- Research population demographics in the area and compare them to those of your target market.

- Research competitors in the area.

- Examine affiliated businesses that you will be able to market with.

In projecting sales figures, you will need to take into consideration —

(a) how much marketing you are planning to do before opening,

(b) how much marketing you plan to do once you are open,

(c) how much money you are planning on setting aside for your marketing efforts,

(d) how good your marketing calendar is (see Chapter 16),

(e) how comprehensive your marketing strategies are, and

(f) how aggressively you plan to implement your marketing strategies.

Once you have projected your income, your next task will be to determine expenses.

## 5.2 Food and paper costs

The biggest cost you will have is food and paper. Your food and paper costs are reflected in the actual cost of the "food" (e.g., the coffee) and the "paper" (e.g., cups, lids, stir sticks) you deliver to your customer. Because coffee is so cheap (only seven to ten cents per cup), many people are lulled into a false sense of security when looking at the food cost of a coffee bar. They forget to take into consideration that there is more than just the coffee to consider — there is the cup and lid, the cream and sugar, and the napkins and stir sticks.

Your food cost percentage will depend on a number of factors, one being your ability to manage your business and control your expenses. We have known some operations to drop their food cost by as much as 7 percent, just by changing managers. While 7 percent may not sound like a huge drop, it can translate into hundreds, if not thousands, of dollars in savings every month. Most coffee bars operate with a food cost of between 25 percent to 35 percent of their sales.

When determining food and paper costs, you should also consider where you will do the bulk of your business. For example, if you plan that 50 percent of your business will be roasting green beans and selling them wholesale, with a food cost of 50 percent, your food cost will be dramatically different than John down the street who is doing 75 percent of his business in liquid coffee with a food cost of 17 percent. Keep in mind that just because you sell more in an area with a lesser food cost, that doesn't necessarily mean you will profit more. Many people make the mistake of thinking that if they focus only on liquid coffee (which has a higher profit margin than a pound of beans) they will make more money. This is not necessarily true. If you get only two customers a day, you are making a lot less money than if you land a large hotel coffee account and make only small margins. Make sure you keep your projections in perspective.

## 5.3 Labor costs

Your second largest cost after food and paper will be labor. During the initial stage of operation, we recommend staffing on the up-side as opposed to the lean-side. This is for a number of reasons. The first is that, while customer service will always be vital to the success of your business, during the first few weeks you are open it will be more than vital. This is because the first few customers will build on the next few customers, and if you lose any of them for any reason — poor service, for example — that base will be more difficult to build.

The second reason is that despite your incredible preparatory efforts, you may have missed something (heaven forbid); by being slightly overstaffed, overcoming a challenge becomes a minor inconvenience rather than a major upheaval resulting in poor service or poor products. If you run out of milk, you can send the extra staff member out to pick some up without disrupting the flow of customer service. If you have to send someone out when you don't have enough staff, you will be left short-staffed and may give your customers poor service.

By staffing on the up-side, you are free to act as the official public relations person who can give your customers that extra special attention that only an owner can give. This helps build the foundation of a solid business.

Coffee bars typically have high labor productivity, known as sales per person hour (SPPH), especially when compared to other fast-food establishments. While a fast-food restaurant usually has an SPPH of $20 to $30, coffee bars can often sustain SPPH of $40 to $50.

To calculate the approximate staffing hours you will require, divide your projected sales by the estimated SPPH for the number of staffing hours needed for that day. Check with your local employment standards branch for minimum shifts. Generally, a minimum shift ranges from two hours for a student to four hours for part-time staff. See Chapter 15 for a discussion on determining staff wages.

## 5.4 Advertising and promotions

We recommend you budget at least 3 percent for local marketing and 2 percent for promotions in ongoing, established operations.

## 5.5 Rent and common area maintenance (CAM)

Rent and common area maintenance costs will vary significantly from site to site. Target sites of 1,500 sq. ft., $19/sq. ft. rent, and $6/sq. ft. CAM (operating costs) mean a monthly combined rent and CAM of $3,125 (1,500 x [$19 + $6] ÷ 12 because the $19/sq. ft. is the cost per year).

## 5.6 Maintenance and repair/electricity

You should usually budget 0.5 percent for maintenance and repair costs and $350 to $400 per month for electricity.

## 5.7 Miscellaneous

Office expenses, permits, licenses, uniforms, and insurance typically run a total of $150 to $250 per month.

## 5.8 Cost of money

The cost of money refers to interest and other financing charges you pay each month to your investors and your bank.

## 5.9 Sign leases

Include the cost of your sign leases, if applicable.

# 6. MAKING AN OFFER

As soon as you have reduced your 20 locations to a shortlist of the four or five best ones, you will want to begin putting in your offers on the leases. Should you use a commercial realtor for this process?

Generally, commercial realtors get paid a percentage of the amount of rent you pay over the term of your lease. This means they may not be very motivated to get you the best deal possible because as the rent drops, so does their commission. However, if you are unsure of the process and don't have access to a knowledgeable consultant who can help you, realtors are an option. To find a good realtor, call the biggest commercial leasing office in town and ask for one of their best agents.

A good commercial lawyer can be helpful in drafting your specific offer. One word of caution: if you do employ a lawyer, do not rely on him or her for site selection assistance unless he or she specializes in coffee bar site selection. While a lawyer may have an opinion on a site, by the time you have researched your concept, finalized your business plan details, and gone through a 20-location site selection process, you will likely be in a much better position than your lawyer to comment on the validity of a site.

Always submit offers on each of your four or five best sites, even if you have already found one to be clearly superior. This does two things:

(a) It gives you strength in negotiating (you can always walk away because there is another site available).

(b) It reduces the odds that you will make an irrational site decision because you will have other sites as a comparison.

In your offer to lease, insert a list of items you would like the landlord to supply, for example, completed washrooms, a rooftop vent opening for a roaster, and a smooth concrete floor. The theory behind a list is that most landlords will scratch off some items, but will be less likely to scratch them all off. The end result is that you can often get not only what you want but some bonuses as well. Don't go overboard with your list, though, as it may end up undermining your negotiating position.

Be sure to include an exclusive use clause, which states that the landlord may not lease space within the same building to another tenant whose primary use is the sale of steam-processed coffee and whole beans; a rent-free clause, stating the length of time you have rent free; and a clause giving your business patio access and approval to use a sidewalk "sandwich board" signage, subject to city hall approval.

As well, be sure to include a clause about tenant improvements, stating the amount the landlord will give you for improvements.

## 7. HOW TO NEGOTIATE YOUR LEASE — STRATEGIES THAT CAN SAVE YOU THOUSANDS OF DOLLARS

The goal of your negotiations is to create a win-win situation for both you and the landlord. You will have achieved this when —

- both sides feel a sense of accomplishment,
- both sides feel the other side cared,
- both sides feel the other side was fair,
- each side would deal again with the other, and
- each side feels the other side will keep the bargain.

In creating this win-win situation, you will need to understand what it is that your landlord wants. Different people want different things and price is not always all-important. For example, a landlord may want a strong tenant in the spot so that he or she doesn't have to go through the lengthy and expensive (through revenue-loss) process of re-leasing the spot. On the other hand, the landlord may be more interested in getting the maximum rent

dollar for the space, regardless of tenant strength.

You may want to consider hiring a consultant to negotiate your lease for you. More often than not, a good lease negotiator will not only save you money but also make you money in the process. Why? Good lease negotiators know what to ask for, when to ask for it, and when to walk away. They will also be familiar with the "fine print" and hidden landlord-protection clauses that can catch you unawares.

If you choose to go about it on your own, here are some tips and techniques used by good lease-negotiators that will help you in your negotiation efforts:

- Don't negotiate on the phone — it is difficult to communicate clearly.

- Try to reduce the amount of pressure you are under (e.g., by having flexible opening dates targeted). In negotiating, the person under the greatest time pressure generally loses.

- If you do have a time deadline, don't reveal that you do.

- Make a big deal of any concession you make, and get a counter-concession for doing so ("I'll do this, but what are you going to do in return?").

- Make your opening offer on the low side, but not so low that it only serves to anger your opponent.

- Make your offer flexible.

- Never say "yes" to the first counter-offer.

- Never be the one to offer to "split the difference" — get your opponent to make the offer to you and then split the difference.

- Never leave the details until later. Deal with them now and in writing.

- Always maintain your "walk away power."

- Don't overnegotiate. The last thing you want to do is frustrate the people you are negotiating with to the point where they throw their hands up and walk away. If you become too much of a nuisance to deal with, the landlord may decide to go with someone else who is less trouble. The other thing to keep in mind is that every day you extend the negotiating process is a day gone by that you could have been selling coffee to customers and making money.

## 8. THE KEY CONSIDERATION IN MAKING YOUR FINAL SITE DECISION

By the time you have completed your site selection criteria checklist, and are ready to start submitting offers and negotiating the leases, it will probably be apparent which site is the best one for you. If this hasn't happened and you're still having a tough time deciding, your final site decision should be based on this question: Is this the best available site, one that provides me with the greatest opportunity to reach my target audience and provides my target audience with the greatest opportunity to reach me when I give them a reason to do so?

---

# COMMITMENT BOX

I, _____, commit to completing site selection criteria checklists for at least 20 sites in my target area.

_____      _____
*(your signature)*                *(today's date)*

---

# 5
# DESIGNING YOUR OWN STORE

*Always do your best. What you plant now, you will harvest later.*

— OG MANDINO

## 1. CREATING YOUR BUSINESS'S IDENTITY

Your business's identity is its "real image." This identity is what you stand for, what you're all about, and part of what your customers will love — or leave — you for. In establishing an identity for your coffee bar, keep in mind this key question: What identity will appeal to your customer profile? There are two important areas you must consider in creating your identity: the look of your coffee bar and the look of your staff.

If you buy a franchise, you may not have any decision-making power in these areas. However, reading this chapter will allow you to evaluate the job your franchisor has done with its design and identity. If you have already chosen or purchased a franchise, reading this chapter may give you some good ideas to recommend to head office.

If you buy an existing business, you will need to evaluate the advantages and disadvantages of redesigning the coffee bar — perhaps you will not want to remodel the interior but will instead focus on staff uniforms, new furniture, and redesigned signage. Many options are available to you — read on.

## 2. YOUR COFFEE BAR'S LOOK

How will you convey your image to your customers through the look of the coffee bar? Do you want:

- Bright or dark surroundings?
- Cozy or cool?
- Contemporary or art deco?
- Large or small?
- Loud or soft?

You may decide to use a design or motifs native to a country from which you will be getting one of your coffees. For example, if you choose Mexico, you could feature a sandy-colored tile floor, lots of terra cotta, and colorful Mexican hats and blankets. Whatever you decide, make sure your coffee bar's look will appeal to the market you are targeting.

Retail store designers can be hired to help you create your coffee bar's look. Keep in mind, however, that experts don't come cheap. You will want to examine the work of a number of designers and ask for detailed proposals before making a final decision. In the end, if you have a flair for colors and are able to do research on design by reading books and visiting other coffee bars, restaurants, and retail stores, you may find that you are better off taking the money that would be spent on a designer and putting it toward your marketing fund instead.

Once you have decided on your target market and the general look of your coffee bar, start to refine and fine-tune your ideas as you settle on design elements for your coffee bar. Checklist 2 at the end of this chapter is a checklist of layout and design elements, as well as equipment, that you should consider when developing your identity and drawing plans for your coffee bar. The items on the checklist are discussed below. Use the checklist as you work on your floor plans and order equipment, furniture, and decorating supplies.

We recommend that you also read Chapter 6 before you begin to plan your design, as it discusses several decisions to be made about smaller items that may affect your overall design.

## 2.1 Interior design

Although details such as the color of paint on the walls and the type of table you will use are those that are put into place after you have drawn up your floor layout plans, you should have a clear sense of how you want your coffee bar to look and the image you want it to convey as you choose the major equipment you will need and draw up the floor plans.

### 2.1a Walls

Stay away from green walls. Studies have shown that green has negative food associations (for instance, green mold!). There are many more appetite-enhancing colors from which you can choose.

Dark colors will create a completely different atmosphere in your coffee bar than will light colors, especially if you have large, unbroken sections of wall that require repair. We prefer lighter shades of earth tones for wall color.

You may wish to contract a faux finisher to create a unique wall design that is difficult for your competition to duplicate. Wainscoting and decorative borders on walls have become popular and can add a dimension of depth to your coffee bar. A high-quality wallpaper is usually not as cost-effective as painting and is more costly to repair or replace.

You might also want to consider slat wall areas for shelving — a good idea for displaying merchandise such as coffee makers and coffee mugs.

Don't forget about the ceiling. An open ceiling painted black often works well. If the coffee bar is small or dark already, though, a lighter color will help make it feel more open. Also consider specific design features such as drop ceilings over counter areas.

### 2.1b Flooring

After owning a store with hardwood floors for a couple of years, we lean toward floor tiles as the best flooring option. Hardwood flooring requires much care and attention and can warp over time, especially if moisture is present.

Carpets are difficult to clean well and quickly become soiled, especially in a coffee bar where food and coffee spills are a daily part of life.

Tiles, on the other hand, are a more permanent option that should serve you well over the long term. Provided the tiles are of good quality, chipping shouldn't be a problem, and a good mopping generally gets them clean. Tiles come in a multitude of different shapes, colors, and sizes, with accompanying differences in price. We recommend speckled tiles as they don't show dirt as much as solid-colored tiles will. A recent trend worth looking at is something called acid-etched floors. Though not cheaper than tile, they have an interesting look, and are easy to maintain.

Don't forget about the kickguard at the counter. You can use either tiles, run up the first foot or two of the counter wall, or a good quality rubber. If you use rubber, a small kickguard is best; anything higher than 5 inches high is overpowering. Incorporate the kickguard into your color scheme.

### 2.1c Lighting

Stay away from fluorescent lights, as they cast a harsh light and can cause headaches

and eye soreness. For evening, "comfortable" lighting is recommended — not dark and gloomy, but soft enough to create a cozy glow and bright enough to read by. Of course, the light fixtures you choose will depend on your personal taste, design, and budget.

We recommend you use as much natural lighting as possible. However, extra windows and skylights can create extra heat in the coffee bar; unless you have a good air conditioning system, the extra heat can cause an uncomfortable work environment.

Determine whether window coverings such as curtains and blinds are necessary; if they are, make sure they match your color scheme. Curtains can have a softening effect; the effect of blinds is cooler, but they are also easier to clean.

Window ledges are another option to consider. Can you use them for some functional purpose?

### 2.1d Entrance door

Carefully choose your entrance door, making sure it fits with your image. Do you want a wood or glass door? Again, match it to your color scheme. Consider design features such as logos etched on wood.

### 2.1e Tables

We recommend a table height of 32 inches. This is the most comfortable table height and most chairs fit it well. Again, the color and finish is your choice, but it should match the rest of your decor. Tables should be laminated on the top, bottom, and sides to prevent expansion and contraction.

There are two basic choices for the support of the table: a nonadjustable table base, or an adjustable base, which will allow you to adjust the table to different levels should you need to.

Look for tables that are easy to clean and repair. Black table bases are easy to touch up with paint when they get scuffed and scratched.

### 2.1f Stand-up bar

The stand-up bar or counter is usually 36 or 42 inches high. Height is a design decision (e.g., if your space has a low ceiling you should have a lower stand-up bar height), but in communities where stand-up bars are uncommon, a lower height can be an easier "transition" for customers unfamiliar with the concept.

You will need to support the bar with either angle iron or poles. Medite (heavy-duty particle board) is a good choice of construction material, since it will not sag.

You will need to laminate the bar or counter on both the top and bottom to prevent expansion and contraction. The color and type of lamination is your choice; match with the rest of your decor.

### 2.1g Seating

The type of seating you have will depend to a large extent on your concept (e.g., coffeehouse versus coffee bar). Comfortable sofas with low coffee tables will appeal to the group that wants to sit back, relax, and enjoy some good conversation and your great coffee. Small, hard-back or no-back stools or chairs will encourage shorter visits, which may be a plus if you plan to run a high volume take-out operation.

Whichever option you choose, you are probably best off making your purchases through a furniture wholesaler, although sometimes good deals can be had from large chain stores.

When buying chairs, check on the long-term availability of the style you choose; your seating will require replacing at some time. If you are using put-together-yourself wooden chairs, for example, they will probably need replacing every couple of years. Also, you'll want to make sure that the seats are easy to clean, resistant to scuff marks (especially from customers' shoes), and that you have some way of making touch-ups (e.g., with paint).

Look for height, back support, and comfort when you are purchasing chairs. The chairs should fit the table height, and the stools the stand-up bar. Chairs with a good back support promote longer comfort. Curved back support is more comfortable. Stay away from cushioned chairs, as they are extremely difficult to clean.

Consider also the chairs' movement along the floor. To prevent scratching a tile floor, stick felt circles under the chair legs.

### 2.1h Signage

The major outside sign you choose will depend on city bylaws, building requirements, and, of course, your budget. Make sure its color, design, and logo are consistent with your image. If possible, include your USP on the sign. The sign should be visible to both walk-by and drive-by traffic.

Make use of any other potential outdoor sign space; possibilities include pylons, signs at the sides of your building, and sidewalk signs. (Sandwich boards are good for getting walk-by attention.) Most additional signage will be negotiated as part of your lease.

Window signs should be visible to both walk-by and drive-by traffic. Ideally, signs should be at eye level for pedestrians, unless that obstructs the view of your customers at the stand-up bar inside.

The color, design, and logo should all reinforce the image and design you are creating for your coffee bar. Use the same fonts for the lettering on your window signs, on your major outside sign, and in other places, such as on business cards and stationery.

### 2.1i Design extras

Consider including your coffee bar's name and logo on walls, tables, chairs, or worked into the floor design.

Statues are a great idea as long as their color and style match the decor. Posters and pictures should be framed properly and suit your concept. Some beautiful coffee-related posters are available.

Live plants will also look great in your coffee bar; use them to fill an empty space, block an unsightly area, or separate seating sections within your coffee bar. They can be hung from the ceiling, too. Choose a plant type that requires low maintenance.

Make sure your design extras complement your decor and appeal to the customers you are trying to attract.

## 2.2 Major equipment

When purchasing equipment, keep in mind several things: the electrical requirements for the particular piece of equipment, the warranty offered on it, the ease of servicing, and your budget. The color, size, and style should all fit with your coffee bar's decor.

### 2.2a Food display cases

The type of food display case you choose — floor model, cooler, or countertop — will depend on your storage requirements and the amount of space you have. Individually covered countertop displays, such as large plates with glass or plastic covers, work well, as do jars.

Should your display case be glass or plastic? Glass is much more scratch-resistant.

If you are buying a refrigerated display case, make sure you get one that doesn't condense on the inside. You will be forever wiping it, and customers won't be able to see the goods inside. A display case that circulates air flow on the front of the glass ensures no condensation.

### 2.2b Cooler

Will you need a cooler to display pop and cold drinks? Pop will likely not be a big part of your business; spending a few thousand dollars to purchase a cooler specifically for pop does not make economic sense; on the other hand, some type of cooler will be necessary to store milk, fruits and vegetables (if you are juicing), and cookie and muffin dough (if you are doing your own baking).

The size and type depends on your storage needs and budget. If the cooler will be in view of customers, a glass cooler with two sliding doors can be blocked off in the middle so that cold drinks are displayed on one side while the other side is used for storage.

Is the cooler easy to service? Look for a cooler with a top-mounted compressor; this kind of compressor has to work less and lasts longer.

### 2.2c Milk fridge

Do you need a milk fridge? Unless the espresso machine is close to the cooler where milk can be stored, you will need one. A small, undercounter or countertop model is usually sufficient.

Electrical requirements need to be considered at this stage of planning.

### 2.2d Freezer

As with the cooler and milk fridge, the size and type of freezer will depend on your storage needs and budget. Stand-ups are a more efficient use of space and are generally a commercial grade in quality (i.e., they're heavy duty), and therefore cost more than chest freezers. Chest freezers are the typical home freezer and, being wider, use more space.

Will you need a separate ice cream freezer? Think about building one right into the counter. This often works well. It must be easy for staff to access and easy for customers to see ice creams displayed inside. A glass front is best.

### 2.2e Prep area equipment (ovens)

The prep area is the area in which food is prepared. The specific tasks that are done here depend on what product lines you will be carrying. However, you will likely need a microwave. If you think you will use the microwave quite often, buy a good quality microwave.

Will you need a convection oven or a toaster? Again, the quality of equipment you buy depends on how often you will use it.

### 2.2f Automatic dishwasher

A high-temperature model of automatic dishwasher is the best and the fastest model of dishwasher. We recommend Hobart models.

Drainage and electrical needs for the dishwasher must be considered as you design your coffee bar's layout. Don't forget to look at the warranties and servicing.

### 2.2g Espresso machine

We suggest you buy an automatic or semi-automatic espresso machine. Check out a variety of models (we discuss different espresso systems in Chapter 11) and buy one you find easy to use. Don't let an equipment salesperson talk you into buying two machines. It's a waste of your money — one will work fine.

The ease of servicing the machine is an important aspect; check with your suppliers about local support (e.g., parts availability, how many service people are available, what hours they work, and how easy it is to get help during an emergency).

### 2.2h Brewing system

We discuss brewing systems in detail in Chapter 10 but, briefly, we recommend a system that brews coffee into thermal carafes, keeping it fresh and hot for up to three hours. The best we've found are called Cafe Barista by Newco. Contact suppliers' existing customers to make sure they are happy with their equipment.

### 2.2i Batch grinders

Batch grinders are commercial coffee grinders that can grind predetermined amounts of coffee (usually set for one pot). You will want two batch grinders, one for flavored coffee and one for unflavored coffee. A less expensive model may be used for flavored coffee, since it won't be used as often as the grinder for unflavored coffee. As usual, check out warranties, support, and customer satisfaction with each potential supplier.

### 2.2j Scales

You will need scales to weigh roasted beans to use in the brewing system and to weigh green beans for sale. Make sure the weighing basket shape makes it easy for you to pour beans into the batch grinder or take-home bag. The scale you buy must be certified "For legal tender."

Many scales have electrical requirements, although some are battery operated. Map any electrical requirements into your floor plan.

## 2.3 Layout

### 2.3a Main serving counter

It is important to consider carefully the location of the main serving counter in your coffee bar. It should be placed in such a way as to create good traffic flow. The number of serving counters you have is a function of both design and estimated volume, but coffee bars generally have one main serving counter. The shape can be either curved or straight.

A counter height of 36 or 42 inches is average. A counter that's 42 inches high will give you storage space underneath, but will cut staff off from customers somewhat.

The color, type of lamination, and trim is your choice: match it to your decor. You may want to try wood or brushed metal trims.

Serving counters can be modified to incorporate major pieces of equipment, such as display cases or lighting systems.

They can also be modified to incorporate specific serving requirements. A money exchange station, for example, can be built right into the counter so that it doesn't stick out and interfere with customer service.

When designing the counter area, consider the location and size of the espresso machine. Ensure there is enough space for staff to work around it and enough serving space on at least one side so that customers can easily pick up their orders. It should also be easy for staff to take drinks from the espresso machine to customers in the seating area if necessary.

It is important to consider the location of your brewing system and batch grinder in the counter area at this stage in your planning, as you will need to allow for the electrical and plumbing requirements. The brewing system, batch grinder, and scales should be close together and easy for staff to access. The brewing system should be near the coffee dispensers.

The coffee dispensers can be placed on a lowered shelf in the counter so that coffee can be poured without the staff having to turn their backs on the customers and without the carafes sticking up so high that customers and staff have to stand on their tip toes to look over them.

Scales should be near the roasted bean storage area and the grinder/brewing system. A scale for green beans should be as close to the green bean display as possible.

### 2.3b Counter area exit/entrance areas

You should close off the entrance to the kitchen or back storage area with either a full or half door.

### 2.3c Money exchange station

You can buy either a computerized register or a traditional cash register. We recommend a computer with customized software if you can afford it; electrical requirements include a dedicated power source (this is critical). Make sure you get a surge-protector if you use a computerized register. (Chapter 15 discusses the pros and cons of cash registers and computers.)

Decide if you want the cash drawer to be part of the cash register or built into the counter, and whether you need a second phone line for a modem so you can access store sales figures from your home computer.

### 2.3d Baking areas and prep areas

As mentioned above, the prep area is the area where food is prepared. When designing the layout of both your prep and baking areas, keep convenience in mind. These areas must be designed so they are easy to work at and easy to clean. They should be as large as necessary to meet the needs of product lines you and your staff will be preparing.

Design as much shelving and cupboard space as size permits; be sure that all shelves and cupboards are properly labeled.

### 2.3e Juice station

If you plan to offer fresh juices, you will need a juicing station. It should be close to the fruits and vegetables in the fridge or freezer. Make sure that it doesn't interfere with other staff activities — staff shouldn't be bumping into each other.

### 2.3f Roasted coffee service area

You will need an area to store and wholesale coffee pouches, labels, and pens with which to prepare customers' orders. These should be stored for easy access near the coffee grinder, scale, and roaster.

### 2.3g Cream and sugar station

The cream and sugar station can be positioned either on the counter or on top of a free-standing structure, but it must be easily accessible to both staff and customers, consistent with the traffic flow in your coffee bar. To be traffic-flow friendly, place it on the right side as your customer would leave the coffee bar area.

The station must be designed to prevent lineups; it should be easy for more than one customer to use at one time.

Its height should be the same as your stand-up bars — 36 or 42 inches.

Consider special design features such as a garbage can hole cut into the center. Make sure the station is finished properly and easy to clean. Its kickguard color and height should also match the decor.

### 2.3h Roasting station/ green bean display

Your roasting station should be highly visible, as it will be a draw for customers. Put it at the front, facing the high traffic area in your coffee bar. Elevating it is a nice design feature.

The color, trim, and type of finishing is your choice to match the rest your decor. The roasting station should also have a kickguard, whose color and height should match the rest your decor.

Don't forget about the electrical or gas needs of and proper ventilation for your roaster and afterburner.

Display the green beans in a highly visible, high-traffic area too — as near the roaster as possible, and also near the scale for ease of weighing.

You may want to add wall displays providing information on the country in which the beans originated.

### 2.3i Merchandising areas

Both racks and shelves can work well; antique shelving units are an option if that fits with your image. The size of your merchandising area depends on the amount of merchandise you have and the amount of merchandising you want to do. Again, color should fit your decor.

Whether you choose to finish the racks or shelves with paint or laminate, pick something that won't show dust and is easy to clean. Extra shelves around the coffee bar are great as mini-merchandisers.

### 2.3j Storage areas

Storage areas should be convenient for the staff to access and easy to work in, if necessary. The size of your storage area depends on your product line.

It is a good idea to have locks on the doors and cupboards. Design this area with as much inside shelving and cupboard space as possible to maximize usage, and make sure that all shelves and cupboards are properly labeled.

### 2.3k Dishwashing area

Make sure this area is convenient for your staff, whether they are dropping off dirty dishes or retrieving and putting away clean ones. It should be shielded from your customer area; your patrons don't want to listen to the dishwasher going through its cycles! This area should be near the storage cupboards for your dishes.

### 2.3l Sinks

You may require a number of sinks in your coffee bar; how many and which ones will be determined partly by your city's health code. Most city health departments require triple sinks. If so, check what type of seam welds are acceptable.

The health department usually sets a particular location for the hand sinks; this is almost always close to food prep areas, but check with the department before you finalize your plans.

A particular location for mop sinks may also be required by the health department.

### 2.3m Restrooms

The local health department will likely also set requirements for the size of the restrooms. Find out what the rules are before you finalize your design.

Don't forget about the accessories. Mirrors are always a good idea; make sure they are securely mounted. Equip the bathroom with toilet paper and hand towel dispensers — they are easy for customers to use. Coordinate the bathroom's color and style to match the rest of your coffee bar.

Garbage cans with swinging tops that hide the contents are best. Plastic containers are easy to clean; tin or metal will eventually rust.

Consider a water-saving toilet and faucets. Your hot water tank should hold sufficient water for your entire coffee bar (minimum 25 gallons).

Don't forget about the door knobs. Make sure they lock. (You will also need locks on office and storage room doors.)

### 2.3n Electrical panels

Your electrical panels must be clearly marked. Make sure you have clear instructions for staff in case a breaker trips. Breakers are not designed to be turned on and off, so try to have all items that are turned off at night on switches.

### 2.3o Patio

Elevated patios are often a nice design feature, so consider adding one of these to your site if it is possible. Hardy, low-maintenance trees or plants are a great idea, but take into consideration changing weather conditions.

Will you allow outside smoking? Bylaws in many cities now prohibit smoking inside food establishments, and a patio may be the only place a smoker can go. If you do allow smoking, make sure you provide enough ashtrays to meet demand, and keep them clean.

Patio furniture should be easy to clean and durable. If you are purchasing umbrellas, consider color, design, maintenance, and durability. Avoid free umbrellas that endorse someone else's product — you want to promote your image, not someone else's.

### 2.3p Office area

If you want to have your office area at the coffee bar rather than at your home, account for this in your design. (A home office is best if you plan to be an absentee owner.)

You may want to design your office differently (e.g., carpeted, different colors) than the rest of the coffee bar, since this is personal space that won't be part of your customers' experience.

The size of your office depends on the coffee bar size and space available; keep in mind that an office won't sell any coffee or seat any customers.

The office door should be lockable, especially if money will be stored there at any time.

### 2.3q General security

Peep holes in the delivery doors at back are a great idea. Doorbells are not necessary in a properly staffed and properly designed store.

An alarm system is always a good idea. You will need to research current systems available on the market. Most alarm companies will supply the hardware for free if you pay the monthly monitoring costs. And note that it's easy to add webcam security cameras if you have a network in your coffee bar.

As we've mentioned above, it's good to have locking door knobs on the office and storage room, and on storage cupboards.

If you expect a large volume of sales in your coffee bar, a safe is a good idea. Keep the safe in the office or in a back storage room. You may want to get expert advice on where to keep the safe — ask the safe retailer for references.

## 3. YOUR STAFF'S LOOK

Once you have created your coffee bar's "look," you will want to present it throughout the entire design of your coffee bar, from the uniform your staff wear to the logo printed on your business cards and letterhead. (See Chapter 2 for more on logos.) Consistency is key to building customer recognition, trust, and loyalty.

Many people don't realize how important staff image is in helping ensure the success of their business. But can you think of any successful business that hasn't taken this element into consideration? A positive staff image ultimately leads to increased sales. Who would you rather have serve you food: a sloppy person with hair hanging down or a sharply dressed, professional-looking person? We think you'll agree that the image created by the latter is a little more appealing.

In addition to enhancing your customers' experience of the coffee bar and the trust they will have in you, a uniform look also conveys to your customers that you care about your business. A uniform is an indication that you have taken time to consider how the staff's look will impact on the minds of your customers and have invested money to ensure this impact is a positive one. Whether consciously or unconsciously, customers pick up on little things like this. Your success will be the result of a multitude of little things all done well.

A uniform look also conveys professionalism, and professionalism converts directly into sales. Simply stated, your customers will buy more from someone who looks and acts professional than from someone who looks and acts unprofessional. People expect that when they see a professional look, they will get reliable professional advice. This becomes a key point as you advise your customers on different coffees, blends, and roasts, or recommend a cookie to go with a cup of your coffee. If you have any doubts, try the following experiment.

Spend a day behind the counter in jeans and a T-shirt. See how your customers respond to you, hear what they say to you. Then spend a day behind the counter in a uniform similar to the one we recommend below. What do you notice? You should find that your customers respond much more positively to you when you are in uniform. They will be more willing to believe what

you say and take you up on any recommendations or suggestions you make.

We recommend your uniform consist of the following:

- apron
- shirt
- black leg wear
- closed-toe, rubber-soled shoes
- neck decoration

## 3.1 Aprons

We recommend a black, above-knee apron with a bib. Bib-less aprons don't provide any protection against the splashes and inevitable stains of working in a coffee bar, and a dark color will not show the dark coffee stains as much as a lighter color. Black is easy to find, so you don't have to special order expensive color matches.

Be careful when choosing your apron length — shorter staff members may trip over aprons that are too long. You want to have an apron that the staff enjoy wearing.

The apron material should be machine washable, heavy duty, and, ideally, should not require ironing. When choosing a material for your aprons, keep the following questions in mind:

- Is the color consistent with my coffee bar colors and design?
- Will the fabric I am choosing wear well?
- Will the color wear well or will it fade after a few washes?
- Does the material have specific wash requirements? (If yes, keep in mind the impact on the environment from bleaches and other toxic chemicals used in the washing processes.)

- Is the material a stock item or special order?
- Will the material be available in one year? Five years?

### 3.1a Washing tips

If your coffee bar is equipped with a washing machine and dryer, you should be able to wash the aprons yourself. If you don't have these appliances, you have three choices.

You can use a linen company. You may be able to find an "all-in-one" linen service that will wash your aprons and cloths, as well as change toilet paper and hand towels in your bathrooms. This type of service is more costly than doing it yourself, but it is a real convenience, especially for a busy coffee bar.

You can plan a weekly wash schedule and take staff aprons and cloths home for washing. Keep in mind that you will go through dozens of wiping cloths per week and these are often difficult to clean properly in home machines. While home washing can save you up to $100 per month, don't let washing aprons take you away from higher priorities like serving customers or marketing your coffee bar.

You could drop off your laundry at a laundromat where you can get it washed and folded. Using a local laundromat is a good way to establish a cross-promotion relationship. (See Chapter 16 for more on cross-promotions.)

## 3.2 Apron logos

Ideally, you will want to distinguish your everyday black aprons from those of your competitors. The easiest way to do this is by displaying your coffee bar's name on the front of the apron. Every time your name is in front of the customer, it brings your business to the forefront and helps reinforce the association the customer will make between the positive experience they are having at your coffee bar and the coffee bar itself. Some options that you might want to explore include:

### 3.2a Embroidery

Embroidery is usually quite costly in small runs, but it will produce a colorful rendition of your logo. Compare prices by contacting several local embroidery shops. You may be able to find an embroiderer who works out of his or her home and who doesn't have the expensive overhead of a large storefront. You might also find someone who is interested in providing embroidery services in exchange for inexpensive coffee. This is a good deal for you, because you end up paying only 30 percent cash for your order (a pound of coffee is valued at $12, but you have paid only $3 for the green beans and packaging), and a good deal for the embroiderer, because he or she gets your coffee at a reduced rate.

### 3.2b Crests

Crests, too, can be quite expensive in small quantities, and you would be well off to do some price comparisons before making a decision.

Also consider that you will need to have the crests sewn on. Some companies charge as much as $2 per apron for this work, although you can always keep the costs down by sewing crests on by yourself.

Going with crests can be a real advantage later if you change your logo and want to remove the crests. If your aprons are made of a good quality material that doesn't fade, you will hardly notice that the crest was there at all. This advantage makes changing crest shape or design easy.

### 3.2c Silk screening

Silk-screened logos can be very colorful. You should contact a company specializing in silk screening to discuss your options.

The biggest drawback with silk screening is that the silk-screen logo will always wear out before the apron. This means you must replace aprons more often than would normally be required.

## 3.3 Name tags

Name tags add a very classy touch to your business. Think of the most successful chain stores in the world. The staff at these stores wear name tags. Name tags work because they can create a more personal relationship between your staff and your customers.

You can have name tags made up for only a few dollars each through your local printer. (One of the cheapest ways to get a quality name tag is to buy a system from Imprint Plus (www.imprintplus.com).) They are available in a variety of sizes and colors. A one-by-two-inch tag with a safety-pin design works well. Choose a color combination and design consistent with your coffee bar's image and color scheme.

You will want to make a list of your staff and order the name tags in plenty of time for your grand opening. After that, you will need to order a name tag every time you get a new staff member. Make sure to order the name tag after his or her trial shift. That way, if the staff member doesn't work out, you won't have to cancel your order or pay for a name tag for someone no longer working there.

Include the cost of the name tags as part of your training budget. Believe us, the extra few dollars are worth it in the long run.

## 3.4 Shirts

While shirts come in a variety of colors, we have always used a basic white shirt. Not only does white convey an impression of cleanliness to the customer, but white shirts are also easy to order and replace. And they work well for both male and female staff.

If you are dead set against white, denim shirts can work well, they look good, and they come in a variety of colors including blues, greens, and tans. You will pay for this look however. You will need to provide approximately two shirts for each of your part-time staff and three or four shirts for each of your full-time staff. Add to this the cost of shirts to replace those that are lost, stolen, or damaged, and you will see how the cost of a simple shirt can add up to hundreds of dollars per year.

You will also need to get shirts of different sizes to fit the different sizes of your staff to maintain a smart-looking uniform look.

One word of caution: whatever shirt you go with, make sure you buy extras. There's nothing worse than finding out two years down the road that the shirts are no longer available and you need to pay to have new ones made or else change your entire uniform.

### 3.4a Collar

We've always liked collared shirts because they give a professional, neat look. They're also necessary if you decide to incorporate ties or bolos into your uniform (see section **3.7**).

### 3.4b Sleeves

Short-sleeved shirts work best because long sleeves tend to get dirty within a matter of hours. Another option is to have staff wear long-sleeved shirts rolled up and held in place with armbands. These can add a unique design feature to your uniform.

Armbands present problems if staff lose the armbands or keep them when they eventually quit, and there is the expense of having them replaced. Also, armbands can be uncomfortable to wear for an extended period.

### 3.4c T-shirts

If you decide to use T-shirts you must provide them for all your staff if you want to maintain a "uniform" look. If you allow your staff to wear any color, any design, any size, and any age of T-shirt, you will create a haphazard, messy look in your coffee bar.

Custom T-shirts work well if they fit in with the design of your coffee bar and promote your coffee bar's name and identity. However, they present many of the same problems as custom shirts in terms of the expense of providing them to your staff, replacement costs, and long-term availability. Also, T-shirts can come to look sloppy over time.

We know of some coffee bar owners who decided to use T-shirts and silk-screened extras to sell in their store as gift items. If you are in a tourist area, you may be able to sell a few this way, but the cost of having them silk-screened and the space they take up in your coffee bar usually isn't worth it. In addition, the margins probably won't be all that great (especially when compared to a cup of coffee) unless you can negotiate a good price on the shirts and the printing. A low profit margin will affect your overall bottom-line profit percentages.

## 3.5 Pants/skirts

We recommend basic black leg wear for a number of reasons. First, a black-bottom dress code is easy for staff to comply with — almost all staff have something black in their closets, whether it be black dress-pants, shorts, or a skirt. Second, it's an easy color for staff to keep clean. Third, black looks great.

Because our top-half uniform standards were always quite strict, we always allowed our staff to wear whatever they liked (within reason, of course) on the bottom — skirts, shorts, or pants — as long as they were black and professional-looking (no sweat pants or work-out shorts). In summer, most staff liked to wear shorts.

## 3.6 Shoes

Generally, closed-toe, rubber-soled shoes are required to be worn by staff in any type of food establishment. The closed toe is for protection against falling objects and spilling coffee. Rubber soles are to reduce the chances of staff slipping on wet surfaces. You may want to enforce a "black only" shoe-wear policy in your coffee bar to further enhance your overall image. Check with your local employment standards branch for workplace safety standards.

## 3.7 Neckwear

We highly recommend neckwear. It is a colorful and creative way to liven up the white shirt/black apron look.

### 3.7a Ties

You can choose a tie theme (cartoon characters, for example, or fancy color combinations) for your coffee bar. Zip-up ties are a great way to overcome the challenge some staff have with tying tie knots. These are usually reasonably priced and can be kept permanently at your coffee bar so they are always available for staff use and no staff member is left without a tie.

You can tie-in tie themes to promotions you are having. For example, red ties or heart ties can be worn leading up to Valentine's Day, Santa ties for Christmas, birthday ties to celebrate your coffee bar's birthday — you get the idea.

### 3.7b Bolos

Bolos add a western touch to your uniform. They can work well with your coffee bar design because they come in a variety of colors. However, they can be expensive to put in place and maintain a supply of.

### 3.7c Bow ties

Colored or cartooned bow ties can be fun and add a creative edge to your look. Unless you are going for the ultra formal look, we recommend staying away from solid-colored bow ties.

Clip-on or clip-up, pre-tied bow ties are the best option because they are easy for staff to take on and off. Because they are small, bow ties tend to get lost easily, so be prepared to have lots on hand.

### 3.7d Scarves

Scarves convey a different image from ties and bolos. Depending on the colors and the way they are tied, they can convey a western theme or a high fashion look. Remember that you will have both male and female staff, and both should feel comfortable wearing whichever scarf you choose. You also don't want to be so different or so unique that the uniform takes away from what you are selling.

---

## COMMITMENT BOX

I, _____ , commit to creating a concept and building my coffee bar to appeal to my customer profile.

_____          _____
(your signature)                                    (today's date)

---

# CHECKLIST 2
# COFFEE BAR DESIGN AND LAYOUT

## INTERIOR DESIGN
### WALLS
- ❑ Color
- ❑ Finish
  - ❑ paint
  - ❑ wallpaper
- ❑ Easy to clean, especially in food areas
- ❑ Special design features
  - ❑ wainscoting
  - ❑ slat areas for shelving

### CEILING
- ❑ Color
- ❑ Special design features

### FLOORING
- ❑ Color
- ❑ Material
  - ❑ tiles
    - ❑ squares
    - ❑ triangles
  - ❑ marble
  - ❑ hardwood
  - ❑ carpet
- ❑ Design
  - ❑ bordered

### KICKGUARD AT COUNTER
- ❑ Color
- ❑ Material
  - ❑ tiles
  - ❑ rubber
- ❑ Height

## LIGHTING
- ❑ Fixtures
- ❑ Brightness
  - ❑ bright for work areas
  - ❑ customer areas comfortable (bright enough to read by)
- ❑ Bulb type (full spectrum, energy-saving)

### WINDOWS
- ❑ Adequate number
- ❑ Height
  - ❑ eye level near tabled areas
  - ❑ eye level for stand-up bars
- ❑ Able to open
- ❑ Opening to a patio area
- ❑ Locks
- ❑ Frame color (match with your color scheme)
- ❑ Coverings
  - ❑ curtains
  - ❑ blinds
- ❑ Ledges

### ENTRANCE DOOR
- ❑ Material
  - ❑ glass
  - ❑ wood
- ❑ Color
- ❑ Design features
  - ❑ logo
- ❑ Knob
  - ❑ material
  - ❑ color
  - ❑ style to match

**TABLES**
- ❏ Height
- ❏ Color
- ❏ Finish
    - ❏ laminate
- ❏ Support
    - ❏ table bases
    - ❏ ability to level
    - ❏ adjustable feet
- ❏ Easy to clean/repair

**STAND-UP BAR**
- ❏ Height
- ❏ Support
    - ❏ angle iron
    - ❏ poles
- ❏ Finish
    - ❏ laminate
- ❏ Color

**SEATING**
- ❏ Height
    - ❏ fits table height
    - ❏ fits bar height
- ❏ Back support
- ❏ Ease of movement

**MAJOR OUTSIDE SIGN**
- ❏ Type
    - ❏ check city bylaws
    - ❏ check building requirements
- ❏ Color
- ❏ Design
- ❏ Logo
- ❏ USP
- ❏ Visibility
    - ❏ walk-by traffic
    - ❏ drive-by traffic

- ❏ Additional signage
    - ❏ Type
        - ❏ pylons
    - ❏ Location
        - ❏ sides of building
        - ❏ sidewalk signs

**WINDOW SIGNAGE**
- ❏ Height
    - ❏ eye level of walk-by traffic
- ❏ Colors
- ❏ Design
- ❏ Visibility
    - ❏ walk-by traffic
    - ❏ drive-by traffic
    - ❏ minimal obstruction of view from inside

**LOGO AND NAME**
- ❏ Location
    - ❏ walls
    - ❏ tables
    - ❏ chairs
    - ❏ floor

# EQUIPMENT
**FOOD DISPLAY CASES**
- ❏ Type
    - ❏ floor model
    - ❏ cooler
    - ❏ countertop model
- ❏ Material
    - ❏ glass
    - ❏ plastic
- ❏ Easy to clean
- ❏ Refrigerated
    - ❏ noncondensing

**COOLER**
- ❑ Size
- ❑ Color
- ❑ Style
- ❑ Location
- ❑ Electrical requirements
- ❑ Warranties
- ❑ Easy to service
  - ❑ compressor top-mounted

**MILK FRIDGE**
- ❑ Size
- ❑ Color
- ❑ Style
- ❑ Type
  - ❑ undercounter model
  - ❑ countertop model
- ❑ Electrical requirements
- ❑ Warranties
- ❑ Easy to service

**FREEZER**
- ❑ Size
- ❑ Color
- ❑ Style
  - ❑ stand-up
  - ❑ chest
- ❑ Type
- ❑ Electrical requirements
- ❑ Warranties
- ❑ Easy to service

**ICE CREAM FREEZER**
- ❑ Size and type
- ❑ Color
- ❑ Design
  - ❑ built into counter

- ❑ Easy to access
- ❑ Easy for customer to view (glass front)
- ❑ Electrical requirements
- ❑ Warranties
- ❑ Easy to service

**PREP AREA EQUIPMENT**
- ❑ Microwave
  - ❑ amount of use
  - ❑ size
  - ❑ warranties
  - ❑ electrical requirements
- ❑ Convection oven
  - ❑ amount of use
  - ❑ size
  - ❑ warranties
  - ❑ electrical requirements
- ❑ Toaster
  - ❑ amount of use
  - ❑ size
  - ❑ warranties
  - ❑ electrical requirements

**AUTOMATIC DISHWASHER**
- ❑ Type (high-temperature model)
- ❑ Drainage
- ❑ Electrical needs
- ❑ Warranties
- ❑ Easy to service

**ESPRESSO MACHINE**
- ❑ Type
- ❑ Ease of use
- ❑ Electrical needs
- ❑ Servicing
- ❑ Warranties

## TABLES
- ❑ Height
- ❑ Color
- ❑ Finish
  - ❑ laminate
- ❑ Support
  - ❑ table bases
  - ❑ ability to level
  - ❑ adjustable feet
- ❑ Easy to clean/repair

## STAND-UP BAR
- ❑ Height
- ❑ Support
  - ❑ angle iron
  - ❑ poles
- ❑ Finish
  - ❑ laminate
- ❑ Color

## SEATING
- ❑ Height
  - ❑ fits table height
  - ❑ fits bar height
- ❑ Back support
- ❑ Ease of movement

## MAJOR OUTSIDE SIGN
- ❑ Type
  - ❑ check city bylaws
  - ❑ check building requirements
- ❑ Color
- ❑ Design
- ❑ Logo
- ❑ USP
- ❑ Visibility
  - ❑ walk-by traffic
  - ❑ drive-by traffic

- ❑ Additional signage
  - ❑ Type
    - ❑ pylons
  - ❑ Location
    - ❑ sides of building
    - ❑ sidewalk signs

## WINDOW SIGNAGE
- ❑ Height
  - ❑ eye level of walk-by traffic
- ❑ Colors
- ❑ Design
- ❑ Visibility
  - ❑ walk-by traffic
  - ❑ drive-by traffic
  - ❑ minimal obstruction of view from inside

## LOGO AND NAME
- ❑ Location
  - ❑ walls
  - ❑ tables
  - ❑ chairs
  - ❑ floor

# EQUIPMENT
## FOOD DISPLAY CASES
- ❑ Type
  - ❑ floor model
  - ❑ cooler
  - ❑ countertop model
- ❑ Material
  - ❑ glass
  - ❑ plastic
- ❑ Easy to clean
- ❑ Refrigerated
  - ❑ noncondensing

**PREP AREAS**
- ❑ Layout
  - ❑ convenient
  - ❑ easy to work at
- ❑ Design
  - ❑ easy to clean
- ❑ Size_____
- ❑ Shelving/cupboards
  - ❑ properly labeled

**JUICING STATION**
- ❑ Near fridge or freezer
- ❑ Layout
  - ❑ convenient
  - ❑ easy to work at

**ROASTED COFFEE SERVICE AREA**
- ❑ Near coffee grinder
- ❑ Near scale
- ❑ Near roaster

**CREAM AND SUGAR STATIONS**
- ❑ Location
  - ❑ counter
  - ❑ free-standing structure
- ❑ Easy staff access
- ❑ Easy customer access
- ❑ Consistent with traffic flow
- ❑ Accessible by more than one customer at a time
- ❑ Height
  - ❑ 36"
  - ❑ 42"
- ❑ Color_____
- ❑ Finishing_____
- ❑ Design features
  - ❑ garbage can hole in center
- ❑ Finished properly

- ❑ Easy to clean
- ❑ Kickguard
  - ❑ color
  - ❑ height

**ROASTING STATION**
- ❑ Location
  - ❑ high visibility
  - ❑ high traffic area
  - ❑ elevated
- ❑ Color
- ❑ Finishing
- ❑ Trim
- ❑ Kickguard
  - ❑ color
  - ❑ height
- ❑ Roaster/afterburner
  - ❑ electrical
  - ❑ ventilation

**GREEN BEAN DISPLAY**
- ❑ Location
  - ❑ high visibility
  - ❑ high traffic area
  - ❑ near roaster
  - ❑ near scale
- ❑ Wall displays
  - ❑ shelving
  - ❑ information
- ❑ Elevated

**MERCHANDISING AREAS**
- ❑ Type
  - ❑ racks
  - ❑ shelves
- ❑ Size_____
- ❑ Color_____
- ❑ Style_____

❑ Finishing
 ❑ paint
 ❑ laminate
❑ Extra wall shelves

**STORAGE AREAS**

❑ Layout
 ❑ convenient
 ❑ easy to work at
❑ Design
 ❑ easy to clean
❑ Size_____
❑ Lockable
❑ Inside shelving/cupboards
 ❑ properly labeled

**DISHWASHING AREA**

❑ Layout
 ❑ convenient
 ❑ easy to work at
❑ Design
 ❑ easy to clean
❑ Size_____
❑ Shelving/cupboards
 ❑ properly labeled

**SINKS**

❑ Triple sinks
 ❑ necessary? (check with city health department)
 ❑ location (check with city health department)
 ❑ what type of seam welds are acceptable?
❑ Hand sinks
 ❑ location (check with city health department)

❑ Mop sinks
 ❑ location (check with city health department)

**RESTROOMS**

❑ Size
 ❑ confirm with health department
❑ Mirrors
 ❑ securely mounted
❑ Toilet paper dispensers
❑ Hand towel dispensers
❑ Garbage cans
 ❑ swinging tops
 ❑ plastic
❑ Toilet type
 ❑ water-saving
❑ Sinks
 ❑ size_____
 ❑ color_____
 ❑ style_____
❑ Faucets
 ❑ size_____
 ❑ color_____
 ❑ style_____
❑ Hot water tank
 ❑ minimum 25 gallons

**HEATING SYSTEM AND AIR SYSTEM**

❑ Necessary? (determined by particular site)
❑ Air flow of system
❑ Sufficient duct outlets for all rooms, especially bathrooms

**ELECTRICAL PANELS**

❑ Clearly marked

## PATIO
- ❏ Design
  - ❏ elevated
- ❏ Trees/plants
  - ❏ low maintenance
  - ❏ suitable for weather conditions
- ❏ Smoking
  - ❏ check city bylaws
  - ❏ ashtrays
- ❏ Furniture
  - ❏ color
  - ❏ design
  - ❏ easy to clean
  - ❏ durable
- ❏ Umbrellas
  - ❏ color
  - ❏ design
  - ❏ easy to clean
  - ❏ durable

## OFFICE AREA
- ❏ Location
  - ❏ home
  - ❏ store
- ❏ Size
- ❏ Lockable
- ❏ Furniture
  - ❏ desk
  - ❏ chairs
  - ❏ filing cabinets

## SECURITY
- ❏ Peep holes in delivery doors
- ❏ Alarm system
- ❏ Safe
- ❏ Locking door knobs
  - ❏ office
  - ❏ storage

## STAFF UNIFORMS
- ❏ Apron
  - ❏ color
  - ❏ length
  - ❏ material
    - ❏ cleaning requirements
    - ❏ durability
  - ❏ design
    - ❏ logo
- ❏ Name tags
  - ❏ color
  - ❏ design
- ❏ Shirt
  - ❏ color
  - ❏ style
    - ❏ collar
    - ❏ sleeves
    - ❏ T-shirts
- ❏ Pants/skirts
  - ❏ color
  - ❏ style
- ❏ Shoes
  - ❏ color
  - ❏ safety requirements
    - ❏ sole
    - ❏ design
- ❏ Neckwear
  - ❏ color
  - ❏ themes
  - ❏ design
    - ❏ ties
    - ❏ bolos
    - ❏ bow ties
    - ❏ scarves

# 6
# GETTING TO YOUR OPENING

Success doesn't come to you ... you go to it.

— MARVA COLLINS

Once you've settled on a design and have a general idea of how you want to set up your coffee bar, you will likely need to do some renovating. This doesn't need to be as scary and costly as it sounds. Once your floor plans are drafted and have been approved by city hall, the general contractor or the tradespeople you hire will go to work on the building, and you can worry about stocking the store and preparing for the grand opening. We discuss hiring and training staff in Chapter 7, but this chapter should give you all the other pointers you need to get to your opening day.

## 1. HOW TO DO COST-EFFECTIVE PLANS

When drafting floor plans for your business, you have three options: do it on the cheap, hire a draftsperson, or hire an architect.

## 1.1 Doing it on the cheap

If you have had some experience preparing plans yourself, and know what information to include, it is possible to draw plans for your coffee bar yourself or to use a basic computer drawing program to prepare the floor plan. Try to get a copy of the "as built" (the original plan for that site) from the landlord. The plans may not be accurate, but they can be useful. Have an erasable vellum copy of them made; with an eraser and significant "elbow grease," you can soon have suitable floor plans.

Drawing the plans for your coffee bar will save you money and usually time. However, if you make an error, it can cost you during construction; if you are not drawing to acceptable building codes, permit approval will be delayed. As well, poor plans will mean that your tradespeople will round up the cost of their bids to allow for your inaccuracy (and cover themselves), and this will cost you more during construction.

## 1.2 Hiring a draftsperson

A local draftsperson can be an excellent alternative to doing plans yourself. Generally, a draftsperson will charge between $1,000 and $2,000 for preparing plans that will be fairly accurate.

A draftsperson is cheaper than an architect and if he or she visits the site and double-checks the measurements, the plans will allow the tradespeople to make accurate bids. Also, you can usually get quick city hall approval with plans drawn by a draftsperson.

Of course, these plans are also subject to errors that are difficult to notice until your coffee bar is under construction. A draftsperson usually has limited accountability if the errors cost you.

## 1.3 Hiring an architect

Hiring an architect is the most expensive but also the most accurate way to go. It will typically cost you $4,000 to $12,500 for the project.

If the architect is good, there should be no mistakes in the finished product. As well, using an architect ensures that the plans are up-to-date on changes to codes and regulations.

An architect will give you detailed specifications that allow for better, more accurate quotes from tradespeople.

On the downside, using an architect will cost you much more money than the other two options. Any changes in mid-course almost always cost extra. If you have any doubts about how to draw your plans, or lack confidence, we recommend you hire an architect; your project will go much more smoothly. That is, assuming the architect has done this type of work. One of our favorite sources for this work is Tom Palm and Design Layout Services (www.design layout.com). They're professionals and really know what they're doing.

Don't forget, once your floor plans are complete, you will likely need a site plan, a ceiling grid, and a mechanical floor plan. Check your city's planning department for its specific requirements in advance.

## 2. HOW TO GET PERMITS AND LICENSES

Always present your plans to city hall yourself. Dress neatly and respectably. It is usually a short (about two to four weeks), simple process to get interior renovations approved. Show respect and never, never argue. If you are positive a mistake has been made, bring it up later; arguing now may delay approval. If you are using a general contractor, he or she can help walk you through this, but unless the contractor has a particularly good relationship with city hall, present the plans on your own.

You will need to pay for a business license and building permits. Costs vary dramatically from a few hundred dollars to a few thousand.

If your plans are ready, submit as soon as you have a signed offer to lease. There is no such thing as having plans approved too early. You do not need to wait for bids from your contractors.

# 3. PUTTING THE JOB OUT TO TENDER

Get "apples-to-apples" bids; when you ask for quotes, be specific about what you want quoted on, give every bidder the same description of the project, and get the quotes in writing.

Always ask for bids to be built to your plans specifications or better, and all equipment to be installed to your desired locations. Also ask for bids to be adjusted to specific site needs as appropriate, without additional costs. Ask for bids to include prep and clean-up of work performed.

If all your specific equipment has not been sourced yet, ask for quotes that are subject to your reasonable equipment specifications, when found, at no additional cost.

Ask for a fixed price bid, with a bonus for early completion and a penalty for late completion (with a one-week window in between the two). This will motivate all parties to be timely. If your lease has been negotiated well, you will get free rent and CAM if you open early, so being fast pays.

## 3.1 Choosing the best bid

When it comes to analyze the bids, keep in mind that the cheapest is not always the cheapest. In other words, a lowball bid will not pay in the long run if the work is of poor quality. Get references. Go check out the bidder's work. Call some of his or her customers. Do your homework.

If references check out and all factors appear to be equal, go with the low bid. If one of the three bids you receive is much lower than the others, ask the bidder why. If the answer checks out, go for it (and then keep a close eye on progress).

## 3.2 Should I use a general contractor?

A general contractor supervises the entire construction process and hires the individual sub-tradespeople. He or she will carry the needed insurance and workers compensation insurance (or should — be sure that you double-check to make sure the contractor has such coverage or you may be liable). While a general contractor generally adds about 20 percent to the final cost of the project, the advantage to you is that the cost to you is guaranteed fixed.

There are numerous other advantages to using a general contractor, including: predictable results, generally speaking (pardon the pun); all the unknowns during construction become the contractor's headache, not yours; the contractor is experienced, and therefore you can expect fewer mistakes; most contractors will guarantee timing; and the contractor knows good sub-trades to use.

Of course, the downside to using a general contractor is that doing so adds that 20 percent to the overall construction part of your budget. Some contractors have a "surcharge" mentality and attempt to add extra costs. Keep an eye on this, and be prepared to question any charge that wasn't part of the quote.

## 3.3 Getting your coffee bar built — while saving money and time

### 3.3a Things you can do yourself to save money

(a) Base painting and priming.

(b) Source your own equipment.

(c) Buy the electrical and plumbing parts and have trades install them.

(d) Demolish all unneeded walls your-self.

(e) Keep the site clean (a clean site gen-erally means less waste).

(f) Arrange all trade bids with a time completion bonus.

(g) Have accurate plans.

(h) Try not to change plans mid-project.

(i) If you use a general contractor, point out concerns to him or her, not directly to tradespeople.

### 3.3b Things you can do yourself to save time

(a) Get the permits and licenses as soon as you can.

(b) Develop a detailed schedule with the trades (or with the general con-tractor).

(c) Set a time goal that is sooner than your real goal, so if the trades miss the deadline, you are still able to reach your goal.

(d) Make sure equipment arrives when you need it (not before and, of course, not after).

(e) Hire the best drywaller you can find (wet or poor "mud" can cause huge delays).

(f) Buy coffees and pop for the trades so they don't take long coffee breaks.

(g) Interview and hire your staff in preparation of opening. (Do this off-site.)

(h) Get all the miscellaneous small wares together well in advance (see section **4.**).

(i) Get any training you need before you open (your equipment sales reps can help here).

(j) Prepare all your marketing items before you open (and never sched-ule a grand opening until several weeks after you are opened, to make sure you are prepared).

## 4. CONSIDER SETTING UP WIRELESS INTERNET (WI-FI) ACCESS

Wireless Internet (Wi-Fi) access is now offered at thousands of locations across North America, including libraries, airports, restaurants, and yes, coffee bars. Depending on your coffee bar's atmosphere and cus-tomer base, consider offering Wi-Fi to your customers. Unlike an Internet café, a café with Wi-Fi offers customers who bring their own laptops access to the Internet. The Wi-Fi "hotspot" café only needs to set up one computer to act as an access point; cus-tomers are responsible for their own per-sonal equipment.

For students and workers who freelance or telecommute, the presence of Wi-Fi can be a draw because it will allow them to work in the communal atmosphere of a café. The advantages and disadvantages of offering Wi-Fi will be discussed in Chapter 16.

The basic equipment needed to set up a Wi-Fi hotspot in your coffee bar is a com-puter (Mac or PC) to act as a server, a router that can deliver wireless connections to sev-eral computers, and cable or DSL Internet access. To ensure your customers a more secure, reliable network, you may wish to consult a computer networking profession-al, or contact one of the many wireless

Internet services that have sprung up to meet the demand for Wi-Fi hotspots. Some issues to take into account when setting up a Wi-Fi network for your customers are:

- *Security*. Will your customers be protected from hackers, viruses, and identity theft?
- *Reliability*. Who can provide tech support if there is a problem?
- *Access*. Who can access your network, and for how long?
- *Appropriateness*. Can sites that are not suitable for children to view — for example, pornography, violence, etc. — be blocked?

Some cafés have also wrestled with the question of whether to charge for access or not. For example, Starbucks has partnered with T-Mobile in the United States and Bell in Canada to provide wireless Internet access to customers who have a subscription. For most café owners, however, free Wi-Fi is a strategy to attract more customers.

You may wish to provide unlimited Internet access in your coffee bar, or you may wish to limit time and bandwidth use. Software is available that will help you manage your Wi-Fi hotspot. One popular program is the Sputnik Control Center (www.sputnik.com) that works with router devices and servers to help you control access to your network. Depending on how the program is set up, it can print out an access code on a customer's receipt that the customer enters to log on to the network. The Sputnik system can also be set up for prepaid or credit card access to your network, if you opt for offering paid access. The cost for routers and software for one Wi-Fi access point is about $500, plus support and access costs.

Once you have your Wi-Fi up and running, you'll want to advertise the service to your customers. Your service provider may give you a sticker for your door. You can also list your business on one of the many online directories of Wi-Fi hotspots, such as AnchorFree (http://anchorfree.com) and Wi-Fi Free Spot (www.wififreespot.com). In addition, list your café in any local directories as Wi-Fi enabled.

For more information on setting up a Wi-Fi access point, check out the Wi-Fi Alliance (www.wi-fi.com).

# 5. ORGANIZING WHAT TO DO AND BUY

Opening your coffee bar is easy if you're organized, and part of being organized means taking care of all the little things. By doing the little things now, you keep your head ache-free. And save yourself a lot of headaches in the weeks to come.

Checklist 3 is a list of things to do and buy as you prepare to open your doors for business. We discuss specifics of some of the more important or coffee-bar-specific items below. As with the heavier equipment discussed in Chapter 5, you should keep the electrical requirements for the particular piece of equipment, its warranty and servicing, and color, size, and style in mind when purchasing.

## 5.1 Food display

If you are selling muffins, you may want to display them in wicker baskets placed either on a countertop display case or on back-wall shelves. Make sure they are easily visible to your customers. The color, shape, and size of the display unit is your choice but should match the rest of the decor.

## CHECKLIST 3
# PRE-OPENING CHECKLIST

**TO BUY**

**DISHES AND KITCHENWARE**

- ❑ wicker baskets for muffins
- ❑ muffin tongs
- ❑ cake plates
- ❑ pie/cake servers
- ❑ cutting boards
- ❑ dry measuring cups
- ❑ wet measuring cups
- ❑ measuring spoons
- ❑ mixing and baking bowls
- ❑ baking pans
- ❑ knives
- ❑ spatula
- ❑ flipper for cookies
- ❑ regular knives (nontarnishing)
- ❑ regular forks (nontarnishing)
- ❑ cutlery separators
- ❑ ice cream scoops
- ❑ chocolate grater
- ❑ plastic containers for flavoring beans
- ❑ sealable containers for fruits, veggies, and other prep
- ❑ bean blending containers
- ❑ steel scoops for green coffee

- ❑ can openers
- ❑ oven mitts
- ❑ dish-drying rack
- ❑ blender
- ❑ juicer(s)
- ❑ 12 oz. mugs
- ❑ 16 oz. mugs
- ❑ 20 oz. mugs
- ❑ 12 oz. cappuccino cups with saucers
- ❑ cold drink glasses
- ❑ teapots
- ❑ teacups
- ❑ 12, 16, and 20 oz. parfait glasses
- ❑ espresso cups with plates
- ❑ double espresso cups with plates
- ❑ small espresso spoons
- ❑ long latte spoons
- ❑ large spoons for scooping foam
- ❑ cream thermos
- ❑ milk thermos
- ❑ shot glass with 0.5, 1.0, and 1.5 oz. measurements
- ❑ bell-shaped steaming pitchers (at least two large and two small)
- ❑ espresso pourers

- ❑ thermometers to steam milk
- ❑ glass bulk sugar dispensers
- ❑ wicker baskets for cream and sugar station
- ❑ glass honey dispensers
- ❑ cinnamon/nutmeg/ vanilla shakers
- ❑ clear squirt bottles for chocolate syrup
- ❑ multilevel rack for syrups
- ❑ napkin dispensers
- ❑ straws
- ❑ straw dispenser
- ❑ garbage cans
- ❑ hand towels
- ❑ soap
- ❑ towel and soap dispensers
- ❑ sound system

**DECORATIONS**

- ❑ flower vases
- ❑ candles and candle holders
- ❑ coat rack
- ❑ magazine or brochure rack

## GENERAL AND OFFICE EQUIPMENT

- ❏ computer and printer
- ❏ fax machine
- ❏ answering machine
- ❏ Velcro for brew cards
- ❏ scissors
- ❏ Scotch tape
- ❏ masking tape
- ❏ duct tape
- ❏ glue and glue gun
- ❏ stapler
- ❏ pens and pencils
- ❏ notepaper
- ❏ clipboards
- ❏ whiteboard or "communications" board
- ❏ daily planner
- ❏ marketing calendar
- ❏ screwdriver
- ❏ hammer

## CLEANING SUPPLIES

- ❏ mini-broom with bin
- ❏ plastic pail
- ❏ dustpan
- ❏ long-handled dust wand
- ❏ large garbage cans
- ❏ broom
- ❏ sponge mop
- ❏ mop

## TO DO

- ❏ Hook up phone
- ❏ Hook up water
- ❏ Hook up electricity and gas
- ❏ Set up Wi-Fi system
- ❏ Change locks on doors if necessary
- ❏ Place initial inventory order for:
  - ❏ green beans
  - ❏ bean flavoring
  - ❏ produce
  - ❏ dairy products
  - ❏ dry goods
  - ❏ liquid coffee-flavoring syrups
  - ❏ baked goods
  - ❏ tea
  - ❏ aprons
  - ❏ staff name tags
- ❏ Order merchandise
- ❏ Order merchandising displays or shelving
- ❏ Order table talkers
- ❏ Order tables, chairs, and stools
- ❏ Design, typeset, and have printed:
  - ❏ business cards
  - ❏ letterhead
  - ❏ envelopes
  - ❏ preferred-customer cards
  - ❏ hours of operation sign
  - ❏ open/closed sign
  - ❏ signage for all products and merchandise
  - ❏ table talker signage
- ❏ Design and order menu boards
- ❏ Design and order bean boards
- ❏ Design and order outside signage
- ❏ Have outside awning/windows washed
- ❏ Make sure all equipment has been ordered
- ❏ Order computer or cash register
- ❏ Arrange for a laundry service (optional)
- ❏ Get initial marketing items in place

Colored cloths squared over the baskets (dark green cloths and wicker baskets look great) make for an attractive presentation. Separate cloth from food items with a waxed paper sheet.

Cheesecakes can be well displayed on plates. Sprigs of mint, orange sections, etc., liven up the presentation. Use a doily to separate the cake from the plate.

## 5.2 Coffee dispensers

Coffee dispensers should be located near the money exchange station and as close to the brewing system as possible. We recommend thermal carafes which have no electrical or plumbing requirements.

## 5.3 Variable grinder

A variable grinder for customer use should be easy for both customers and staff to access. It should also be as close to the roaster as possible.

## 5.4 Espresso grinders

Espresso grinders should be placed beside the espresso machine, as close as possible while still allowing easy arm movement.

## 5.5 Small prep-area equipment

Will you need a toaster in the prep area? The quality of toaster you buy depends on how often it will be used. Consider buying a high quality toaster if you think it will get a lot of use.

The ease of cleaning and sterilizing cutting boards is an important point to consider when purchasing them.

## 5.6 Baking supplies

Stainless steel is the best material for measuring cups and spoons, pans, mixing bowls, and mixing utensils.

## 5.7 Juicing equipment

If you plan to offer fresh juice, you will need a juicer and blender. A top-of-the-line home version may suffice in the beginning stages of your coffee bar.

## 5.8 Glasses and cups

You will likely need 12-, 16-, and 20-ounce sizes of coffee mugs, cappuccino cups, specialty coffee mugs, and cold drink glasses.

Make sure you get heavy-duty coffee mugs that won't break easily. Keep in mind that they must be also be cheap enough to replace constantly, as they do break or go missing despite your best efforts.

Buy heavy-duty cappuccino cups and saucer combinations. Buy taller versions of the cappuccino cups for specialty coffees. Latte bowls will need to be at least 20 ounces and have a handle.

Cold drink glasses should be ones that can be chilled without breaking or chipping.

You will need both single- and double-size espresso cups. Single size should be a heavy-duty cup and saucer combination with small espresso spoon, and double size should also be a heavy-duty cup and saucer combination.

## 5.9 Cream and milk containers

We recommend Nissan stainless steel cream and milk containers. When you are shopping for these containers, be sure to ask yourself:

- Are they easy to sterilize?

- Do they keep the cream and milk fresh? Some health departments require that milk is stored on ice or with plastic ice cubes inserted into the containers.

- Are they easy for customers to use? Try to reduce the twisting, turning, twirling confusion that so often happens as customers struggle to figure out how to get the container open.

- Are they durable? Will they still look good after extended use? We recommend painted stainless steel.

- Do they have drip protection? If not, your cream and sugar station will always be messy.

## 5.10 Bulk sugar dispenser

Whether glass or plastic, a see-through bulk sugar dispenser is best both for customer convenience and for staff so they know when to refill. Free-pour containers are better than the measured type.

## 5.11 Condiment holders

Will your condiment holders be built into the cream and sugar station? We recommend that they are, but if they're not, placing them in a container of plastic, wicker, or any other material that suits your coffee bar's image will do.

When you are buying, consider how easy the holders will be to fill and how much stock they will hold. They must be large enough that you don't need to refill them every five minutes.

They also must be easy for customers to use. The plastic, squeezable type works best

for honey, but also consider the pancake syrup style.

Condiments and syrups needed by staff during coffee preparation should be placed close to the espresso machine and the milk fridge. Keep them underneath the counter if there is shelving.

A multilevel rack to hold syrups will free up counter space. Racks can be wood or metal wine racks, or specific syrup racks purchased from the syrup manufacturer.

## 5.12 Napkin dispensers

Despite the cost, we recommend recycled napkins. To reduce waste, you might place a "tree friendly" sign, requesting that your customers take only what they need, on the dispenser. Dispensers are much better than loose stacks of napkins for reducing usage abuse.

Again, consider color, ease of restocking, and customer use when purchasing dispensers.

## 5.13 Straws and dispenser

We suggest you stock milkshake straws, as the smaller straws are difficult to suck through. Studies by Coca-Cola have shown that customers will buy larger drinks over time if the straw size is large.

A straw dispenser can reduce use, but it must be easy to use. Also some city health departments require that you use individually wrapped straws — check with your local department.

## 5.14 Garbage cans (trash bins)

You can buy either countertop or floor models. We think built-in garbage cans are best, followed by a countertop garbage can built into your cream and sugar station, and then floor models.

Garbage cans must be placed for customer convenience and be easy for customers to use, so you aren't always picking waste off the floor. The cans should also be easily emptied and easily sterilized.

## 5.15 Hand towels and soap

You will need hand towels and soap for each hand sink.

The health inspector will require sanitizing soap in a dispenser (rather than a bar soap, which can spread bacteria from user to user) and will also likely require a hand-towel dispensing system for either paper or linen rolls (for the same reasons).

## 5.16 Menu boards, daily roasts sign, and specials boards

Your choice of backlit or chalk menu boards for inside the coffee bar must be consistent with your image and concept. Also make sure that, whichever system you go with, it's easy to change the pricing.

You should have a daily specials board and a daily roasts sign inside, either on your countertop or separately mounted on the wall, as long as both can be seen clearly by your customers. If you are not using a chalk board for the daily roasts, make sure that it's easy to change the names of the coffees on the sign (e.g., by inserting tabs into a glass or plastic stand). One client recently installed a brand new system with projection-screen menu boards, so who knows, the best ideas may only be a test program away.

A daily specials board outside is also essential. A V-shaped sandwich board is best, although you may need to secure it if it's in a windy area. Chalk doesn't work well in the rain or snow; if you choose to use a menu board outside, cover it with Plexiglas.

## 5.17 Educational material

Consider having an area in your coffee bar where you can display pamphlets on your product and environmental coffee organizations such as Coffee Kids. The Specialty Coffee Association of America has a good series of pamphlets for sale (see the Appendix for contact information).

You can put the pamphlets either on the countertop or hang them in a holder on the wall, depending on space. Just make sure the pamphlets are accessible to customers.

## 5.18 Sound system

If you're going to have background music, we recommend you buy equipment with a well-known brand and a good warranty. Today it pays to get a wireless music system installed from one of the big suppliers. Great sound at a great price.

Speakers should be placed so that the sound is balanced throughout the coffee bar. However, the focus should be on the customer seating areas, pointing away from the servers.

# 6. SUPPLIER CONSIDERATIONS

Once you have decided on your products and product lines, your next step will be to choose a supplier for these products. Take into account the suppliers' reputation and length of time in business, as well as the quality and price of its product. Find out about —

- delivery schedules,
- delivery schedule flexibility,
- approachability of sales reps,

- point-of-sale material (see below), and

- minimum dollar volume for each order.

You can find suppliers' names by asking other store owners or by checking the Web or the Yellow Pages in your area. The Appendix lists suppliers we recommend in each category. Your next step is to call and speak to the sales representative for your area and arrange a meeting or have product samples and price sheets mailed to you.

## 6.1 Meeting your sales rep

It is important to establish a strong relationship with your sales rep; a good relationship can be a great benefit to you.

For one thing, sales reps are often a source of information. They can give you the "inside scoop" on the products they are supplying and how they are selling in other locations. They will also have a good understanding of their competitors' products and the research they have done can save you a lot of time and effort; you won't waste time meeting with suppliers whose products are not suited to your concept or target market.

Sales reps can help you with signage, point-of-sale (POS) material (e.g., material displayed at the point of sale, including information on various coffee products), merchandising ideas, display tips, and product information for your staff and customers.

Finally, your sales rep can help you build your product sales by offering to supply free product or sample sizes for a special promotion.

The first thing you will want to do is meet face-to-face. Call the company and ask for the salesperson in your area. (You may discover that he or she is a fellow entrepreneur.) Explain that you are opening a new business and would like to set up a meeting to discuss the possibility of doing business. Arrange a time and place to meet.

Start the meeting by finding out a bit about the sales rep and the company he or she represents. (You may end up doing business with these people for many years to come so it's nice to get to know them a little.) Once you've had a chance to build some rapport, explain what it is you are doing. Tell the rep a bit about your concept and the market you are targeting, as well as your pricing and markup strategies. Giving him or her these guidelines will help the sales rep determine which products and/or product lines are best for your customers. Usually sales reps will bring product samples along and you will have a chance to do some sampling.

At some point during the meeting, you will also want to ask the sales rep:

- What makes your product(s) unique?

- Why do you think your products will appeal to my target market?

- What are the suggested markups (percent profit)?

- Do you provide point-of-sale material?

- Do you have nutritional information on your products?

- What do you offer for special occasions such as Valentine's Day or Christmas?

- Are you willing to do in-store taste-testing sessions?

- Do you provide free product if I want to do a special promotion to promote your products?

- Do you give price breaks for larger volumes?

- What is your delivery schedule and what is your minimum dollar volume needed for each order?

- How flexible is the delivery schedule?

- Are you open after hours or weekends?

- What happens if I run out of product on Saturday or Sunday?

- What are the names of three current customers I can call for a reference?

When making a decision on which products to carry, ask yourself these two key questions:

(a) Will they appeal to my target market?

(b) Will the markup cover the price I need to charge to maintain my profit margins?

## 6.2 Build supplier relationships that pay off

As we mentioned above, building a strong relationship with your suppliers can benefit you later.

Here are some tips to building and maintaining those good relations with your key suppliers or sales representatives:

(a) Invite suppliers and sales reps to your grand opening.

(b) Offer complimentary coffees to the delivery person.

(c) Follow up free product promotions with a thank-you letter.

(d) Pass along positive customer comments about the product.

(e) Get permission from the supplier to add its logo to flyers or coupons when it is donating product for a promotion.

(f) Pay your bills on time.

(g) Always be pleasant with suppliers and sales reps on the phone or when they drop in to your coffee bar.

(h) Offer to supply coffee to the supplier at a discounted price or even in exchange for product. (This does not work for your coffee suppliers!)

Remember that goodwill creates goodwill.

## 6.3 Credit applications

Credit applications give your suppliers assurance that you will pay them if they extend credit to you. Having credit is handy because it frees up your cash so you can use it to generate additional business during the time for which you have credit (generally 7 to 15 days). It also means that you are not constantly writing checks or counting cash for suppliers, but can write one check for multiple purchases.

The downside to credit is that it is easy to let the invoice pile grow big and you can soon find yourself behind in payments.

As a new business, your suppliers generally require that the first order is paid with cash on delivery (COD), while subsequent orders can be paid on credit provided your credit application is approved.

You will want to have your credit applications filled out in plenty of time before your doors open. It can take up to two weeks for a supplier to approve credit, so a little preparation can save you some hassle during the often hectic time just before your coffee bar opens.

On most credit applications, you will be asked for —

- your business name,

- the name and address of your business,
- the amount of credit you want to receive, and
- credit references.

You will almost always be asked to sign a personal guarantee so the supplier has backup protection should you fail to pay its invoices.

### 6.3a Asking for credit

The amount of credit you ask for generally depends on the size of the orders you will be placing. Your sales rep will be able to help you determine this. You may want to ask for a larger amount of credit than you think you are going to need so you don't need to ask for credit limit increases in future.

### 6.3b Credit references

When your business first opens, you likely won't have any credit references. Ask your sales rep if you can use personal credit references such as credit card or bank references. If you can, make sure you make careful note on the credit application that these are personal references and are under your personal name.

When your references are called, the supplier typically verifies that you have credit, asks what your credit limit is, and confirms that you are dependable in your payments — that you always pay your bills on time.

If you aren't approved for credit, find out why. Not being approved may indicate a problem with your credit or may be a miscommunication (you may have given a wrong phone number or contact name). You may be refused because you do not have a long enough history in business for

the supplier to consider you a good investment. Respect this. Many businesses do fail and a supplier is only protecting itself against being stuck with bad debt. Feel free to ask for credit in three months or so, once you have had a chance to build up a solid track record and a good relationship with the supplier.

## 6.4 Ordering inventory

### 6.4a Preparing your opening order

Most suppliers provide ordering sheets that will help you prepare your opening order. Your sales rep may be able to help you figure out what your first order should be. (Be warned: we've seen some coffee bars open with far too much stock and end up throwing the stock away, all because their sales rep was overly optimistic.)

First orders are difficult to prepare because you will not have an accurate record of how much product you will need. You will have to guesstimate, based on the homework you have done while preparing to open your own coffee bar — all those hours sitting in your competitors' stores will really pay off now. (Chapter 15 discusses proper product management, including maintaining inventory levels once you have a better idea of your coffee bar's sales cycles.)

While overordering can result in product wastage, underordering is even worse. The last thing you want is to be apologizing to customers, within the first few days of opening, that you don't have any food. If you run out of product you will either disappoint customers who had the product before and have come back for it, or you will miss exposing new customers to the product and they will leave not knowing you carry the product. If that product was really important to a customer and he or she thinks you don't carry it, the customer may not come back to your coffee bar. The long and short of it is a lower average check (or average purchase per customer) and lower sales.

If you do run out of necessities such as milk, you or one of your staff will need to leave your coffee bar to get more. Unless you have ample staff, this can result in poor customer service.

In summary, it is better to order a little extra, especially if a weekend is coming up and you won't have access to suppliers for a couple of days.

### 6.4b Getting the best price

The best pricing will come with time and it isn't always a good idea to ask for a price break right away. What you need most in the beginning is service and flexibility.

Service is important because you are new to the business and it will probably take you a while to get organized. You'll want your supplier to be willing to make an emergency delivery if you run out of product or forget to place an order.

Flexibility is important because you may not meet minimum order requirements, for example, and you will require the supplier to be somewhat flexible as you build your business. Both of these elements are much more important than price, especially in the early stages.

Even once you have built your volume up, you are often much better off asking a supplier for free product for a promotion or marketing campaign that helps build your sales rather than squeezing for a 5 percent reduction in price.

### 6.4c Recording your order

It is important that you carefully record exactly what you ordered and when, not only with your opening order but throughout your years in business.

Records help you analyze overordering and underordering so you can reduce waste and/or disruptions in service because of lack of product. A good recording system will also help sort out shipping discrepancies should one occur. We highly recommend a computerized inventory and ordering system for ease of ordering, to reduce ordering errors and to make month-end statement production easier. In Chapter 15 we discuss the inventory order form, which is a good way to keep track of both your ordering and receiving. If you do not have access to a computer, the supplier may have ordering sheets you can use.

Whatever system you use, be accurate in your recording method. For example, distinguish clearly on your order between one case and one box; it can make a huge difference in the amount of product you end up with, as a case consists of a number of boxes. One of our managers once ordered a case of Ajax cleaning powder. We had that stuff for years!

Check with your supplier on whether large amounts can be ordered in smaller amounts. For example, you may want a wide variety of syrups, but want only one of each with extras of the most popular type. However, some syrups are available only in boxes of six 26-ounce (750 mL) bottles, so double-check before placing your order.

If your orders are COD, make sure you have a check for the supplier ready. Most suppliers will happily tell you the total amount before the delivery to make the delivery smooth and easy.

## 6.5 Receiving your opening order

When you receive your opening inventory, confirm and record that the amounts received are the amounts ordered. This will serve as a check against any dumping of extra quantities and will quickly earmark any short shipments.

Always check your order against your record of what you ordered, what you were billed for (if the order is COD), and what you actually received. If you are invoiced later for the order, check the invoice against both your ordering record and receiving record.

When receiving the order, inspect all items to ensure that you are getting the products you ordered. Look for substitutions, bent or bloated cans, and torn containers. Inspect all produce for evidence of rot, freezer burn, and deterioration.

Items that are unacceptable in terms of type, quality, or quantity should be refused at the time of delivery. Mark it clearly on the invoice and make arrangements for a correction on your invoice. Remember that once the invoice has been signed, you have accepted the order and items are considered bought.

When receiving green beans, examine your shipment for water damage or damage to the packaging sack.

Most suppliers are very careful about what they deliver — a mistake on their part is a hassle for them, too. You will quickly find out who the reliable suppliers are, but it is always a good idea to get into the habit of checking deliveries. If the delivery person appears impatient, turn a negative into a positive: offer him or her a complimentary coffee for the road. It will take only a couple of minutes to check an order, and by the time the delivery person has added cream and sugar, and put a lid on his or her cup of coffee, you are all done.

If you do notice a discrepancy, first ask the delivery person if he or she knows anything about it. Give your delivery person the benefit of the doubt; he or she may have forgotten the case of chocolate syrup in the truck. On the other hand, it may be your mistake, so you want to be careful about accusing someone else until you find out what has really happened. Because a number of people are often involved in getting your order to you, human error is not uncommon, so be patient.

We have had experiences, however, where a company repeatedly messed up our orders. If this ever happens to you, make sure you keep a record of the occurrences and then arrange to meet the sales rep or the owner to figure out the best way to solve the challenges you are facing. While switching suppliers is always an option, it is not necessarily one you want to pursue. In our case, we really loved the products we were being supplied with (when we got them), and there were no alternative suppliers producing the same items. Sitting down to iron out any crinkles in the system is usually the best thing to do. (That is what you would want your customers to do, isn't it?)

Once your coffee bar is up and running, you will want to try and schedule your orders to arrive on quieter days, at quieter times, if possible, although often you won't have much say in when shipments will arrive. Deliveries can disrupt the flow of business and it takes time for the order to be inspected and completely put away.

Once your coffee bar is open, you may want to do a quick count every Friday morning as a check to verify that all products ordered in that week have arrived and to spot products that have been under-ordered so you are fully prepared to handle your weekend volume.

Note that the orders you place will be subject to the delivery schedules of your suppliers. Some products may be delivered daily while others are available weekly or biweekly.

# 7. STORING YOUR ORDER

## 7.1 Plan ahead

Carefully plan where your stock is going to go before it arrives. When it arrives (and it always comes at the busy times), you will want to put it away immediately, especially refrigerated items, and you don't want to be running around humming and hawing about where the cinnamon should go. Once your coffee bar has been up and running for some time, stocking is a simple, routine job.

The general rule of thumb is to place everything as close as possible to the place you are going to need it. Everything that is required to stock the cream and sugar station, for example, should go in the cupboard below the cream and sugar station; cups, lids, and anything you need to stock the specialty coffee toppings are in a cupboard underneath the espresso machine. While this sounds logical, you would not believe the number of coffee bars that are set up inefficiently.

### 7.1a Label stock areas

It is a good idea to clearly label stock storage areas, especially the storage area for take-out cups. It is often difficult to distinguish between cup sizes, unless they are clearly differentiated. When you or your staff are in a rush, the last thing you want to do is pull out one sleeve of cups after another, trying to figure out which size is which. Keep the cups in one area, clearly marked. This will also save you a lot of time when you do your ordering. You will be able to determine at a glance what needs to be ordered for the following week.

## 7.2 FIFO — first in, first out

The rule when stocking is FIFO. No, not Jack and the Beanstalk — first in, first out. Store and use all products in accordance with their arrival time. Use up your oldest stock before moving on to use stock that's arrived more recently. Stock rotation is important from a product quality and a product waste point of view.

## 7.3 Disposable goods

Disposable goods such as film wrap, paper cups, and tinfoil have indefinite shelf life and need only be stored in clean, dry surroundings at least 8 inches off the floor to prevent rodent attacks. Rip the lids off cardboard boxes, or take items right out of cardboard boxes, to reduce the amount of space taken up in your freezer, fridge, or cupboard. Doing this also makes the items easier to access. In a busy coffee bar, every second counts. If you can make your life a little easier at the start, you'll be that much better off when you're in a rush later.

## 7.4 Frozen goods

Put frozen goods away first. Stock large amounts in the back and smaller amounts near the front of your freezer. This makes it easier to access the smaller items. Place items in easy-access containers. Frozen strawberries, for example, are much easier to get to if they are in a wide-mouth plastic container.

## 7.5 Dairy and produce

Put refrigerated items away next, especially dairy products, which generally have a shorter shelf life than, for example, oranges or apples. Dairy products must always be refrigerated with expiry-date stamps facing out so they can be easily checked by staff.

Produce requires very special handling. It must be kept in a cooler that is able to maintain a temperature of 34°F to 40°F (1°C to 4°C). Colder temperatures will do cellular damage, while warmer temperatures will accelerate the process of rotting that naturally begins at the time of harvesting. Make sure you place thermometers in all refrigerated equipment so that you can maintain proper temperature control. This is almost always required by health inspectors as well.

## 7.6 Baked goods

To retain freshness, breads and buns must be frozen (never refrigerated) immediately on delivery. Packing them in a freezer requires care, as these products can be crushed if stacked incorrectly. If your coffee bar sells bagels, try to have them delivered daily, to avoid having to freeze them, as true bagels will stale within 24 hours of baking.

## 7.7 Beans

All roasted coffee beans should be kept in Ampac bags until needed (see Chapter 9). Green beans must be stored in clean, dry areas off the floor.

## 7.8 Canned goods

Products that are canned can be stored for extended periods of time (up to six months) in clean, dry storage areas on shelves 8 inches or more off the floor. Canned goods, once opened, should be refrigerated in a clean, covered container.

## 7.9 Condiments

Buying condiments such as sugar in bulk is the cheapest way to go, but the product must be transferred to a rodent-proof container — a large one if you are buying 20 pounds at a time. Use a smaller wide-mouth plastic container or scoop to transfer the condiment from the bulk container to the serving jars.

## 7.10 Cleaning products

Cleaning products must be kept away from food products and should be placed in a separate, designated area.

## 7.11 The customer comes first

As a final point, always remember that the customer comes first. If you are putting an order away and a customer is waiting to be served, it is important that you immediately leave what you are doing and help the customer. If your delivery driver won't wait, explain that your customers must come first.

## 8. HOW AND WHEN TO OPEN YOUR DOORS

You will want to open the doors of your business as soon as you are ready to — once you have passed the building inspections and as soon as your staff is trained and your initial order has arrived.

We recommend doing a "soft" opening, which means opening the doors for business at the time you are ready and gradually building up the business without a lot of hype. This allows the kinks to get worked out. It is better to make a mistake once with one customer than repeatedly with many customers.

Make sure you have a lot of staff on hand to help you spoil your customers. Welcome them to your new coffee bar and help them become familiar with your menu items and your business practices such as in-store roasting and organic bean buying. Offer all customers a complimentary sample of beans hot out of the roaster to take home and try, along with a special offer to bring the bean package back for a discount on their first pound. (See Chapter 16 for more information on marketing strategies.)

Once your business is running and you have your initial marketing strategies in place, you will want to plan for your grand opening. By this stage you will have survived the initial stages of owning your own business and now it's time to celebrate!

## 8.1 The purpose of a grand opening

A grand opening is a chance to take time to enjoy, recognize, and reward this achievement in your life. You can also use the grand opening as an opportunity to draw attention to your coffee bar with the intention of exposing new customers to your concept, as well as reinforcing relationships with people who can help support you, your business, and your marketing efforts in the future. These people might include local business owners, community leaders, and local media.

## 8.2 The format of a grand opening

You have two choices when planning the format of your grand opening.

You can hold a small event on an afternoon, from about 4 p.m. to 7 p.m. The idea is to catch people on their way home from work. It will be more difficult to get a good turnout if you hold your grand opening later in the evening because you will have to pull most people from their homes.

The alternative is to hold a larger event on a weekend, making it a big event that draws people to your business in a major way. (See below for some suggestions on how to make your grand opening a major event.)

Whichever option you choose, you will want to have all-day specials such as 50 percent off everything in the store.

## 8.3 The first steps in planning your grand opening

The first step in planning your grand opening is to visualize what you want the event to look and feel like. The second step is to run backward through what you will need to do to reach that outcome. Then research the costs involved and total them. Spend some time weighing the pros and cons of the options available to you in terms of dollars and time and the return you expect to get.

## 8.4 Who will attend?

You must know who you are targeting to come to your event and why. A low-key event may have a few of your closest friends and relatives popping by with warm wishes, while a heavily promoted event may have your town's mayor stopping by to try a few sips of that great coffee!

Attendance at your grand opening will vary, depending on how much promoting you do. Once you know who you want to come, you must get their attention, create interest about the event, create desire to come to the event, and motivate those people to take the time to come to the event.

(a) If you are targeting potential customers:

- Offer complimentary lattes
- Give them an opportunity to win prizes
- Offer complimentary food

(b) If you are targeting the media:

- Do something unique and interesting
- Get a celebrity to come to your event
- Offer a complimentary cappuccino lesson to food writers
- Have a media award for the fastest latte drinker (e.g., the winner has 10 pounds of coffee donated to that media outlet's favorite charity)

(c) If you are targeting businesses in your area:

- Offer complimentary coffee and cheesecake to business owners
- Offer $10 gift certificates or gourmet coffee gift baskets for every business owner that shows up

(d) If you are targeting public figures in your area:

- Arrange a ribbon-cutting ceremony for the mayor and/or other dignitaries

## 8.5 How to let people know about the event

You can use any one or a combination of the following methods to promote the party, depending on your budget and how much time you have available for promotion:

- Distribute fliers
- Post posters
- Hand out tickets to existing customers the week before the event
- Arrange a radio remote (see Chapter 16 for more details)
- Advertise in local newspapers or community newsletters
- Word of mouth
- Hand out, mail, or email invitations to friends, family, media, equipment suppliers, community groups, local chambers of commerce, and other networking groups

## 8.6 Sixteen steps to planning your grand opening

Here are 16 steps to planning your grand opening:

(a) Decide on the date. Allow a couple of weeks for preparation. Plan to have a grand opening at least three weeks after you have opened.

(b) Decide on your budget.

(c) Decide which ideas for increasing attendance (above) you will pursue.

(d) If you choose to do a radio broadcast on site (a radio remote), you will need to research the local stations' prices, broadcast ranges, and target markets. Find out how many prize giveaways and on-air mentions they will give you, who the disc jockey will be, and how long they will spend at your coffee bar. Radio remotes are usually expensive unless they are done for charity or in conjunction with other businesses in your area that will share costs with you.

(e) Decide how you will let people know about your event.

(f) If you are doing any print advertising, you will need to research each publication's target market and prices and decide which one(s) you want to advertise in. Insert the advertisement a day or two before the event (too much before that and people will forget about it). Make sure your ad attracts attention and arouses the reader's interest.

(g) Develop a plan of action (e.g., photocopy fliers, hand out tickets to customers, mail out invites to suppliers).

(h) Set out a specific timeline for your plan of action (e.g., drop off invites to printer on Wednesday morning, mail invites on Thursday afternoon).

(i) List the items you will need (e.g., coffee, food, red ribbon and scissors for ribbon-cutting ceremony, balloons, prizes to give away).

(j) Make a mailing list or email list of specific people you want to invite.

(k) Mail or email invitations out one week prior to the event.

(l) If you will be distributing fliers or handing out tickets, make sure they're ready to distribute about one week prior to your event.

(m) Follow up with your ticket distribution centers (e.g., local businesses to which you gave tickets). Call three days before the event to see how their customers are responding and if they need more tickets.

(n) Do a press release.

(o) Fax press releases out as a follow-up to the invitations, three days prior to the event.

(p) Follow up press releases with a phone call to ensure that a representative from that newspaper, magazine, or coffee trade publication will be attending.

# COMMITMENT BOX

I, _____ , commit to hosting a grand opening celebration a few weeks after I open to recognize my great accomplishment and have some fun!

_____          _____
(your signature)                         (today's date)

# 7
# BUILDING A WINNING TEAM

All successful employers are stalking [people] who
will do the unusual, [people] who think, [people]
who attract attention by performing more than is
expected of them.

— CHARLES M. SCHWAB

## 1. HOW TO FIND GREAT STAFF

Finding great staff is important because
great staff can save you a lot of money.
Hiring a poor staff member, on the other
hand, can cost you literally hundreds of dollars in wasted labor costs, as you pay not
only the person you hired but also the trainer. Training can also cost you money if it
disrupts customer service. Reducing the
number of people you have to train ultimately contributes to how much money
you make.

## 1.1 Finding staff through paid advertising

Small ads placed in the employment section
of your major local paper are wonderful for
finding staff. One of the nicest things about
a local paper is that you tend to attract people in your immediate area who can easily
bike or walk to work. These people are often
more available for emergency shifts and
tend to stick with you longer because they
don't have lengthy travel times to consider.

The response rate to an ad depends on a
number of factors, including the paper's
distribution, what day you place the ad
(weekends generally get higher responses),
the time of year (e.g., when school is letting
out, a lot of students are looking for work),
and, of course, the ad itself.

Give yourself plenty of time to find staff
in case you get a low response to the ad and
need to run it again. On the other hand,
don't run the ad so far in advance that the
people you hire end up getting other jobs
because they won't wait for your coffee bar
to open.

### 1.1a Tips for writing a great ad

Here are some tips to follow if you want to write a great ad:

- Keep it short and simple — you are likely paying by the line.

- Focus on what's in it for the employee — what are you offering staff? A fun place to work? Good wages?

- Give people an idea of the type of person you are looking for (cheerful, outgoing, friendly).

- State a specific date and time that interested applicants should come by your store or home office.

- Don't put your phone number in the ad — if you do, you will be inundated with disruptive phone calls that are of no help to you. If people do track you down by phone, it is a good sign that they can't follow instructions!

### 1.1b Interviewing

Have applicants come in for interviews during a set time, say from 4 p.m. to 6 p.m., on a particular day. This is a much more effective use of your time than interviewing as people drop by at random.

Don't ask for résumés ahead of time. Résumés are difficult to evaluate without meeting in person with the applicant as well, and you should have your own application form for the applicant to fill out.

Have an extra person on hand to help with interviewing in case a lot of people apply. This is especially important when your business isn't open yet and you are doing your initial hiring of many people. Once you have experience with the response you get from an ad, you will be in a better position to determine how many people you need to help with interviews.

## 1.2 Finding staff by word of mouth

You can often get good staff by word of mouth once you're established. Be cautious, however, about hiring friends of existing staff. This can lead to trouble when they all want to go to the same movie or they are all in the same school play and you're stuck with no one to work. Having said that, however, two of the best staff members we ever had were best friends for the two years they worked for us.

## 1.3 Finding staff through in-store advertising

A cheap way to find great staff is to put a notice up in your coffee bar asking people to fill out an application form.

Always provide your own, customized application forms. You will want specific questions answered that aren't usually provided on a résumé or a standard form such as the ones you buy at an office supplies store. Our coffee bar application forms ask permission to call references, as well as ask why the person left their last job. Sample 4 is a customized application form.

## 1.4 Finding staff online

Another way to find great staff is by using online placement services, such as Monster .com and Craigslist. These online resources are getting better and better at helping employers find great employees. Running ads may require a one-time fee, but you can include as much detail as you want, and

# SAMPLE 4
# STAFF APPLICATION FORM

Last name: _____ First name: _____
*(please print)*

Phone: _____ Birthdate:* _____ / ____ / _____
                                                    *(m)*        *(d)*      *(y)*

E-mail: _____ Fax: _____

Address: _____
                                            *(Street)*

_____
    *(City)*                    *(State/Province)*              *(Zip code/Postal code)*

Are you currently employed?    [   ] Yes    [   ] No

What is your present occupation? _____

When are you available to start work? _____

What is your past coffee experience?         What is your past education?
1._____         _____
2._____         _____
3._____         _____

Please list any volunteer work you do:       What do you like to do in your spare time?
1._____         _____
2._____         _____
3._____         _____

Please list two previous places of employment:

_____     _____
*(Business name)*                            *(Business name)*

_____     _____
*(Employer's/Manager's name)*                *(Employer's/Manager's name)*

_____     _____
*(Phone number)*                             *(Phone number)*

Why did you leave? _____         Why did you leave? _____

Can we call for a reference?                  Can we call for a reference?
    [   ] Yes   [   ] No                          [   ] Yes   [   ] No

*Note: In some areas, you may not ask for the applicant's date of birth until you have hired him or her. Check with your local employment standards office.

**References**

Please list at least two references (other than family):

_____
(Name)

_____
(Position/Occupation)

_____
(Phone number)

Can we call for a reference?

   [   ] Yes   [   ] No

What are the top three reasons why you would like found to work here?

1._____

2._____

3._____

At this job, constant cleaning is required. Is this something that you will mind doing?

We have a strict uniform policy. Are you Prepared to adhere to our dress code at all times?

We also require that you maintain a positive mental attitude with staff and customers whenever you are at work. Do you feel that you would be able to do this?

Five years from now, what do you see yourself doing?

_____

Is there any other information about you that you feel we should know?

_____

_____

_____
(Name)

_____
(Position/Occupation)

_____
(Phone number)

Can we call for a reference?

   [   ] Yes   [   ] No

What are three characteristics you believe are in a great staff member?

_____

_____

_____

Are you confident that you either possess these characteristics or have the ability to learn them?

   [   ] Yes   [   ] No

   [   ] Yes   [   ] No

   [   ] Yes   [   ] No

   [   ] Yes   [   ] No

I, the undersigned, declare that the statements made in this application form are to the best of my knowledge true and correct.

_____
(Applicant's signature)

Today's date:_____/_____/_____
             (m)     (d)     (y)

Thank you for taking the time to complete this application. We look forward to having you work with us some day!

that means you can really narrow down what you're looking for.

## 1.5 Hire staff using a Hiring Seminar™

One of the tools we've developed to hire our own staff involves screening for "Core Values" rather than skills. This amazing technique not only saves you money and time, but it allows you to match new employees to the core values and guiding principles you believe are most important. (For a free report on how to hire using this tool, send us an email with "Hiring Seminar" in the subject line to info@startandrunaprofitablecoffeebar.com.)

# 2. EMPLOYMENT STANDARDS

Before you begin to interview, we recommend you contact two agencies. The first is your state's or province's council or commission of human rights. Ask for the employers' guide to human rights in your area. This guide will cover topics such as employers' rights, employees' rights, and recruitment procedures.

The second agency you should contact is your state's or province's government office dealing with employment and labor. Here you should obtain information on, or a copy of, the employer's guide to the current employment standards or fair labor act in your area. These publications cover topics such as minimum wage requirements, shift lengths, and overtime.

# 3. HOW TO INTERVIEW

Once you are familiar with hiring guidelines, you will be ready to start your interviews. Our recommended interviewing procedure — and one that we have found to be successful in hiring dozens of employees over the years — is broken into six parts. Sample 5 is the interviewer's form we use for hiring. (A PDF of this is available on the CD-ROM.)

First, though, make the applicant feel welcome. Take him or her into your office and shut the door to avoid interruptions. Begin the interview by building rapport; ask some conversational questions such as, "Did you have any trouble finding the coffee bar?" Glance at the applicant's application form and ask questions relating to the information on the form, such as "Oh, I see you're in grade 11 — how do you like it?" that will help the applicant relax and give you both the opportunity to get settled in.

Explain that the interview takes about half an hour and has the following parts:

(a) A description of the position

(b) A question period when you ask the applicant questions, during which you may be taking notes

(c) An explanation of job details (e.g., pay structures, hours)

(d) Information about the date and time when successful applicants will be called by to come in for a trial shift (if applicable)

(e) A question period where the applicant can ask you questions

Now proceed with the interview.

## 3.1 Qualifications

The first part of the interview deals with the applicant's qualifications. This gives you the chance to expand on the qualifications that you have already indicated (e.g., in an ad or the in-store poster) are required for the job.

## SAMPLE 5
# INTERVIEWER'S FORM

Date: _____ Interviewer's name: _____

Applicant's surname: _____

Applicant's first name: _____

### 1. QUALIFICATIONS

"As you know, we are looking for cheerful, outgoing, positive people to serve the most important person in our business — the customer.

"Our only requirements are that you are willing to learn the skills necessary to become great at what you do, have a positive attitude, and commit to having fun at work!"

### 2. QUALIFYING QUESTIONS

What made you want to apply for this position? _____

_____

What is most important to you in a job? _____

_____

Think back to a time when you were late for work — how did your boss handle it?

_____

What did you like most about your last boss? _____

_____

What did you like least about your last boss? _____

_____

What do you think are your strongest skills and attributes? _____

_____

_____

What do you think are your weakest skills and attributes? _____

_____

Assuming you come to work with us, there may be times when someone gets sick or a mistake is made in the schedule and we need you to come in right away — it may be a Friday night and you may already have plans. What would you do?

_____

You'll be required to do a lot of cleaning as part of your job — how would you feel about this?

_____

You are also required to wear our standard uniform and conform to our dress standards — are you comfortable with that?

_____

Most importantly, in a customer service position like this, it is vital that you are consistently cheerful and pleasant with customers, even when you don't feel happy — how do you think you would do in this regard?

_____

_____

Where do you see yourself one year from now? Five years from now?

_____

If you could have the ideal job, what would you be doing?

_____

We will be interviewing many people for this position. Some will have more experience, some will have less — tell me why you think we should hire you over someone else. (Be quiet and let them answer!)

_____

_____

Tip:   If you want the applicant to expand on any of his or her answers, ask these open-ended questions:

| | |
|---|---|
| Will you please tell me about it? | How did that make you feel? |
| What did you do differently the next time? | Why do you think that is important? |

## 3. EXPLAIN JOB DETAILS

General duties: serving, cleaning, selling

Number of hours per week _____ Shift times and length _____

Starting pay per hour _____ Training pay per hour _____

Performance reviews are conducted every three months with raises based on your performance.

## 4. SHOULD APPLICANT BE SUCCESSFUL

Explain that training takes about 20 hours and is paid.

Explain what parts of the uniform he or she will be provided with.

## 5. ALLOW APPLICANT TO ASK YOU QUESTIONS

## 6. CONCLUDE INTERVIEW

Thank the applicant for taking the time to come in for the interview.

This doesn't necessarily mean previous coffee or customer service experience. Sometimes people with experience are the worst people to hire because they have learned someone else's system and they may not be willing to change and adapt to your system. On the other hand, if they are willing to adapt to your system, they can become a big help to you, especially in the initial stages of your business.

You may find that people who have never had a job before are motivated to do well and excel because it is their first job and they are eager to prove themselves. On the other hand (yes, there is usually another hand), they may be ill-prepared for the hard work and demanding environment of a busy coffee bar.

Our experience has shown that someone who is outgoing, cheerful, smiles a lot, and seems happy and eager during the interview can be the most rewarding staff member to have.

Part 1 of the interviewer's form is an example of what you might say to the applicant.

## 3.2 Qualifying questions

As you can see in Sample 5, we have designed the qualifying questions to determine how suitable applicants are for the job. The questions also give you a hint of the applicant's future behavior. For example, asking a question about how he or she feels about wearing a uniform suggests to the applicant that he or she will be required to wear a uniform. You can then judge from the applicant's reaction how he or she feels about doing so.

## 3.3 Job details

Part 3 of the interviewer's form gives you the opportunity to explain exactly what the job entails, including the hours and times of shifts, and the wage. Remember to be familiar with the employment standards legislation governing your jurisdiction.

## 3.4 Information for successful applicants

We recommend that you have a date and time in the near future where you will call successful applicants and have them come in for a trial shift (see section **4.** below).

Call only successful applicants so that you don't spend hours on the phone calling dozens of people to deliver the bad news that they didn't get the job. Not only will you be the bearer of bad news but you often find that the person you are calling isn't home and you have to call again and again. If you reach an answering machine and leave a message, you may potentially embarrass the applicant in front of others. Sometimes you get the applicant's parent and have to explain that the son or daughter didn't get the job — another awkward situation.

It is much easier to say to all applicants, "I'll call you by noon this Friday if we would like you to come in for a trial shift. Otherwise we will keep your application on file for possible future consideration."

However, if you are doing your initial hiring, a trial shift won't be possible, as you will need to have staff hired before the coffee bar is set up and open. You will have to bring in a group of staff to start training, and you will have to make final decisions from there; hire staff on a probationary period if possible. Again, check with your local government office about particular requirements in your area. Section **6.** discusses training techniques for both preopening staff and staff you hire after you have opened your doors for business.

## 3.5 Questions

Part 5 of the interview gives the applicant an opportunity to ask you questions. The hiring process is a two-way street: you must like the person, and he or she must like you and the job. The questions (if any) that the applicants ask will give you a reflection of the type of people they are and will give you clues about what they tend to focus on or what is important to them.

If you explained the requirements and job details fully and clearly, it is not uncommon for the applicant to have no questions.

## 3.6 Conclusion

Finish the interview by thanking the person for applying and taking time to come in for the interview. You may want to restate that you will call by noon Friday (or whatever time you choose), if you wish them to come in for a trial shift.

# 4. HOW TO MAKE HIRING DECISIONS YOU WON'T REGRET

The best way to ensure you make a hiring decision you won't regret is to bring the applicant in for a trial shift.

A trial shift is an opportunity to observe the person "in action." Often a person who does well in an interview doesn't work well in a busy and sometimes high-pressure coffee bar. Check with your local government employment or labor standards office, and set the trial shift for the minimum number of hours you must pay for. These few hours are plenty of time to assess and observe each person's work ethic.

For the trial shift we recommend you assign a simple task to the applicant, one that doesn't require a lot of training (and thus time and effort) on your part. The task may involve clearing tables or weighing out coffee to include in a gift pack.

During the trial shift you will want to determine the following:

- Does the applicant work well with staff?
- Does the applicant follow instructions?
- Does the applicant ask questions when he or she doesn't understand something?
- Does the applicant go above and beyond what he or she has been instructed to do?
- Does the applicant take initiative?
- Is the applicant eager or cautious?
- Is the applicant cheerful or serious?
- Is the applicant outgoing or shy?
- Is the applicant enthusiastic or dispassionate?

# 5. DECIDING HOW MANY PEOPLE TO HIRE

How many people you hire will depend on the following factors:

(a) Your hours of operation

(b) Your sales (projections or actuals). If your coffee bar is not yet open, the accuracy of these numbers will depend on the amount of research you have done and the amount of premarketing you are planning to do.

(c) Your coffee bar's traffic flow patterns

(d) Your sales-per-person-hour (SPPH) goals

(e) The amount of emphasis you place on roasting and the amount of roasting you do for retail and wholesale

(f) The number of part-time versus full-time staff you employ (an 8-hour day requires one full-time person or two part-time people)

(g) The number of hours each of your staff want and the times each is available to work

(h) The number of hours *you* will work, either behind the counter or as the roast master. Keep in mind that you will want to spend a large part of your time marketing and building your business.

We have seen some coffee bars open up that fly from the start and need four or five people on at one time, as well as the owner. We have seen other coffee bars open up that have only a few customers trickling in over the first few days of business, thus requiring only one person behind the counter and one roast master. The roast master will be the staffperson who talks to customers, asks customers questions about their current coffee habits, gives customers samples of your coffee to take home, sells customers coffee beans hot out of the roaster, makes suggestive sales and add-on sales (discussed in Chapter 16), and educates the customers about coffee, grinding, and brewing the perfect cup of coffee.

When determining how many staff members to open with, keep in mind that understaffing often results in poor customer service. People are generally tentative and cautious about trying something new. They will try it once and if they have a negative experience you can be sure they won't be back, no matter what you do. It is easier to get customers and keep them than to get customers, lose them, and try to get them back again.

On the other hand, being overstaffed can have a negative impact on your cash flow.

What does this mean in terms of the number of people to hire? To help you make that decision, let's look at the following scenario.

If you are open at 7 a.m., you could run two 8-hour shifts from 6:30 a.m. to 2:30 p.m. with the second 8-hour shift starting at 2:30 p.m. and running till 10:30 p.m. Part-time shifts could then be worked in to meet your traffic flow requirements. This might involve an extra 7 a.m. to 11 a.m. shift to help cover the morning rush and an extra 7 p.m. to 11 p.m. shift to help with the evening rush and closing activities. You would need three or four Monday-to-Friday full-time workers and five or six part-time workers, as well as yourself, acting as roast master.

If things are slow at the beginning, go out and build your sales. You are in the business of building sales (not cutting back staff), especially in the first weeks, months, and even year that your business is open.

Unless you are really off in your projections, think of using your staff more effectively rather than letting them go home early. Get them to drop off fliers in the area or make phone calls. Get them to do PR in your coffee bar or hand out bean samples to customers walking by on the street.

Ask your staff for their ideas about things they can do to help build the business. If you notice a slow pattern, do something to build it up. For example, coffee bars tend to slow down around the lunch period (unless you are serving lunch items), so this is an opportunity to get out and do some marketing. It also allows staff to get caught up on prep work from the morning and prepare for the evening. It allows you time to build wholesale bean volume for your coffee bar and it gives you time to think up ways to build the business during this time — promotions such as "complimentary lunch latte when you bring a friend."

# 6. HOW TO TRAIN YOUR STAFF

Training your staff will be an ongoing process. The coffee industry is an ever-changing one; as new technologies are invented and new discoveries are made, you will want to pass the information on to your staff so that they are able to offer better customer service.

Many of the basics of your business will remain static, however, and it is important that you develop a way to communicate these basics to the many people who will pass through your business over the years. The best way to do this is through the development of a series of manuals and checklists.

We recommend that you develop, at a minimum —

(a) a staff manual with corresponding quiz,

(b) a manager's manual with corresponding quiz,

(c) a staff training checklist, and

(d) a manager's training checklist.

In the following sections we outline a basic training program that covers the major areas of working in a coffee bar. You will want to modify, add, and even delete sections to fit the needs of your business. You can carry out this training yourself or hire an outside trainer to follow your program.

## 6.1 Pre-opening training

Before starting your pre-opening training with new staff members, make sure you are familiar with the training techniques you will be teaching. If necessary, spend one or two days in your coffee bar without your staff, testing and trying for yourself the methods outlined below. If you have never foamed milk before, now is the time to practice. The last thing you want is a staff member showing you how to make a cappuccino! That would not instill staff confidence in your abilities.

Be aware, too, that you will be asked a lot of questions by both staff and customers, and you must be able to answer them accurately. As you spend time learning these new skills, think of potential questions that you may be asked. By anticipating questions, you will avoid potentially embarrassing situations throughout the training process. However, if you are asked a question you don't know the answer to, admit it. Find out the answer as soon as you can, and tell the staff member or customer what you have learned. Encourage questions as much as you can: they give you an opportunity to learn.

Plan your training schedule so that staff know what time frame they are dealing with and what topics they will be covering. Put into practice the public speakers' motto: "Tell them what you're going to tell them, tell them, then tell them what you told them."

### 6.1a Step 1

One week before the staff begins training, give each person a copy of your staff manual. This will give them all a good idea of what your coffee bar is about and the expectations you have of them.

Number your manuals on the back page or inside cover and have the staff sign out the manual. This will allow you to keep tabs on who has manuals and who doesn't. It also reduces theft and loss, as well as preventing a manual from falling into your competitors' hands.

Ask the staff to bring the manual with them on the day you start the official training.

### 6.1b Step 2

Begin the first day of training by giving your staff a quiz on the manual. This quiz is not really a test but rather a way to reinforce what the staff has read in the manual. A quiz helps assist with the learning process.

### 6.1c Step 3

Go through the correct quiz responses with the staff members as a group. We recommend that staff members correct their own copies and fill any answers they have missed. Get the group involved by asking them to read out their answers (it can get boring if you read all the answers). This also reinforces the learning process and makes things a bit more interesting.

### 6.1d Step 4

Use videos. There are some excellent videos on the market today that can introduce your new staff to the exciting world of coffee. Make sure you have watched the videos in detail first. There will likely be discrepancies between the way the video states or shows something and the way you are doing things. Make careful note of these and then as the video plays for your staff, stop it at these points to clearly point them out. Pointing out these discrepancies is important, especially when they involve drink recipes. There are many variations in the measurements and techniques for making specialty coffees, and you will want to ensure complete consistency among all your staff members.

### 6.1e Step 5

By now the staff should have a good understanding of the company they will be working for and what is expected of them, as well as an introduction to the world of coffee. They are now ready for hands-on work.

The best way to handle hands-on training is to think of your coffee bar as being made up of various "stations." Outlining specific stations helps distinguish the roles and areas of expertise that are required in your coffee bar.

We recommend a core of the following stations:

- Roasting station
- Gourmet coffee station
- Specialty coffee station

• Money exchange station

Additional stations might include a dishwashing station, baked goods/food items prep station, fresh squeezed juices station, baking station, and tea/coffee equipment sales station.

The responsibilities at each core station are outlined below.

**Note:** All stations are responsible for greeting customers, keeping the coffee bar clean, providing the highest quality service to customers, creating a WOW! experience for them (see Chapters 14 and 16 for more on how to create a WOW! experience), and serving the highest quality products.

(a) **Roasting station.** Whereas the highest priority of the people behind the counter is the customer, the highest priority for the roast master is roasting coffee and promoting roasting to customers. The roast master is responsible for helping customers select and/or blend the beans they wish to have roasted, roasting green beans for customers, packaging the beans, and ensuring the customer receives the beans with accurate care and handling information. We highly recommend that the roast master be stationed right at the roaster rather than behind the counter, and assists staff members behind the counter only if absolutely necessary.

Failing to enforce this is a major mistake we have seen many businesses make in the past. If you do not promote your in-store roasting, you are missing the whole point of having it in the first place and it will affect your sales negatively.

While roasting gives you huge revenue potential, that is all it is — potential — until you promote it to your customer. One of the best ways that we have seen to promote it is to make this station the focus of your entire operation.

We also recommend that once they have completed training for the roasting station, your staff be awarded with "Roast Master" status. This awarding process should take the form of a certificate and a "Roast Master" name tag that the staffperson wears when he or she is on shift. The roast master will be a major key to your success.

(b) **Gourmet coffee station.** The person assigned to this station is responsible for filling liquid coffee orders and ensuring that your "on tap" coffees are kept freshly brewed.

(c) **Specialty coffee station.** The staff-person assigned to this station is responsible for preparing specialty coffee orders (for cappuccino, for example). He or she typically serves them over-the-counter-style to the customer. This person is also responsible for keeping the espresso machine clean and in good working order.

(d) **Money exchange station.** The person assigned to this station is responsible for one of the most important functions in your coffee bar: taking and suggesting orders, and accepting money in exchange for the products being served. This person may also be responsible for "backup" duties such as order preparation and serving. Because of this station's importance to the profitability of your coffee bar, the person at the money exchange station is often a senior staff member or manager.

Depending on how many staff members you start with, it is probably easiest to break your training group into two. This is more time effective than training one large group (using time efficiently is important because you will be paying your staff for the time they spend getting trained), and the groups will learn more effectively as well. Having a large group usually results in someone not being able to see or hear properly; by investing the extra time now, you will save yourself needing to go over everything again one-on-one with staff members.

If you are doing all the training on your own and the group is large (over six people), you will want to schedule the two groups for different times.

Alternatively, if you still have a lot of instore cleaning and organizing that needs to be done, you can place one group in charge of this while you take the other group and start training. As yet another alternative, you can have one group write the manual quiz while you start training the other group and then switch.

If you have a partner or associate to help you, you will take one group while the partner takes the other. (Make sure your partner or associate is also fully trained beforehand.)

### 6.1f Step 6

Go through the tasks of each station until they have all been successfully completed. "Successfully completed" means that each staff member has satisfactorily practiced the task.

Each task should be divided into three parts —

(a) explanation,

(b) demonstration, and

(c) practice.

## 6.2 Training once you're open

You will be hiring only one (or maybe two) staff members at a time once you are open, so group training will be unnecessary. Depending on how comprehensive your training checklist is, you may be able to have your manager or even a trusted staff member conduct the training for you. The only word of caution here is that any uncorrected bad habits a staff member has picked up along the way will be passed along to the new staff member. However, it is often through training someone else that a staff member realizes his or her mistake and corrects it.

## 6.3 The importance of a training checklist

If you do not create a training checklist, or if it is not comprehensive, your training will not be systematic or able to be reproduced.

There are several advantages to a training program which can be reproduced. For one thing, you don't have to do all the training yourself. Training the first few staff members may be fun, but three or four years and dozens of staff members later, the fun tends to wane.

Secondly, a comprehensive training checklist allows for easier expansion should you decide to open additional locations or to franchise.

Thirdly, a training program which can be reproduced means you can leave others to run your business for you with the assurance that the standards you expect to be upheld actually are being upheld because they are clearly understood by everyone involved — staff and managers.

If you have a systematic training program, you are using your time and your money more effectively. Your time is used more effectively because you are not running from here to there remembering this, remembering that, forgetting this, forgetting that. Instead, you are packing as much as you can into a given minute or hour, which makes you, your staff, and thus your business, more productive. Increased productivity means increased profits. By having a systematic training program, you can dramatically cut your training time, saving the extra wages you would have to pay for haphazard training.

A systematic training program allows you to measure the costs of training so you can build them into your pro formas and your cash flow projections. This is very helpful in controlling your expenses and, thus, increasing profit.

If your training is systematized, you can also plan your training. Planning your training means scheduling it to occur during a quieter time of the day, for example, so there is minimum disruption in customer service and the staff members (both the new one and the trainer) can better focus on the training, making your training sessions more productive and effective, and again saving you time and money.

In the end, a training checklist system assures you that all your staff has the same basic level of understanding. This is of utmost importance if you want to consistently deliver high quality service to your customers.

## 6.4 Training certificates

Once staff members have been trained at all stations, it is a great idea to award (and reward) them with a training completion certificate (see Sample 6). Inexpensive 8.5" x 11" blank certificates can be purchased at your local print shop or office supplies store, or you can use the sample provided on the CD-ROM.

By recognizing your staff members' achievements, you will be helping to instill a sense of pride in your staff that will shine through in all aspects of their work.

## 6.5 Training follow-up

Three months after your staff have completed the training checklist, and every three months from that point on, we recommend you complete a staff performance review for each of your staff members. This will help keep your staff motivated and focused on ways they can improve, and, in turn, will motivate them to offer even better service to your customers.

The staff performance review should outline each of the tasks required at each station and measure the performance standard. For example, one task of the money exchange station is "greeting the customer." The description of the task would be "Staffperson uses honored guest greeting procedure" (see Chapter 16). And the performance standard would be "Greets customers within five seconds of their entering the coffee bar."

## TRAINING COMPLETION CERTIFICATE

# Congratulations!

This is to certify that

_____

has completed The Coffee Bar staff training program.

_____          _____
*Signature of owner/manager*                    *Date*

## 7. STATION DESIGNATION

It's a good idea to give your staff designated stations for their shifts. That means one staff member is in charge of a particular station for the duration of his or her shift. Make sure, however, that you encourage your staff to work together with staff at other stations in the coffee bar. The idea is to serve customers as quickly and efficiently as possible, not to just "do your job" by remaining at one station. Instruct your staff to ask for help if it is needed.

Below we have listed some pros and cons of station designation.

For more information on how performance reviews can be tied to raises and bonuses, see Chapter 15.

### 7.1 Pros

- One person is accountable. If coffees are not kept properly brewed, for example, you know who is responsible and you can deal easily with the situation. If multiple staff members are in charge of brewing coffees, often no one will take responsibility.

- Personalities can be matched with tasks. Some staff members will really shine in customer relations and may be best suited to the money exchange station where good rapport skills are necessary. Other staff members may be more technically oriented and shine in areas such as product preparation. They may be better suited to the specialty coffee or gourmet coffee stations.

- Station designations can make work more efficient because staff aren't running around, bumping into each other.
- Staff may be happier because they are doing something they are well suited to and enjoy.

## 7.2 Cons

- Station designations can be inefficient if they are inflexible and one station requires more staff than another. For example, if one staff member is stationed on the specialty coffee station but there are no orders for that station at that moment, he or she may be standing at that station with nothing to do while the staff member at the money exchange station is run ragged. This is obviously not the way to provide your customers with WOW! customer service.
- Staff may get bored if they are on one station for a long time.

The best thing to do is to designate stations but encourage flexibility so that they can help each other as necessary. For example, the responsibility of the staff member at the gourmet coffee station is primarily brewing coffee. This may or may not be a full-time job, depending on how much liquid coffee your coffee bar uses. If it is a part-time job only, you could assign this staff member to be responsible for preparing other orders such as teas or baked goods.

# 8. HOW TO FIND A GREAT MANAGER

At some point, your personal lifestyle and/or your coffee bar's profits may dictate the need for someone other than you to run the coffee bar. This person must be someone you can rely on to take responsibilities off your shoulders and competently deal with day-to-day challenges as they arise. He or she will likely be one of your existing staff members or assistant managers rather than an outside manager brought in from off-site. This will be for a number of reasons:

(a) A person with management experience outside your coffee bar may be groomed under another management style and may not fit into your management mold, be compatible with your management style, or live up to your expectations.

(b) An outside manager will have no more than a general knowledge of your coffee bar's day-to-day operations and functions. This means that his or her training must begin at step one.

(c) It will be difficult to tell from just an interview how well he or she will interact with your staff.

(d) Staff may resent an outsider coming in and telling them how to do their job. This could lead to low staff morale, which in turn results in poor service to customers.

When choosing a new coffee bar manager, ask yourself:

- Is this person consistent in his or her behavior, moods, and thought processes?
- Is this person well liked and respected by other staff members?
- Is this person a high achiever?
- Does excellence shine through in the service he or she delivers to customers?

- Does the person show characteristics of leadership?

- Does the person have the qualities, or the ability to develop the qualities, that will make him or her a good manager?

- Do you think the person will have a positive influence on the coffee bar and staff?

- Does the person enjoy learning and taking on new challenges?

- Does the person thrive on additional responsibilities?

- Does he or she plan to be around in a year? Two years? Five years?

Also take into consideration the managerial candidate's —

(a) current abilities,

(b) commitment to the business,

(c) commitment to your principles of operation,

(d) ability to promote your business in a positive way,

(e) long-term goals and objectives,

(f) ability to learn, grow, and accept additional responsibility,

(g) ability to be organized,

(h) ability to manage financial responsibility, and

(i) willingness to accept the position of manager with all the responsibilities that go along with it.

When you are ready to think about promoting your manager, follow these 11 steps:

**Step 1.** Once you have decided who you would like as manager, find out if that person is interested in the promotion —

sometimes a person is great with the customers but is not a business or people manager.

**Step 2.** Explain to your candidate that the time has come for the responsibilities of manager to be passed along and that you would like to offer them this opportunity.

**Step 3.** Explain your reasons for choosing them. For example, you could say: "Mary, I feel that you exhibit many of the talents that this job requires. You're looked up to by other staff members, you are well organized, you set and accomplish goals, you take action, you have high service standards and give ten times more to the customers than they expect. You are responsible, dependable, and trustworthy — and I think you'd make a great manager."

**Step 4.** Explain what changes this would mean to the person with regards to:

- daily schedules
- responsibilities
- pay structures

**Step 5.** If your candidate is willing, ask other staff members their thoughts on what you're proposing.

**Step 6.** Allow them to ask questions.

**Step 7.** Allow for decision time (if required). If the decision requires a location transfer, for example, your candidate may need to talk to his or her partner before making a decision.

**Step 8.** If the staff member immediately accepts, congratulate him or her with a handshake and pat on the back.

**Step 9.** Set changeover date.

**Step 10.** Plan for changeover:

- Explain the manager training program to the new manager and set goals for what areas will be covered over what period.

- Decide on the best way to notify other staff members of the changes — individually or in a group meeting?

- Outline to staff how the changes will affect them; discuss possible challenges as a result of the changes, ways to overcome them, and ways to make the change a positive experience for everyone involved.

**Step 11.** Take action.

---

# COMMITMENT BOX

 I, _____ , commit to building an all-star customer service team, creating and using training checklists for my staff, and awarding staff with training recognition certificates on completion.

_____          _____
*(your signature)*                              *(today's date)*

---

# 8
# HOW TO KEEP YOUR COFFEE BAR CLEAN

I cleaned the windows and I swept the floor
And I polished up the handle of the big front door
I polished up that handle so carefullee
That now I am the Ruler of the Queen's Navee!

— W. S. GILBERT

You've set up your coffee bar the way you dreamed about it, hired great staff, had your grand opening, and now you're enjoying the excitement and bustle of day-to-day operations.

One of the most important daily chores will be keeping your coffee bar clean. This is not only for the enjoyment of your customers but also for their health and the health of your business. Any establishment that serves food and drink must maintain stringent cleanliness standards. Otherwise it risks having customers walk away in disgust or, worse, being shut down by the health department.

There's lots of equipment to keep spotless in a coffee bar. We give you some pointers below.

## 1. KEEPING YOUR COFFEE BAR CLEAN

Keep the coffee bar uncluttered and organized. Keep paperwork, boxes, and cartons out of your customers' line of sight.

Ask your staff to be clean-aware; they should take the initiative on cleaning tasks such as wiping out a fridge, washing a fruit container, wiping out a shelf, dusting a light fixture, or cleaning the areas and items listed below:

- Seating-area tables and chairs
- Stand-up bar
- Kickguards
- Counter areas
- Mats and/or carpets

- Windows and window ledges
- Roaster and roaster ventilation systems
- Front floors, back floors, storage area floors
- Cream and sugar station counters
- Straw, napkin, cream, sugar, stir stick, lid, and honey containers
- Garbage cans, especially those that the customers use
- Sinks
- Storage areas
- Kitchen/prep areas
- Fridges, freezers, display cases, and other equipment
- Exterior patio or seating areas
- Outside walkways and parking areas

# 2. CLEANING TIPS

## 2.1 Floors

Give your floors a good sweep and mop every night after closing or, if you are open 24 hours, at least once within the 24-hour period. If mopping must be done when your coffee bar is open, ensure that a "Caution — Wet Floor" sign is in full view of customers walking in so they know to be careful. Try to time your mopping for less busy periods so that you don't inconvenience customers.

Sweep floors before washing. Then mop with hot water and the appropriate cleaning solution (ideally an environmentally friendly type) for your type of flooring.

## 2.2 Dusting

You will need to keep your coffee bar well dusted, focusing particularly on merchandise areas, all counter and shelving areas, and ceiling light fixtures (you don't want dust falling from the ceiling and landing on top of someone's latte). One helpful tip is to use Pledge on laminate counters. It minimizes the dust and fingerprints on these surfaces that are tough to keep clean.

## 2.3 Restrooms

If your coffee bar has restrooms, you will want to ensure that they are kept absolutely spotless. Customers will judge the cleanliness of a restroom more critically than any other area of the coffee bar: a clean restroom can only enhance your customers' WOW! experience. Here are some bathroom cleaning tips:

(a) Keep a restroom check record and ensure that restrooms are checked at least once every hour, depending on how busy your location is. (McDonald's, for example, has a 20-minute restroom check policy.)

(b) Keep this record in full view of customers as a way of making a statement about your commitment to cleanliness and to making their visit a pleasant one.

(c) Keep towel racks and toilet paper well stocked.

(d) Keep mirrors shiny and free of fingerprints and dust.

(e) Keep sinks and faucets shiny and clean.

(f) Keep counters clean and free of soap and water.

(g) Keep floors and walls clean.

(h) Empty and thoroughly sanitize garbage cans regularly.

(i)   Keep hand soaps topped up.

(j)   Keep the restroom doors shut at all times (this may mean installing a door spring closing system).

(k)   Keep the bathroom fan on at all times.

## 2.4 Linen supplies

Use white cloths, thoroughly dampened, for cleaning in customer areas. Remove excess moisture from the cloth by folding it once and then twisting.

If cloths are not badly soiled, you can rinse them with water or soak them in hot soapy water, rinse, and use them again. Be sure to store soiled linen in covered containers, out of sight of your customers, as it can get quite smelly and unsanitary. Most linen supply companies supply large bags with a hanging rack for easy storage and removal.

Arrange a regular pickup time with your linen service company. You'll probably want them to come by once or twice per week, depending on your volume.

## 2.5 Roaster and bean display

Keep the walls behind your bean displays free of dust and chaff, and make sure the coffee sacks are neatly rolled down at all times, with clean scoops inside.

## 2.6 Hygiene

It is very important that staff wash their hands before handling or prepping any food items, especially after going to the bathroom, touching their face or hair, or handling money or toxic cleaning products.

# 3. THE IMPORTANCE OF DISHWASHING

A dirty dish is a definite turn-off for customers and leaves the impression that other items in the coffee bar may be unsanitary as well. In addition, a dish that has not been cleaned properly can transfer germs to a customer, which could have serious consequences.

## 3.1 Dishwashers

If your coffee bar has a dishwasher, follow the manufacturer's recommendations for precleaning, loading, and washing. Rinse any large food particles off dishes before putting them in the dishwasher, and use a brush to take off hard-to-remove lipstick.

## 3.2 The three-step method of dishwashing

If your coffee bar is busy, you will need to invest in an automatic dishwasher. If you do not have a dishwasher, or for items that are washed by hand, a triple sink will be required. Use the three-step method of dishwashing to properly sanitize dishes. Although it is called the "three-step method," the procedure actually involves five steps:

(a)   Rinse off food particles

(b)   Wash in sink 1

(c)   Rinse in sink 2

(d)   Sanitize in a water and bleach solution in sink 3

(e)   Drip dry

Check with your local health inspector for guidelines on water temperature and bleach requirements.

### 3.3 Putting dishes away

Double-check that dishes are clean before putting them away. Look especially for lipstick residue.

Check for any chips or cracks. If a chip or crack is found, you must discard the dish immediately for health and sanitation reasons.

When putting dishes away, put the cups used for cold drinks in cold places and the cups for hot drinks in hot places (e.g., on top of the coffee brewing system or the espresso machine). Of course, these places should be clean before you put clean dishes there. It's a good idea to put the dishes on bar mats and this may actually be required by the health inspector in your area.

### 3.4 Dish handling

When handling mugs, cups, or glasses, do not touch the rim of the cup with your hands. This contaminates it and you will have to wash it again.

When handling cutlery, make sure to touch only the handle.

## 4. SPECIFIC DISHWASHING INSTRUCTIONS

### 4.1 Baking pans

Make an extra effort to clean hard-to-get-to areas such as the corners of the pan. If a pan is washed carelessly once, the result is often a black crust that is almost impossible to remove later. Use steel wool to remove baked-on particles.

Baking pans will rust if left in water for an extended period, so don't soak them too long. Once they're washed, place them upside down and allow them to drip dry in a warm place.

### 4.2 Milk steaming pitchers and foaming spoons

As milk heats during steaming, it adheres to the walls of the pitchers and to the spoons, making simple scrub brushing ineffective. You'll need to scrub them with steel-wool at the end of each day.

### 4.3 Espresso machine group handles

Group handles hold the stainless steel brew baskets on your espresso machine. If you don't want *really* strong coffee, follow these steps to clean them.

(a) Pop off the filters using a spoon or other utensil as leverage.

(b) Use steel wool to scrub both screens and inside the group heads to remove all espresso stains.

(c) Return the proper screen to the proper filter (the small single screen fits on the single-spout handle; the larger double-capacity screen, on the double-spout handle).

(d) Pop the screens securely back into place.

(e) Allow water to drain through for a few seconds to rinse away any soap residue — otherwise it might end up in someone's coffee.

(f) Run water through the group handle first thing in the morning to clean it of any cleaning residue left over from the evening cleaning.

## 4.4 Thermal carafes

Thermal carafe coffeemakers must not be submerged in water, but the outsides can be wiped off and the insides scrubbed with a long-handled brush and then thoroughly rinsed with hot water. You can use baking soda or other soap solution. Remember to let clean water drain out the spout to clear out any soap residue.

## 4.5 Cream and milk containers

When washing out cream and milk containers, disassemble and thoroughly sanitize all parts. If cream and milk find their way under rubber seals and into cracks, bacteria can grow and become a health threat to staff and customers. At closing, store leftover cream and milk in back-up containers, and be sure to use that cream and milk first, upon reopening the store.

## 4.6 Sugar and toppings containers

When washing sugar and toppings containers (e.g., for cinnamon), ensure that the container has thoroughly dried before refilling it. Otherwise the contents may lump together and cause your customers inconvenience before you end up throwing it all away.

The best time to wash these items is at the end of the day when the containers can dry overnight. Put them on top of the espresso machine to dry; the morning shift can fill them.

## 4.7 Display case and serving platters

Keep all serving platters and serving utensils for baked goods clean at all times.

Clean all areas of the display case, especially those that will be seen by customers from the front. Be sure to remove uncovered baked goods from the display case when you are cleaning the glass so that you don't get cleaning product on any food item.

## 5. KEEPING YOUR COFFEE BAR WELL STOCKED

Part of your staff's cleaning duties should include stocking — for example, filling the sugar containers and making sure there are enough napkins out. Making sure all areas of your coffee bar are kept well stocked increases the level of service given to your customers and reduces customer inconveniences. Keep a constant eye on the level of stock at —

- the cream and sugar station (includes sugar, honey, cream and milk, lids, stir sticks, and napkins),
- the display cases,
- the baked goods areas,
- the drink coolers, and
- the specialty coffee station (includes condiments such as nutmeg, cinnamon, vanilla, and chocolate).

## COMMITMENT BOX

I, _____ , commit to keeping my coffee bar spotlessly clean and properly sanitized at all times.

_____          _____
*(your signature)*                          *(today's date)*

# PART 2
## THE PRODUCT

# 9
# ROASTING COFFEE

That is a perfume in which I delight; when they roast coffee near my house, I hasten to open the door to take in all the aroma.

— JEAN-JACQUES ROUSSEAU

## 1. COFFEE

### 1.1 What is coffee?

Coffee beans are actually the "pits" (like a cherry pit) of the red berries that grow on a coffee plant. These plants are evergreen shrubs.

There are two major types of beans: arabica and robusta. Arabica beans are grown at high elevations and are characteristically hard beans with superior flavor and aroma, and a rich taste. Robusta beans are grown at lower elevations and typically have a harsher taste and up to double the caffeine content of the arabicas.

Different strains of coffee beans have their own characteristics that vary from country to country, region to region, and season to season.

### 1.2 Growing coffee

Growing good coffee is a lot like growing good grapes for wine: you need the right climatic condition, altitude, soil, and care. The ideal growing conditions are moderate rainfall, volcanic soil, and moderate sunshine.

Coffee plants are started from seeds, usually planted in a protected environment such as a greenhouse. At about six months, the seedlings are planted in rows outside on the plantation. Within about five years, the plants — which are pruned to about six feet for easy picking — bloom with jasmine-scented flowers. Within months, small green cherries appear and soon ripen to a bright red color. At that point they are ready for picking. The cherries must be hand-picked since they ripen at different times, and care must be taken in the picking process: if underripe cherries are picked, the coffee will have little flavor; if overripe cherries are picked, the coffee will have a strong, harsh flavor.

## 1.3 Processing

After picking, the coffee cherries are processed by one of two methods: dry or wet.

Three-fifths of the world's coffee is processed using the dry method. The cherries are laid out to dry in the sun for three to four weeks, after which they are put into tumblers where the dried outside shell is rubbed off, leaving the clean, green coffee bean.

In the wet method, the cherries are fermented in large vats of water for 24 to 48 hours to loosen the cherry mucilage from the beans. The beans are then washed and either sun- or machine-dried. This method has been criticized because of the huge amounts of water used and the burden it puts on local waterway systems. "Semi-wet" processes are slowly being introduced that use up to 90 percent less water.

## 1.4 Grading

Whichever method is used in the processing, the coffee beans are then graded by size to ensure even roasting. If beans are not sorted to some degree in terms of size, you would have smaller beans burning during roasting, while larger beans would not be roasted enough.

Two beans that have grown as one are called pea berries and are said to have a more delicate flavor than their halved counterparts.

## 2. DECAFFEINATING

Caffeine is a mild stimulant that naturally occurs in hundreds of plants, including coffee. While the research on caffeine is controversial, the general consensus seems to be that caffeine is good for you in moderation and is bad for you in excess. Arabica beans generally have less caffeine than the robustas; this is one of the reasons customers often comment on how the side effects linked to caffeine are reduced when they drink a higher-grade coffee.

Caffeine can be removed by one of two methods: indirect or direct.

In the indirect method, beans are soaked in hot water to dissolve the caffeine and the water is treated with a chemical solvent to remove the caffeine. The water is then sprayed back on the beans so the flavor constituents can be reabsorbed.

In the direct method, the beans are soaked right in the chemical-laden water. The chemical solvent is then removed from the water and the beans are put back in the water to soak up the flavor.

The four main decaffeinating processes are —

(a) Methylene chloride

(b) Ethyl acetate

(c) Supercritical carbon dioxide

(d) Swiss water method

## 2.1 Methylene chloride (DCM)

Methylene chloride (DCM) is usually used in the direct method. It is the least expensive process for decaffeinating green coffee beans, and many people think it produces the best tasting beans. Although DCM is carcinogenic (as are all solvents used in chemical decaffeination), the trace amounts left in the coffee are low enough to be acceptable to governing agencies. Also, any residual

DCM on the beans evaporates during the roasting process because of its low flash point. There is, therefore, virtually no DCM on roasted beans.

DCM is an ozone-depleting gas, however, and — at least in the European Union — all DCM plants have had to change over to different solvents because DCM can escape during manufacturing, transporting, or use.

## 2.2 Ethyl acetate

Ethyl acetate exists in fruits in minute quantities. For this reason, many people consider this method of decaffeination "natural." However, ethyl acetate is commercially prepared for decaffeinating coffee from ethyl alcohol and acetic acid.

## 2.3 Supercritical carbon dioxide

This process uses liquid carbon dioxide that has been compressed to 200 times the standard atmospheric pressure. It takes between five and eight hours for the carbon dioxide to extract the caffeine from the water. This is slightly faster than DCM or ethyl acetate. Since carbon dioxide is highly selective for caffeine, it creates no toxicity hazards.

Liquid carbon dioxide is chemically stable, and since it is a natural component of roasted coffee, as well as being in the air we breathe, residual amounts remaining after the decaffeinating and the roasting processes are indistinguishable in the final cup.

This process is used for large-scale decaffeination only and is not yet widely available for top-grade beans.

## 2.4 Swiss water process

The Swiss water process (SWP) is a chemical-free process of decaffeination. The SWP trademark is owned by Kraft; the SWP decaffeination plant is located in Burnaby, British Columbia.

The process involves a number of steps. First, a starter batch of unroasted green beans are soaked in water. The water absorbs both the caffeine and the flavor components of the beans. The caffeine-laden water is then passed through carbon filters that remove the caffeine but not the flavor components, resulting in water that has flavor but no caffeine.

Next, a new batch of beans are soaked in this flavor-charged water. As in step one, the caffeine leaches into the water. However, because the water has absorbed as much flavor constituent as it can hold, the flavor stays inside the beans.

This process is unique because the bean is left with its original flavor.

# 3. ROASTING

## 3.1 What is roasting?

In its green state, the unroasted bean has an earthy smell and exhibits none of the attractive, aromatic characteristics of the roasted bean. You will be amazed at the number of customers who will pick up a handful of green beans and exclaim, "Oh! Is that what coffee looks like?"

Roasting is the process of transferring heat from one area (your roaster) to another (your coffee beans). During the roasting process, certain flavor oils, waxes, and acids are burned off the beans, while others develop. This is why you get such different tasting cups of coffee when the same kind of beans are subjected to two different roasts, a mild and a dark, for example. (For a discussion of the different roasts, see section **4**.)

## 3.2 History of roasting machines

Early roasting machines tumbled the beans over gas flames in a perforated cylinder that often reached temperatures over 1,000°F. Because it was so hot, this method had a number of problems. It tended to char the outer portion of the bean, and the coffee would not be uniformly roasted. As well, the high heat roasted away many of the coffee's flavor constituents. The result was a burnt-tasting cup of coffee.

It was later discovered that far fewer flavor constituents were dissipated if the coffee was roasted at about 500°F; new roasters were designed to roast quickly at lower temperatures by rapidly circulating the beans and the heat.

But even the gas-fired roasters of today are fraught with problems. For one, the hot air from a gas-fired roaster is high in aldehyde, ketone, alcohol, acid, and other organic vapors. These are very reactive and readily combine to create smog and smoke. In addition to the pollution problem, this smog and smoke can get on the bean and affect the end coffee taste.

There are also problems with stack fires caused by the tarry coating built up on the insides of venting cylinders. Most tars in today's commercial roasters, however, are passed through afterburners at temperatures of 800°F to 1,800°F, which reduces the pollutants.

## 3.3 Our roaster of choice

Today's large, gas-fired roasters (also known as batch roasters) are very expensive and require extensive training periods.

For this reason, we recommend hot-air roasters such as the one sold by Universal Coffee in Vancouver, Canada. This electric roaster eliminates many of the challenges of a gas-fired roaster by roasting the beans in a column of heated air. Air currents levitate the beans 50 feet per second. This method allows heat to pass through the thin film on the surface of the beans without burning it. The heat enters the body of the bean. The bean's internal temperature rises more or less uniformly. This uniformity results in better flavor development and a smoother, richer tasting cup of coffee.

(Technology is changing rapidly, so drop us a line for our latest recommended in-store roaster, with the words "roaster recommendation" in the subject line, at info@ startandrunaprofitablecoffeebar.com.)

## 3.4 Eight simple steps to roasting

Many of today's commercially available roasters reduce the complicated roasting process to eight simple steps:

(a) Weigh the beans.

(b) Check roasting chart for approximate roasting time.

(c) Check roaster temperature.

(d) Place the beans into the roaster.

(e) Start timer.

(f) When timer sounds, compare bean sample colors.

(g) If beans need additional time, reset timer.

(h) If bean color matches that of the sample, pull release lever.

## 3.5 Results of the roasting process

The roasting process draws out the qualities inherent to the particular bean being roasted. The changes that occur as the green bean transforms to its brown state are called its "development." This development is influenced by —

(a) the length of time the coffee is roasted,

(b) the temperature the coffee is roasted at,

(c) the means of heat conveyance, and

(d) the rate of cooling.

### 3.5a Weight loss

There is significant weight loss during roasting. Depending on the water content of the bean and the roasting method, mild roasts can lose anywhere from 10 percent to 12 percent of the green bean weight, while the darker roasts can lose as much as 20 percent.

You will want to factor this weight loss into your pricing strategy. If you base your price on the cost of a green bean pound, you will need to add 10 percent to 12 percent to the price for medium roasts and about 20 percent for dark roasts in order to get the accurate roasted weight price.

### 3.5b Caramelization

During roasting, the sucrose in the bean is altered to form caramel and decomposed sugars. This alteration results in the change of color seen in the bean (it's just like baking a cookie). If a coffee is roasted too dark, the carbohydrates actually convert to charcoal, hence the burnt taste of over-roasted beans.

### 3.5c Cell wall destruction

The bean becomes brittle as it roasts. The internal gas pressure created by the heat can cause the bean to swell to twice its original volume, causing a softening of its cell walls and brittleness.

This brittleness is important because the more brittle the bean is, the easier it is for water to penetrate the ground coffee particles to draw out the flavor. This is part of the reason that a mildly roasted coffee does not taste as strong as a dark roasted coffee.

You can test brittleness by crushing a bean between your fingers. You will find that dark roasted coffee breaks quite easily, while the milds are much harder to break.

### 3.5d Revelation of chaff

As the bean roasts there is a revelation of the chaff that can be seen at the bean crevice. The chaff dries out and detaches itself from the bean. This chaff is drawn away from the beans to the back of the roaster by a fan. Crevice development is one of the clues indicating how far the bean is in the roasting process.

### 3.5e Acid formation/depletion

Some acids are burned off during the roasting process while other acids are formed from the thermal decomposition of carbohydrates. This is why the same bean can produce such different tasting cups of coffee when it is roasted for different lengths of time.

### 3.5f Decrease in acidity

Acidity refers to the liveliness or verve that a coffee has, and is characteristic of arabica coffees. As a coffee roasts, its acidity decreases. Coffee without acidity is generally dull and flat.

### 3.5g Oils come to the surface

Coffee becomes more oily as it roasts because of the increase in cell wall destruction. The cell walls act as a protective layer for volatile aromatics locked inside the bean; as swelling occurs and the cell walls are destroyed, the oils are released and become more apparent on the surface of the bean.

### 3.5h *Caffeine burns off*

Dark roasting does not necessarily make the coffee's caffeine content stronger. Caffeine levels are nearly identical in all shades of roasts and are slightly lower in very dark roasts.

## 3.6 The cooling process

Beans in most gourmet roasters are cooled using an air method rather than the water method, which "quenches" the beans.

In quenching, the beans are sprayed with water to stop the roasting process. As the water hits the beans, it absorbs the heat and is carried away in the form of steam. One criticism of quenching is that the steam may also carry away with it certain flavor characteristics of the bean. A second criticism is that the amount of water used can be abused by roasters. In other words, they use more water to create false weight in the beans to result in a higher yield for them. In North America, any bean containing more than 12 percent water must say "water added" on the package.

After roasting, the beans lose 0.5 percent to 1 percent of weight in the form of carbon dioxide gas that continues to be released after roasting. Unfortunately, the gas also carries away flavor. This is why beans begin to stale within hours of roasting.

## 4. THE DIFFERENT ROASTS

There are six roasts generally recognized by roasters. These are —

- Cinnamon
- Medium high
- City
- Full city
- French
- Italian (also called espresso)

We recommend, however, that you focus on three only, using the following terms:

(a) Mild

(b) Medium

(c) Dark

There are a number of reasons for this. First, three terms are simpler. It is easy to train your staff about these roasts and their terms. Instead of having your staff (and your customers) memorize six different roasts and terms, they need to remember only three.

Second, because you will be doing your own roasting, you want to have a system that is consistent and easy for staff to remember. By focusing on three roasts, you (and your customers) will be able to tell the difference between them.

Third, you will need color samples of every bean you carry in order to properly test your roasts. It is very tedious to maintain six different roasts in potentially dozens of different bean varieties.

Fourth, it is much easier to pinpoint the type of roast your customers enjoy. It is easy to supply them with samples of each roast — mild, medium, and dark. You will find that one roast will typically stand above the rest. This makes recommending coffee a much easier task for you and your staff. As your customers become more educated and sophisticated in their tastes, you can easily start custom roasting a "medium high" or a

"French" by roasting mild-mediums, or medium-darks.

When determining whether a coffee is a mild, medium, or dark, you will want to take into consideration:

- Color
- Color distribution
- Weight
- Crevice development
- Bean surface (dry versus oily)
- Brittleness
- Aroma

## 4.1 The three roasts

### 4.1a Milds

Many roasters use the term "cinnamon" to label their mildest coffee, but we have found the term "cinnamon" confusing to customers: "I don't want flavored!" they often exclaim. As well, saying the word "cinnamon" creates a feeling of that taste on the palate, which can influence the tasting decision and leave customers unsatisfied when they find that the roast does not in fact taste like cinnamon. "Mild" is a less loaded term.

The mild roasts can be difficult to roast well because of the danger of under-roasting. Under-roasted coffee tastes tart and weak, and is highly undesirable.

A mild roast is an even, light-brown shade. If the color is speckled or blotched, or if the bean is very heavy and hard, it may be under-roasted. The surface of the bean will be dry and will smell slightly tart.

You may notice that the crevice is still flaky, since the chaff has not fully separated from the bean. If the crevice is underdeveloped, the beans may be under-roasted.

### 4.1b Mediums

Medium roasts should be a medium-brown shade. The beans will be lighter in weight than their mild counterparts and the crevice will be more developed. The chaff at the crevice will likely have separated from the bean. The surface of the bean may be slightly shiny as oils start to come to the surface. The bean will be more brittle than a mild, but not as brittle as a dark. The roasted beans will have a pleasant and rich aroma.

### 4.1c Darks

Dark roasts are also difficult to do well because if they are under-roasted they are mediums and if they are over-roasted they taste burnt. We recommend a dark, chocolate-brown shade. This is not black, but rather a deep brown. You should still be able to see brown nuances shining through. Dark roasts will be heavier than the mediums, and the crevice will be fully developed. The surface of the bean will be very shiny as the oils have come to the surface of the bean. The roasted beans will have a strong, somewhat smoky, aroma. Dark roasts are suitable for espresso.

## 4.2 The ideal roast

The ideal roast in terms of fully developing the character and quality inherent in the bean differs from coffee to coffee. There is no single shade of roast that is ideal for all coffees, but generally, if a coffee is roasted too dark, the oils, waxes, and other flavor elements are driven to the surface and are partially dissipated in roasting. Also, the smoke created in a dark roast coffee will undermine the aromatic constituents, resulting in a harsher, smokier tasting cup of coffee. The burnt taste introduced by dark roasting masks shortcomings in flavor that a mild roast would reveal. This explains the reason why many cheap coffees are roasted dark.

# 5. ROAST SAMPLES

With every new crop or new coffee you receive, you will want to prepare samples of each of the roasts you offer in your coffee bar. You must do this for three reasons: to determine the roast colors; to determine the roasting times (depending on the roaster model and the number of pounds that you are roasting, one pound will take anywhere from 6 to 12 minutes); to determine weight loss of the different roasts so you can incorporate that into your pricing strategy.

Use a small screw-and-nail sorter (you can pick one up at any local hardware store) for your roasting samples container. Find one with multiple, clear-plastic drawers. Be careful not to put hot beans in the drawers because they will melt the plastic.

Write the roasting times for each bean and roast on colored stickers and stick them on the outside of the roasting containers. Colored dot stickers work well because they can be removed or new ones placed on top of them as the roasting times change for each new crop.

# 6. COFFEE FLAVORING

## 6.1 The art of flavoring

According to the Coffee Association of Canada, flavored coffees represent up to 40 percent of the gourmet coffee market, and this segment is staying strong. There are a number of difficulties with flavoring however.

It is difficult to flavor in a way that improves and enhances the flavor of the coffee beans, rather than masking or covering up the flavor. It's also difficult to ensure uniform application of flavor, especially when flavoring small quantities, and this may result in inconsistent flavor. Another difficulty involves applying the right amount of flavor for a particular bean at a particular roast. For example, a mild roasted Mexican bean will require a different amount of flavoring than a dark roasted Guatemalan.

There are two basic methods of flavoring: flavor solutions and flavor extractions.

Flavor solutions are applied by soaking the beans. This method is preferred by large, commercial roasting houses because uniform treatment of the beans is easier and the weight of the bean is increased. However, shelf life is dramatically decreased and these commercially available coffees are often stale.

We recommend that you purchase flavor extractions to use in your coffee bar. Flavor extractions are applied by spraying a thin layer directly onto the beans. This method is best for small batches because the flavors can be quickly applied and shelf-life is not compromised. A number of North American companies specialize in coffee flavorings. The sales reps from these companies will help you decide on a variety of flavorings to begin with. Some of the most popular flavors include hazelnut, vanilla, chocolate, pecan, and Irish cream.

## 6.2 The easiest way to flavor

The easiest way to flavor beans is to weigh them in a plastic-lidded container, apply the flavoring using an eyedropper or other measuring tool (approximately 3 percent flavor by weight of coffee), then close the lid and shake the contents well.

Check with the manufacturer to determine how much flavor to use with a particular bean and a particular roast. Allow the beans to cool after roasting before you flavor them. If you apply the flavoring while the beans are hot, some of the flavoring will evaporate and the taste will be altered.

Flavors work best with medium roasted coffee. Mild coffees are often acidic and don't mix well with flavors, while the strong taste of dark roasted coffees can overpower the flavoring.

Most flavoring manufacturers recommend that you give the beans a curing time — up to six hours — to allow them to absorb the flavoring. If you are preparing an order for a customer and you don't have time for curing, ask the customer to let the beans sit for a few hours before brewing at home.

After each flavoring, completely clean and sterilize all utensils and containers used to prevent cross-contamination. Label the containers holding the flavoring clearly.

# 7. STORING BEANS

## 7.1 Storing green beans

Most green beans will arrive at your coffee bar in 150-pound sacks. Provided they are not exposed to moisture or heat, the beans will store for years. In fact, some coffee connoisseurs say the coffee improves as the beans "age."

Decaffeinated green beans have a shelf life of approximately six months.

Sacks of beans should be kept on boxes or on shelves elevated from the floor. Open coffee sacks by finding the string that opens the entire sack when you pull it (it takes some skill to find the right one). You shouldn't have to use scissors or a knife to open the sacks if you can find the magic string.

## 7.2 Storing roasted beans

Once coffee has been roasted, it stales quickly and will stale faster the more it is exposed to air or heat. Coffee reaches its peak of freshness approximately six hours after roasting — from there it's all downhill.

Coffee loses its taste as the gases escape, taking the flavor with them. Storing coffee in an airtight container isn't a good idea because the gases are not able to escape. We have actually had five-gallon glass jars explode in a flurry of beans and glass because of gaseous build-up.

We recommend storing coffee in containers that allow the gases to escape but do not expose the coffee to air. The best containers we know of are coffee packs produced by a company called Ampac. These high-quality plastic bags have multiple layers that are heat-sealed together. Multilayers are an important feature to look for when shopping for storage containers. The multilayers are more resistant to heat than single-layer bags, so you are able to package beans that are still warm.

Ampac bags come in sample-size, half-pound, one-pound, and two-pound bags, so they can be used to store beans in the store and to sell to customers. The bags can be reused and are a good, environmentally friendly option for customers. You might want to offer a financial incentive, such as 50¢ off a pound of coffee, for customers who bring their bags back to reuse.

Coffee should be stored in a dark, dry place. Not the fridge — this is one of the worst places to store coffee. Fridges increase the staling process and the coffee can actually absorb food odors in your fridge.

If you are not going to use your coffee within two weeks, storing it in the freezer can help slow the staling process as long as it is not removed from the freezer so often that moisture on the bean condenses.

# 8. CUPPING

## 8.1 The best part of the job

Beans have up to 450 flavor characteristics our senses can detect (by comparison, red wine has only 150), including floral, sweet, mellow, tart, sour, wild, woody, and buttery. The length of roasting time helps determine which characteristics you detect. The longer the coffee is roasted, the more characteristics are burned off. True coffee connoisseurs prefer mild roasts because they can better taste and smell the unique characteristics of the bean.

To be sure you can taste the true characteristics of the bean, you should "cup" each sack of beans you receive.

During cupping, coffee is tasted in its purest form, without going through any filtering processes that may influence its taste. Cupping is always done the same way so that the experienced cupper is able to discern differences between beans and roasts that will not be influenced by differences in the amount of coffee used or the temperature of water used.

## 8.2 The cupping method

When you cup a sack of beans, you take a quarter ounce of coarse ground roasted coffee, heat 5 ounces of water to just below the boiling point, and pour the water over the coffee in a circular motion. (If you are cupping several types of coffee at one time, be sure to sample them in the order they were poured so that they are all sampled at approximately the same temperature and length of brewing time.)

The first step is to do a smell test. With your nose close to the cup, dip a spoon into the cup at an angle to break the top layer of grinds that have floated to the top, while at the same time sniffing the vapors that escape.

Then take up about half a spoonful of the liquid and quaff the liquid with a loud slurping noise. This noise is made for a reason: the object is to mix the liquid with air and spray it directly over your entire tongue where it is savored, rolled, or swished once, then spat out.

By slurping the coffee from the spoon to the back of your mouth, the hot coffee is not only cooled but the aroma reaches the nasal passages again and the complete structure of fragrance and flavor can be assessed. The back part of the tongue is sensitive to bitter nuances and reveals the liveliness of the coffee. The sides of the tongue detect staleness. The tip of the tongue reveals specific flavors.

## 8.3 Glossary of cupping terms

Describing the taste of coffee is like describing the taste of wine, and many of the same terms are used. The descriptions are generally divided into smell, taste, and body.

Some examples of the more common terms used in cupping are described here:

(a) **Fragrance:** The smell of the actual dry coffee grinds.

(b) **Aroma:** The odor of the prepared, brewed coffee.

(c) **Body (mouthfeel):** The tactile impression of weight and texture in the mouth.

(d) **Mellow:** Refers to a fully developed flavor and aroma, not harsh but balanced.

(e) **Rich:** Indicates a coffee has more than body and aroma; it is buttery and satisfying.

(f) **Acidity:** Refers to the verve a coffee has. Acidity is a (very desirable) characteristic of arabica beans. A lack of acidity produces dull, flat coffee. **Note:** Alkaline water counteracts acidity and therefore in areas where there is a high alkaline content in the water, recommend that your customers have their beans roasted at slightly lighter roasts so the coffee will not taste overly flat. Ideally, all coffee and espresso should be brewed with purified water.

# 9. SELLING ROASTED BEANS TO YOUR CUSTOMERS

If you are roasting in-store, one of your staff's most important responsibilities is to promote the custom roasting service your coffee bar offers.

Not all customers will buy right away; it may take them some time to absorb this new and exciting roasting procedure before they purchase their first pound to take home. You may need to give them a sample of the coffees, let them sniff some newly roasted beans, or have them see the beans roasted in front of their eyes. People will be motivated by different reasons: for some, the freshness will appeal; for others, taste will tell; and for still others, the environmentally and socially responsible elements of the beans will be the appeal.

No matter what the motivating factor is for each customer, keep in mind that customers will purchase beans from you only if they trust you. Trust comes from the care you and your staff show your customer, how professional you look in your uniform, and the information you pass along. The last thing you want is customers walking out of your coffee bar thinking, "Those people don't know anything about coffee."

## 9.1 The Bean Club

We recommend that you create a Bean Club for your coffee bean customers. The purpose of the Bean Club is twofold. It creates increased customer loyalty, and it builds a valuable database that can be immensely helpful for mailouts and for defining your target market so that you can better meet its needs.

Membership in your Bean Club would be free; the only effort on your customer's part would be filling in a membership form that gave you the customer's name, address, phone number. Let customers know you will be keeping track of their purchases so that you are able to give them better service — you will know what roasts they liked or didn't like and so will have a better idea of what to recommend, or steer them away from, in the future. Regular customers can also call your Call Ahead Bean Roasting Service and say "Give me a pound of what I had last time."

Other Bean Club benefits might include a quarterly newsletter with helpful hints and tips on coffee, and information on draws for prizes, discounts on products, or a free delivery service.

You can keep track of each customer's sales history using a computer software program or even just by writing the information on a recipe card. File the cards alphabetically by the customers' last name. Each purchase should be recorded with the date or purchase, description of purchase (e.g., the bean, roast, and grind), and the quantity. (Good software allows you to manage this process simply and easily.)

## 9.2 Seven steps to selling roasted beans to new customers

### 9.2a Opening question

Ask your customers one of these two questions: "Do you drink coffee at home?" or "Have you tried our coffees at home before?" Why is asking these questions important? They allow you to break the ice with a customer and let you inform him or her of your coffee bar's roasting services, the organic or sustainably grown beans you carry, and your commitment to organizations like Coffee Kids. These questions also form the basic roadwork that will lead you into the rest of the sales process.

### 9.2b Offer a complimentary sample

If customers have not tried your coffee before, offer them a complimentary sample of a mild, medium, or dark roast. Ask which they prefer: "How strong do you generally like your coffee — light, quite strong, or more of a full-bodied coffee somewhere in the middle?"

Don't ask customers if they like mild, medium, or dark roast coffee since most won't know the difference. The strength of the coffee, however, is something that people do understand and their answer will give you the information you need to provide a sample.

### 9.2c Find out if the coffee should be ground

Ask customers if they have a grinder at home. If not, ask what kind of brewing equipment they do have so that you can grind for the correct basket. Chapter 10 discusses grinding in more detail.

### 9.2d Encourage customers to become Bean Club members

Ask customers to fill out a Bean Club membership form while you prepare the sample. Make sure to explain the benefits to them and let them know it's free to join.

### 9.2e Give customers the sample with brewing instructions

Hand the customers their sample as you give them verbal instructions on how to brew the perfect cup. Also hand over a copy of your coffee bar's newsletter or a brochure on your coffees and your in-store roasting service.

### 9.2f Encourage customers to come back

Encourage customers to return for more coffee beans by offering a discount when they bring the empty sample pouch back (e.g., give them $2 off their first pound). If you want to get aggressive and build up your bean business quickly, offer $5 off or a complimentary half-pound with the first pound purchase.

### 9.2g Follow up

Since you now have each customer's name and phone number on the Bean Club membership form, give them a call to find out how they enjoyed their samples. This is a very crucial step that will affect how much money you make in the coffee business. You will lose the majority of your customers between the sample and the purchase stage unless you phone them up. Here is a sample script:

*Staff member:* "Hi, this is Karen, the roast master from The Coffee Bar. I am calling to find out how you enjoyed your coffee sample. Do you have a minute?"

*Customer:* "Sure."

*Staff member:* "Have you had a chance to try the coffee yet?"

*Customer:* "Yes, we had it last night after dinner."

*Staff member:* "How did you enjoy it?"

*Customer:* "It was good, though I found it a little strong."

*Staff member:* "Do you remember how much coffee you used?"

*Customer:* "No, that was part of the problem — I just put the whole sample in, it seemed to be about the same amount as we usually use."

*Staff member:* "Well, look, why don't I mark your card here so that next time you come in we'll give you a complimentary half-pound of our milder roast when you buy a pound of the medium that I gave you. That'll give you a chance to try another roast. Does that sound okay to you?"

*Customer:* "That would be great! Thanks."

*Staff member:* "We look forward to seeing you soon. Make sure you give the staff member your name so they can look up your Club Member card if I'm not here."

You will notice a few elements of this script that are important to remember when creating your own script. The first is to mention that you are the roast master: you are the expert!

Then make sure you ask the customer if you have caught him or her at a good time; you want to make sure you are not intruding.

If the customer has not had a chance to try the coffee yet, mention that you will call again in a couple of days, once they have had time to brew the coffee. Make a note to call back on your Day-Timer or customer call-back sheet.

If customers found the coffee either strong or weak, find out how much coffee they used — they may not have followed your instructions. (You may want to provide customers with a complimentary measuring spoon when you give them their free sample. This can be a great gift and serve as a sales-builder if it has your coffee bar's name and Call Ahead Bean Roasting Service phone number on it.)

It is important to distinguish between coffee that customers find too mild and a coffee they find too weak. If mildness is an issue, you will want to recommend a darker roast. If the coffee is too weak, they will need to use more in the brewing process.

Restating an offer or upping an offer (e.g., reiterating they get a discount if they bring the sample bag back, or offering the discount plus a complimentary half-pound as in the sample script), especially if they were not entirely happy with the coffee, is a good reinforcer and will increase your response rates.

Finally, make sure you mention that you will write customers' specific requirements on their Club Member card. This reinforces their decision to join the Bean Club by emphasizing a benefit of the Bean Club — customized service.

## 9.3 Seven steps to selling roasted beans to existing customers

### 9.3a Ask opening question

Ask the customer one of these questions: "What do you usually buy?" or "What did you buy last time?" or "Are you a Bean Club member?" If the customer is a member, check his or her card or computer record to find out what they usually buy.

### 9.3b Ask customers whether they want the same roast/bean

"Did you want to have the same bean or would you rather try something different today — we just got in a crop of Sumatra that is really delicious at a medium roast." If customers decide to try a different bean, ask how they liked the coffee they had before and how they would change it. Would they like something darker? something milder? something livelier? something smoother? something more full-bodied? From there you will be able to choose the coffee that they will enjoy most.

**Note:** Your customers — especially those who are new to the world of gourmet coffees — may be easily baffled by the terminology and choices, so try to simplify the process by offering a couple of basic choices. Maybe offer a sample from what you have on tap that day or use a one-cup coffee plunger to make a sample.

### 9.3c Ask if customers will wait while roasting

Find out if customers have time to wait while you roast their coffee. Depending on how many orders are waiting, this may take anywhere from ten minutes to ten hours. Let the customer know how long the wait will be. If it's substantial, suggest customers go for a walk, do some shopping, sit and read the paper, have a latte, or come back tomorrow — whatever their preference — while the beans are roasted. Suggest that they call ahead next time to place their order.

Not all customers want to have their coffee custom roasted. Many are content to take the beans you just roasted that morning — beans you roasted as back up for customers such as these who don't want to wait.

### 9.3d Roast the beans

We recommend that your roast master keep a record of what is to be roasted. Include information on the type of bean, the type of roast, the amount, the customer's name (and phone number if the order was placed over the phone), the name of the person who made the sale (usually the roast master) or took the order, the date and time the order was placed, whether the order is to be ground or whole bean, whether it is regular or flavored, and what time the customer is expected to pick the order up or have it delivered.

### 9.3e Give customers their order

Hand customers their order and a copy of your coffee bar's latest newsletter or a brochure on your coffees and in-store roasting service. Confirm that they know how to brew the perfect cup.

### 9.3f Encourage customers to come back

Encourage customers to come back to your coffee bar by mentioning next week's feature-of-the-week and the discount you offer when customers bring their bag back to reuse for their next order.

### 9.3g Enter the order on the customer's Bean Club record

Have the staff member at the money exchange station record the order on the customer's Bean Club file if you have a computerized system, or manually if you don't have a computerized system.

## 9.4 Packaging and labeling

As mentioned, we recommend you use Ampac bags, with a customized sticky label, to package roasted coffee for your customers. Using a label allows you to write the name of the customer (or the person receiving the coffee as a gift) right on the bag. This adds that little bit of customization to the sale.

You can also include the date the coffee was roasted and the name of the roast master. Putting the date the coffee was roasted will help customers keep track of how fresh the coffee is. Putting the roast master's name on the label will help identify the staff member who roasted the coffee should there be any problem (e.g., under-roasted coffee).

## 9.5 Closing the sale

Before closing the sale, suggest the customer purchase flavored decafs for after dinner, or grinders and brewing equipment such as plungers. (See Chapter 16 for more on suggestive selling.)

Ring the sale in before the beans are roasted. This is important: we have often had customers pop their heads in and order coffee, then pop back out, never to return. Giving customers the receipt to hold on to will make them feel secure about giving you their money up front.

## COMMITMENT BOX

I, _____ , commit to using the seven steps to a successful sale and to make sure all my staff do too!

_____
(your signature)

_____
(today's date)

# 10
# MAKING AND SERVING COFFEE

Coffee should be black as hell, strong as death, and sweet as love.

— TURKISH PROVERB

## 1. WHICH COFFEE SHOULD YOU SERVE?

We recommend that you feature three to four daily roasts. These should include a signature blend medium roast that remains consistent from day to day (this appeals to your customers who can't start or end the day without their same familiar coffee), a dark roast, and at least one flavored coffee. Flavored coffee, especially fresh-roasted, will give you another competitive edge to the Starbucks and "Starbucks wannabes" out there.

We don't recommend keeping a mild roast on tap; we have found that we throw out more than we serve. Milds often have a tartness that not everyone appreciates (although, as we mentioned earlier, true

coffee connoisseurs often prefer milds). You may want to offer a mild initially, and monitor customer response.

Coffee drinks should be offered in three sizes: a 12-ounce "small" size (sometimes called "regular"), a 16-ounce "medium" size, and a 20-ounce "large" size.

In our experience, offering a decaffeinated coffee as a daily roast usually isn't worth it. You end up throwing out much more than you sell. If you find that you do get a lot of decaf orders, you may want to run with it for a month and keep a record of how much you sell versus how much is wasted. However, you may be better off boosting the average customer check by recommending a decaf latte or even a decaf espresso Americano to your decaf drinkers.

## 2. GRINDING

Grinding increases the surface area of the coffee bean, allowing water to penetrate more easily and increasing taste. Grinds range from a powder-like consistency used for brewing Turkish coffees to a very coarse consistency for percolating.

You are more likely to use coarse rather than fine grinds in your in-store brews. Coarse is generally used for drip coffeemakers that have a flat basket, while fine is used for drip coffeemakers with cone-shaped filter baskets.

In a cone-shaped filter, the water does not have much time to mix with the coffee and thus extract the flavor of the coffee since it is dripping through the filter quite quickly. Therefore, coffee used in these filters should be finely ground so that the water comes into contact with more flavor constituents. (An espresso uses very fine grinds for an extremely quick 30-second extraction.)

With a flat basket, the water has time to mix with the coffee and hence doesn't require as small a surface area as cones. Therefore, coffee can be more coarsely ground.

A note on grinders: You will want two grinders — one for regular coffee and one for flavored. Flavor extracts penetrate everything, and it is next to impossible to remove flavor from a grinder. The only solution is to run regular coffee beans through the grinder to try and clear out as much of the flavor as possible. This, however, is a time waster, is expensive, and doesn't always work, especially with exceptionally strong flavors such as cinnamon. Having a grinder just for flavored coffees will allow you to keep your flavored coffees together, at least.

## 3. MEASURING — HOW MUCH COFFEE FOR HOW MUCH BREW?

How much coffee do you need for how much brew? Approximately two heaping teaspoons of coffee are recommended for an 8-ounce cup (adjust the amount to individual taste). Most carafes, including the Cafe Barista carafes that we recommend (see section **4.** below), hold 2.25 quarts of liquid. We recommend that you use 3 ounces of a mild or medium roast. People who prefer darker roasts also usually prefer stronger coffee. Add a little extra so that the coffee has that added "kick" that dark-coffee lovers love. We use 3.5 ounces.

Flavored drinks require less coffee (e.g., just under 3 ounces), though this depends on the strength of the flavor. You may want to increase the amount slightly if you find that the coffee is not strong enough.

## 4. BREWING EQUIPMENT

### 4.1 Which brewing system should you use?

We recommend a thermal carafe brewing system called Cafe Barista, which is distributed by Newco Enterprises, located in Missouri. It is the only coffee brewer graded by the SCAA as "Gold Cup" certified, ensuring great coffee flavor. For more details, visit www.newcocoffee.com.

The Cafe Barista brewing system brews coffee directly into an airtight thermal carafe with no burner, which keeps coffee as fresh as possible for as long as possible. Heat and air are coffee enemies. A properly preheated carafe will keep coffee fresh for at least three hours, greatly reducing waste. The Cafe Barista system also brews at a very hot temperature, extracting more flavor than other brewing systems. This will save you money and make better-tasting coffee.

If you choose to buy a brewing system other than the Cafe Barista, ensure that the coffee brews into thermal carafes, and check the brewing temperature.

There are two main brewing system models: in-line or pour-over. In-line models are plumbed straight into a water supply whereas the pour-over models are not. Instead, water is measured, then manually poured into the top of the machine. Consider whether other systems offer in-line models. Pour-overs will not be efficient in a large volume location.

When comparing brewing system models, we recommend that you call the suppliers' existing customers and ask how happy they are with the system, and what problems they have had.

Once you've got your system, you should show staff where the machine is plugged in (in case the cord is accidentally unplugged), as well as where it is plumbed in. We had an enthusiastic cleaning crew mistakenly turn the water release valve off, resulting in water not being able to get into the system. Of course, if your brewer stops working, service to your customers will be affected.

## 4.2 Carafes

In the Cafe Barista system, coffee is brewed into airtight thermal carafes. These can be preheated either by swishing a few ounces of hot water around the inside and then dumping it out, or by steaming with the wand from the espresso machine. Preheating keeps the coffee hotter longer.

You will need to explain to staff how the carafe works. In the Cafe Barista system, for example, the large top of the carafe unscrews for preheating and dumping out old coffee, while a smaller top contains a little bobble that floats as the coffee brews into it, then drops down to seal the hole shut when the coffee finishes brewing.

The carafes also feature a clear sight pipe up the front that allows you to see how much coffee is inside the carafe. Initially, the liquid you will see as the coffee brews appears clear and watery, but as the flavor is extracted from the coffee, it gradually deepens in color.

Coffee is dispensed from the carafe using a spout that holds about 0.5 to 1 ounce of liquid. The liquid held in the spout will cool if left to sit for too long. Therefore, when offering coffee samples to customers (or doing a taste temperature test — see section **4.2d** below), make sure you use at least 2 to 3 ounces of coffee, not just the one cold ounce. Also remember that this spout will need to be cleared of any cleaning solution used when you wash the carafe. You don't want to serve that into someone's cup.

### 4.2a Carafe differentiation

It is important to differentiate your coffee carafes because each will contain a different roast or flavor. Unless they are clearly marked, they can easily get mixed up. You don't want customers to discover after leaving your coffee bar that they got French Vanilla when they ordered a dark roast.

Distinguish your carafes by marking them permanently with a dot or letter system. Name tags hung over the spout don't work as well because it is too easy for staff to mix them up. Dots can be drawn with a permanent marker on the upper front of the carafes so staff can easily see them. You can, for example, use one dot to denote your mild roast coffee if you offer one, two dots to denote your medium roast coffee, and three for your dark. A large "F" will indicate flavor; if you have more than one flavor, write the flavor on the carafe with a water-based pen that will wash off easily and won't stain the carafe, or label the carafe with sticky tape so that staff can easily distinguish which carafe holds which flavor.

Don't ever brew regular coffees into flavored coffee carafes (your customers will be able to taste the flavor). As well, try to brew the same flavor into the same pot whenever possible. If you change flavors daily, you will likely have to use the same carafe for different flavors, so make sure the carafe is carefully cleaned. Some flavors, such as cinnamon, may be so strong that they are impossible to eliminate and will contaminate other flavors. If this is the case, we recommend discontinuing that flavor or, if it is popular, using one carafe exclusively for that flavor.

### 4.2b Backup carafes

You should have a backup carafe of each coffee, especially the flavors, during busy times so that you never run out and a customer never has to wait for a coffee to finish brewing. Look for a brewing system that offers multiple-carafe stands.

Cafe Barista supplies two types of carafe stands — one is a single unit and another holds eight carafes. The eight-stand system is fantastic. Four carafes are in a front row and four are elevated in a back row so you can tell how low the coffee is by looking at the level displayed on the pipe (or by lifting the carafe by the handle to feel the weight).

You can have the carafe you are using at the front; as it begins to deplete, you take the carafe from the back and move it to the front. Then brew into the first carafe and move it to the back. In this way, the carafes are constantly rotated and you never run out of coffee.

### 4.2c Brew records

When you first open, and until your coffee volume grows, you may want to use a brew record sheet. Sample 7 shows a sample brew record. Staff members write down the time they brew each daily roast (e.g., medium, dark, and flavored) to ensure that a customer doesn't end up with cold or stale coffee.

### 4.2d Taste test for temperature

If a brew record has not been done and no one is sure when a carafe of coffee was brewed, do a taste test for temperature. Make sure that the first release of coffee — the coffee that has been sitting in the carafe's spout — is flushed out before you do a temperature test, as that coffee will be cool.

How hot the coffee stays and how long it stays hot depend on the quality of the carafe's insulation, whether the carafe was preheated before the coffee was brewed into it, and the temperature of the liquid coffee itself. For example, a full carafe may keep hot for up to 12 hours. Does it stay fresh for that long? No, definitely not — it may be hot, but it will also be stale. On the other hand, a carafe that has been partially used and is only half full will cool down more quickly. This time will vary between brewing systems. Cafe Barista, for example, will keep a half-full carafe of coffee hot, on average, for about 2.5 hours.

# BREW RECORD

| Mild | Medium | Dark | Flavored 1 | Flavored 2 |
|------|--------|------|------------|------------|
| 6:05 *a.m.* | 6:00 *a.m.* | 6:10 *a.m.* | 6:15 *a.m.* | 6:20 *a.m.* |
| 7:30 | 6:25 | 6:30 | 8:00 | 9:00 |
| | 6:45 | 7:10 | | |
| | 7:00 | 7:15 | | |
| | 7:05 | | | |
| | | | | |
| | | | | |
| | | | | |
| | | | | |
| | | | | |
| | | | | |
| | | | | |
| | | | | |

Taste temperature tests should be done at the 2.5 hour mark, and then every half hour after that. Be aware, though, that if you have a high volume of liquid coffee sales, a carafe may be only one-quarter full by the 2.5 hour mark and may be too cold to serve. Vary the timing of your temperature taste tests to accommodate volume.

## 4.3 Cleaning guidelines

### 4.3a Brewer

The top of most brewing systems is quite warm and can be a good place to store coffee mugs and cups. It must, of course, be kept free of dust and water. If you do keep dishes here, most health departments require that cups are placed upside down on top of bar mats rather than right on the surface of the machine.

### 4.3b Carafes

Carafes need to be thoroughly cleaned at least once a week, if not more frequently. Check their cleanliness by looking inside; if the glass is clear and shiny, the carafe is clean. If brown residue is beginning to build up along the sides, it needs to be cleaned.

Carafes can be cleaned by brushing them out with hot soapy water and a long handled brush. Alternatively, fill the carafe with a baking soda and water solution and leave it to soak overnight to remove any buildup. If a carafe is left to stand, attach a large, clear note to it so that other staff don't think the contents are coffee to be served to a customer.

Rinse carafes thoroughly before using them to brew again, and clear dirty water out of the spout by opening the spout over a sink and allowing clean water to run through it until it is clear of any baking soda or other cleaning solution residue.

# 5. THE STEPS TO BREWING SUCCESS

## 5.1 Preparing to brew

### Step 1: The carafes

Preheat the carafe using a steaming wand or hot water from the brewing system. (This will make a big difference in how hot the coffee will be.) Next, look inside the carafe to ensure that there are no grounds at the bottom. If in doubt, add a bit of hot water and drain it out the spout over a sink.

### Step 2: The brew basket

Take the brew basket and check for smell (e.g., leftover flavor) and for any grounds. Because the water level rises during brewing, it is common for grounds to float up over the paper filter and wind up in the basket. You can check for grounds by running your index finger around the inside.

If there is flavor residue in the basket, wash the basket out with hot, soapy water. If there are leftover grounds, rinse the basket under hot water. Make sure you use hot water to wash the basket, otherwise the basket will be cold and will cool the coffee as it brews through.

If you have to stop to wash the basket, it can interrupt customer service, so have your staff get into the habit of always checking the basket immediately after brewing.

Set the basket, ready for the coffee filter, aside.

### Step 3: Weighing

Take a single coffee filter and place it on the scale. (Separating your coffee filters ahead of time can save time when you're busy.) Weigh out into the filter the appropriate amount of coffee for the brew.

Unless your coffee bar is very busy, you will not want to prepare brewing portions of coffee ahead of time because this will expose the coffee to air and speed up the staling process. If you do pre-portion, be sure to set the filters somewhere dry, and away from steam. Don't stack the weighed-out filters one on top of each other, as coffee grounds can attach to the bottom of the filter above and end up in someone's cup.

### Step 4: Grinding

Check to make sure there are no beans left in the hopper from the grind before. Although you can train your staff to let the grinder run for a second *before* grinding to make sure no grounds from the previous batch are left inside the grinder, it is more efficient to have them check that nothing is left *after* they grind a batch.

Place the weighed-out beans in the hopper, and place the filter underneath on a clean surface. As with stacked filters, if the filter is placed on a surface with grounds on it, grounds will stick to the bottom of the filter and likely end up in a customer's coffee.

Turn the grinder on and wait until all the coffee has ground through. If you have a batch grinder (see Chapter 5, section **2.2i**), you can adjust the settings to match your measurements.

Note that even when the hopper looks empty, beans are still being crushed inside. Have your staff watch until no more grounds come out. They can also listen for changes in pitch and volume of the grinding as the beans are ground and run out.

### Step 5: Brewing

Place the filter full of grounds inside the brew basket, ensuring that all sides of the filter are snug up against the sides. If the sides are not lined up properly, the water spray could catch an edge of the filter, causing it to fall over and fill your coffee with coffee grounds. A pot of coffee's retail value is about $10, so you don't want this to happen.

Put the brew in place under the water spout. Make sure the basket is straight and as far back on the machine as it will go. Put the empty, preheated, free-of-grounds carafe underneath, ensuring that it is lined up properly with the brew basket hole. Double-check to make sure the carafe is empty and that carafes weren't somehow switched while you weren't looking.

Push the "on" button. Brewing should start almost immediately. If you are using a brew record, write down the time.

## 5.2 Post-brewing

Place the full carafe in position on the stand. Take the filter out of the brew basket by pinching one corner of the filter together with thumb and forefinger and sliding the filter out into a garbage can. If you use this technique, grounds are less likely to fall into the basket.

Look for grounds left in the basket, and also check for them by running your finger around the edge of the basket. If you have just brewed a flavor, thoroughly wash the basket in hot, soapy water. Replace the clean basket in its proper position.

If you are using a brew record, double-check to make sure you wrote the time down. You are now ready to brew your next batch.

---

### SEVEN STEPS TO BREWING A CUP OF COFFEE YOUR CUSTOMERS WILL LOVE

1. Use clean equipment.

2. Use the proper grind for your brewing system.

3. Use filtered water.

4. Make sure the water is at the proper temperature.

5. Use the proper amount of coffee for the amount of water you are using.

6. Brew into a carafe system — remember that heat and air destroy coffee; by brewing straight into a thermos you eliminate these two coffee enemies.

7. If you don't have a carafe brewing system, pour the coffee into a preheated thermos immediately after it is brewed.

---

## 5.3 Troubleshooting

All sorts of things can go wrong. Here is a list of some of the more common problems:

(a) **Your brewing system won't brew.** Is it in auto brew mode? Has it come unplugged? Has a breaker tripped? Does it need servicing?

(b) **Your grinder won't grind.** Is a foreign object stuck inside? Are the burrs too close together to grind (i.e., are they out of adjustment?)?

(c) **The carafe is overflowing.** Check your manual for the emergency water turn-off procedure. Place an empty carafe underneath to catch any remaining drips and clean up the mess. If overflow happens on a continuous basis, the water level may need readjusting.

(d) **The coffee is weak.** Are the beans under-roasted? Was the proper amount of coffee weighed out? Was the grind correct (e.g., too coarse a grind means there isn't much surface area for extraction, which makes the coffee weak)? Does the water level or water temperature need adjusting?

(e) **There is clean water in the carafe tube.** During the first stage of brewing, the water will appear clean because full extraction hasn't yet taken place. However, if the carafe tube is filled with completely clear water, check to make sure the coffee was brewed with coffee in the basket and/or that coffee was weighed out properly.

(f) **The coffee is cold.** When was it last brewed? Has the water temperature dropped on the brewing system? If coffee is cold and new coffee has to be brewed, and you don't have a backup, offer the customer a complimentary coffee of another blend. Commit to keeping coffees properly brewed.

(g) **Carafe lever will not press down.** It is possible that the carafe has been "locked" — a safety feature that is handy when you are transporting coffee (e.g., to an office for a staff meeting). Unlock by flicking the "lock" switch.

# 6. HOW TO SERVE YOUR COFFEE

## 6.1 Three steps to serving coffee

### Step 1: Take the order

Find out which roast and size customers would prefer and whether orders are to stay or go.

Make sure customers can easily see the different cup sizes. "Small," "medium," and "large" could mean any size: it is important to show the customer the cup size.

### Step 2: Prepare the order

If there is a staff member on duty at the gourmet coffee station, pass the order on to him or her.

Coffee should be served in hot coffee mugs or cups. Place the cup directly underneath the carafe spout and press the dispensing lever. While you are filling the cup, watch for steam. Steam should be visibly rising as you pour. If there is no steam, it is possible the coffee is cold. Double-check (and see troubleshooting, above).

Leave about a half-inch at the top of the cup so customers can add cream and sugar without spilling. Those who drink it black will still feel that they got good value for their money.

### Step 3: Serve the order

Staff at the gourmet or specialty coffee stations should also serve the coffees. If they are exceptionally busy, the staff member at the money exchange station can act as backup.

Hand customers their coffee, explaining where the cream and sugar are located. This is very important for first-time customers who otherwise will be forced to look around the coffee bar until they find what they need — a small inconvenience but an inconvenience nonetheless. Keep lids at the cream and sugar station as well so that customers can help themselves.

## 6.2 Serving tips

- Never tell your customers, "This coffee is better; I just brewed it." This destroys their image that you have fresh coffee all the time — an image you want your coffee bar to have.

- Take care when making drinks. Customers will often watch and will notice the care with which you prepare the order, so don't just throw the thing together and slosh it across the counter.

- Never handle the tops of the cups with your hands when passing to customers (or at any other time).

- Place the cup or mug directly down onto the counter — never hand it to a customer in the air. That increases the chance of spillage.

- Be very careful when serving coffee near pieces of vulnerable equipment such as computers or the cash register. (A customer at one of our stores once spilled a whole cup of coffee onto our keyboard. Luckily we were able to hang the thing upside down to dry it out and it worked fine for the next two years.)

---

## COMMITMENT BOX

I, _____, commit to brewing and serving only the highest quality cups of coffee in my coffee bar.

_____        _____
(your signature)                               (today's date)

---

# 11
# THE SECRETS OF ESPRESSO SUCCESS

Coffee is a fleeting moment and a fragrance.

— CLAUDIA RODEN

## 1. ESSSSSPRESSO
### 1.1 What is espresso?

The first thing you should know about espresso is that in English-speaking countries it is pronounced "eSpresso" not "eXpresso." (In French an espresso is called *un express*.)

Espresso is produced when water is forced through a very fine coffee grind under high pressure so that the delicate essence of the coffee is extracted very quickly — 1.5 ounces of espresso should be brewed in 15 to 20 seconds for maximum flavor, taste, and aroma.

Prolonged contact between water and coffee that occurs during an extended brewing time draws out unpleasant bitter chemicals and destroys flavor and aroma.

## 1.2 The best roast for the best brew

The best roast for an espresso is generally dark. The deep, rich flavor of a dark roast is more easily extracted in the short time that the grounds are in contact with the water. Of course, make sure the beans have not been over-roasted. A smell test works well: espresso should never smell burnt or charred.

## 1.3 The best bean for the best brew

You will decide on a bean or a blend of beans to feature as your espresso by testing and trying the coffees that you plan to carry. A dark roast Mexican coffee can work very well, especially if it is blended with a dark roast Peruvian, which smooths out the sharpness that is characteristic of many Mexican coffees.

Whatever bean you decide on once you've found a great taste, stick with it for the long term. You must not change your choice of espresso bean and roast once it is in place. Your products' consistency will be the key to your success, and switching the espresso whenever you feel like it or because a bean is not available year-round can be damaging to your product sales.

## 1.4 The best grind for the best brew

The grind for espresso is very fine. This means there is more surface area from which the water can extract the flavor. As well as a brew test, use a feel test to check for appropriate grind size. Take a pinch of grounds between your thumb and forefinger and slide it between them. Espresso should feel like tiny grains of sand. If it feels like sugar, it is too coarse. If it feels like flour, it is much too fine. During training, let your staff actually feel the difference between the different grinds so they can experience it for themselves.

## 2. THE ESPRESSO GRINDER

### 2.1 Types

There are many espresso grinders on the market; you will want to purchase one that releases the correct amount of grinds for an espresso. The exact amount you will want is a quarter ounce (7 grams) for each shot of espresso. Many grinders, however, will not release this much, and so you must halve the amount — set the grinder for an eighth of an ounce (3.5 grams) and then release

twice. We have seen many grinders that do not release this small an amount, so you end up with either too much or too little. This is a major problem because your espresso ends up either too strong or too weak. Make sure you purchase a grinder that can be set to release one of these amounts.

The beans for the grinder are stored in a hopper. You should purchase a grinder that allows you to remove the hopper for cleaning.

## 2.2 Grinder adjustments

Most grinders release equal portions of grinds through a spoked system at the bottom of the machine. Each pull on the release handle moves the system one spoke over and releases coffee. Most grinders have two adjustments to adjust the amount of coffee released. The first is a leveler that levels off the amount of coffee being released. The second adjusts the size of the release hole. Instruct your staff not to make adjustments on the grinder. Because making a perfect espresso is an exact science, having many staff members adjusting this and that can result in a real espresso mess.

## 2.3 Troubleshooting

Here are some common problems you might experience with your espresso grinder:

(a) **Small amount of grinds released.** Is the spoke system completely covered with grinds? If not, the full amount won't be released. Get into the habit of checking the level often and even turning the grinder on for a few seconds before making each espresso. Turning the grinder on often creates an image of freshness for the customer (the customer "hears" the freshness of his or her espresso). Turn it on many times during a day for small amounts rather than once for a long time.

If your grinder has an automatic volume level sensor, check to see if it is functioning.

(b) **No grinds come out.** Check to see if a bean or other particle is stuck in the hopper. Depending on how well your coffee has been processed, you may find rocks, pieces of corn, or wood in your beans. Check your manufacturer's recommendations on how best to remove these objects. Often it involves unplugging the grinder and dislodging the object with a sharp knife.

If the hopper has been removed and replaced, check to see if the hopper gate is still closed.

(c) **No power.** Check power cords and breakers.

# 3. THE ESPRESSO MACHINE

## 3.1 Types

Espresso machines are automatic, semi-automatic, or manual. The manual system usually involves pulling a handle down to make the espresso; semi-automatic machines require that you push a button to start and to stop the amount of water flowing through; fully automatics require only the push of a button to start the process.

We recommend automatic machines because they can be programmed to make the perfect espresso every time, so you end up with consistently good specialty coffee products.

Most machines are also equipped with a steaming unit on the top of the machine to steam glasses — this will impress customers as they wait for their specialty coffee.

Espresso machines come in two-group, three-group, or four-group models; you will choose the one that suits your projected sales and your budget.

## 3.2 Features

### 3.2a Standard features

A typical two-group espresso machine has the following features on both the right and left side of the machine:

- Single espresso button
- Double espresso button
- Short espresso button
- Double short espresso button
- Hot water tap (sometimes only on one side)
- Steaming wand
- Steam start mechanism (this can be either a button, lever, or knob)

### 3.2b Brass eagle

Some models feature a brass eagle dome, designed to draw attention to the espresso machine. According to our experience, the addition of a brass eagle can increase specialty coffee sales by up to 40 percent, especially if you're in a market that's new to espresso-based drinks. A customer once said to us: "I see that brass eagle on top of a machine and I come straight in. You must have good coffee here."

### 3.2c Group handles

The stainless steel coffee brew baskets that hold espresso are attached to what are called group handles. On the underside of the brew baskets are one or two spouts to dispense the liquid espresso as it is brewed.

There are two types of group handles, used to make either single shot or double shot espressos. You can identify the single shot group handle by its single spout and by its smaller capacity basket. The double shot group handle has a double spout and a large basket. We recommend a two-group espresso machine.

Group handles must be kept in place, attached to the espresso machine, at all times. This is one of the clues by which experts in the field will judge how good your specialty coffee products are and how well educated you are in the coffee business. If the group handles are not kept in place they become cold; this lack of heat causes the espresso to lack flavor and crema, the foam on a freshly-dripped espresso.

Another mistake many coffee bar owners make is to rinse the group handles after each espresso. Running water — even hot water — through the group handles causes water to pool inside and then drip into the next espresso you make. There is no need to clean the group handles with water during the normal course of business. If there is a buildup of espresso grinds that cannot be pounded out on the pounder stick, use the handle of a spoon to scrape your grind recycling container. Apparently some of the great Italian coffee bars haven't cleaned their group handles in years (a little extreme, we feel)!

If you are the first person in the morning to use the machine, it is a good idea to run water through the group to clean it of any cleaning residue left in it from the night before. (Group handle cleaning is discussed in detail in Chapter 8.)

### 3.2d Steaming wand

In most models, steam is released through four small holes at the bottom of the steaming wand. It is crucial that the pipe and the holes are cleared of milk residue both *before* and *after* steaming milk. This is because the pipes can quickly grow bacteria, which can be transferred into the next pitcher of milk being steamed. Also, the holes can become clogged with small hard milk particles, which are then steamed into someone's milk. Not only is it unsanitary, but it is also a real turn off for customers who see brown, crusty milk particles on the wand with which you are about to make their latte. Finally, if the wand is not properly cleaned, the steam that condenses and then cools in the wand will end up as cold water in the milk pitcher.

To keep the outside of the wand clean, have a damp cloth nearby that is designated to be used for this purpose only. To clear out the inside, turn on the steam for a couple of seconds once you've finished steaming the milk, to clear any debris left in the four small holes.

## 3.3 General cleaning

The staff member who is at the specialty coffee station is responsible for keeping the machine clean and polished during his or her shift. This is a simple job of keeping the steaming wands clean and any glass or metal parts shiny by using Windex or an environmentally friendly alternative such as a vinegar and water solution. Check with your sales rep or equipment manual for specific cleaning instructions.

Clogged filters will impede the water as it filters down through your espresso. This can result in uneven or weak extractions. These filters are easy to replace by removing the center screw and replacing the clogged filters. Always have an extra set of filters on hand because you will need to change them regularly. One word of caution: When replacing screens, ensure that you don't tighten the center screw more than a quarter turn or it will strip.

You can burn off the oily residue buildup that clogs the filter screen by placing the filter on the element of a stove burner at a high setting. The filter can then be used again.

## 3.4 Troubleshooting

Here is a list of some of the more common problems you may encounter with your espresso machine:

(a) **No power.** Check to make sure the machine is turned on; check to see if the breaker has been tripped.

(b) **Little or no steam.** Check pressure gauges and water lines.

(c) **Water sprays out in all directions.** Filters need replacing. Your staff should notify you immediately if they notice this.

# 4. SIX STEPS TO A TERRIFIC ESPRESSO

## 4.1 Step 1

Have single shot holder in hand. Make sure any espresso that may have stuck on it from a previous use has been cleaned off. If there is any espresso in the bottom, use the handle of a spoon to quickly scrape it out.

## 4.2 Step 2

Check that there is enough ground espresso in the grinder hopper to ensure you get a full pull.

## 4.3 Step 3

Rest holder in place under grinder opening and pull once to release 7 grams of espresso into the handle. Make sure you got a full pull. If you didn't, lift lid, dump espresso back in grinder hopper, and pull again.

## 4.4 Step 4

Take hand tamper (a small device used to compress the espresso grounds) and use it to even out the espresso if it is off to one side. It is important to do this, otherwise you will not get an even extraction. Tamp once firmly — do not use any kind of twisting motion and do not tamp more than once. (Don't use the tamper that is part of the espresso grinder because you need to feel the pressure you are putting on the grinds; you can't do this if you are using the upward motion that is required for a fixed tamper).

Brush off excess espresso around the edges of the basket using one swipe with the palm of your hand — do it quickly, decisively, and, again, only once.

## 4.5 Step 5

Firmly place the group handle in the espresso machine. It is important that you do it firmly or else the extreme pressure will push water and grinds out the sides, and they will drip into the cup of espresso. If you need to, brace yourself by putting one hand on the side of the espresso machine, then take your other hand and pull the group handle toward you. (Don't do it so tightly that you can't get it back out again. Also, if you do it too tightly, you will damage the rubber seal that seals the connection and your group handle will keep moving to the right until you need servicing to replace the rubber seals.) Be careful to place the group handle level when fitting it into the machine.

## 4.6 Step 6

Place a preheated espresso cup directly underneath the spout if the espresso is to stay, or place the espresso pourer underneath if the espresso is for takeout, and push the single espresso button.

**Note:** It is important for the quality of your espresso to brew it straight into a preheated cup. Remember that an espresso is only 1.5 ounces of liquid and cools quickly.

You will want to watch the espresso as it brews to monitor three things:

(a) Length of brew (should be between 15 and 20 seconds)

(b) Color of brew (should be a caramel color)

(c) Consistency of brew (should be an even, foamy-looking stream)

## 5. CREMA

The final characteristic of a well-brewed espresso is the color and amount of crema on top. Crema is the creamy foam that lines the first quarter-inch of a good espresso. Some Italians believe that a perfect espresso is one with crema so thick that you can place a full teaspoon of sugar on top and the sugar will not sink.

Creating crema is an art and you must always be finding the perfect balance between —

- the grind,
- the length of extraction time,
- the temperature of the water, and
- the amount of espresso being dosed (e.g., 7 grams).

Good crema is also influenced by the temperature of the group handles and of the espresso cups.

The perfect crema should be a golden caramel color and a quarter-inch thick. Have staff practice making crema, checking how fast the liquid is dispensed, its color, and the other elements involved. Once staff knows what to look for, they can notify you or the manager if the crema standard seems low so that changes, e.g., to the grind, must be made.

## 6. ESPRESSO TROUBLESHOOTING

(a) **Grinds getting into the espresso.** You will probably see water and grinds dripping down the sides of the group handle or left at the bottom of the cup. Check that the group handle is firmly in place or has not been inserted at an angle.

Also check the rubber seals to ensure they have not been breached.

(b) **Dark crema color.** An espresso with dark crema color will be bitter and strong. Check the amount of espresso being used (more than 7 grams for a single espresso or more than 14 grams for a double is too much).

Check extraction time. Is it too long because of —

(i)   too much espresso,

(ii)  too much water (more than 1.5 ounces), or

(iii) too hard a tamp?

(c) **Not enough crema.** An espresso with not enough crema will taste weak and watery. Check the amount of espresso used (less than 7 grams for a single espresso or less than 14 grams for a double is not enough).

Check extraction time. Is it too short because of —

(i)   not enough espresso,

(ii)  not enough water (less than 1.5 ounces), or

(iii) too light a tamp?

Is the water hot enough?

Is the espresso grind fine enough?

(d) **Watery espresso.** A watery espresso will have little if any crema and a watery appearance because of either one or a combination of the following:

- Not enough espresso grinds at the start
- Not a firm enough tamp
- Too coarse a grind
- Water temperature not hot enough
- Group handles not hot enough
- Espresso brewed into a cold cup

(e) **Extraction takes too long (more than 20 seconds).** Have you used too much espresso? Too firm a tamp? Too fine a grind?

(f) **You are getting less or more than 1.5 ounces of water.** Provided you have the correct grind, correct tamp firmness, correct amount of espresso released from the grinder, and the correct water temperature, you may need to reset the espresso machine's water calibration levels.

Check water levels by brewing into a shot glass clearly marked with measurements ranging from 1 ounce to 2 ounces. You will want the espresso (including the crema) to brew to the 1.5-ounce mark exactly. On an automatic machine, recalibration is a simple procedure of pressing two buttons at the same time, then pressing another to stop it at the correct time. Use a stopwatch or egg timer to help you time the brew time.

# 7. TRAINING TIPS

When training your staff in the art (and science) of making espressos, you will want to demonstrate what happens when you use too little espresso and when you don't tamp enough:

- The espresso gushing out of the spout will look watery
- The espresso will taste weak and watery
- There will be slightly more than 1.5 ounces of espresso because there has been little absorption of moisture

As well, demonstrate what happens when you use too much espresso and tamp too much:

- The espresso will drip slowly

- The crema will be dark
- The espresso will taste bitter
- There will be slightly less than 1.5 ounces of espresso because the espresso has absorbed a certain amount of moisture

Allow your staff to taste test each of these espressos, and compare it to an espresso that's done just right.

## 8. ESPRESSO MENU ITEMS

We recommend that all to-stay espressos be served in espresso cups on a small plate with small spoon. You may want to include a spiral of lemon peel on the side. The toppings for cappuccinos are not used for espressos.

Espressos should be available in two sizes: single and double. The Americano should be made available in three sizes: 12 ounces, 16 ounces, and 20 ounces.

Here are some different espresso drinks:

- **Espresso.** A strong shot or shots of straight-up espresso.
- **Espresso con panna.** An espresso topped with whipped cream.
- **Espresso macchiato.** An espresso topped with foamed milk.
- **Americano.** An espresso to which hot water is added. (Basically a strong-tasting cup of coffee.)

---

# COMMITMENT BOX

I, _____ , commit to using the six steps to a terrific espresso and to always strive for a quarter-inch-thick crema.

_____          _____
*(your signature)*                              *(today's date)*

---

# 12
# SPECIALTY COFFEES

One sip of this
Will bathe the drooping spirits in delight
Beyond the bliss of dreams.

— JOHN MILTON

## 1. WHAT ARE SPECIALTY COFFEES?

Specialty coffees are variations of the same base of espresso and steamed or foamed milk. They include cappuccino, latte (often mislabeled café au lait), and mocha, and for our purposes, will also include items such as true café au lait (made with gourmet coffee rather than espresso), hot chocolate, and flavored steamed milk. Specialty coffees can also be cold (e.g., iced or blended coffee drinks like the Starbucks Frappuccino, or various mochaccino-like products).

## 2. FOAMING VERSUS STEAMING

Steamed milk is simply milk heated using steam. Heating milk by steaming alters the proteins of the milk in a way that creates a distinctive, unforgettable flavor. Steamed milk is usually used in lattes.

Foamed (sometimes referred to as "frothed") milk is milk that has been "foamed" using the steaming wand of your espresso machine. It is used primarily in cappuccinos. The steaming wand injects air along with the steam into the milk. As the steam heats the milk, the injected air forms bubbles that rise to the top. Milk will not foam when it is hot, so you must remember to always use cold milk.

Be careful not to scorch the milk; this will result in an unpleasant smell and undesirable taste. When foamed properly, milk will have a pleasant smell and almost sweet taste.

157

# 3. SIX STEPS TO STEAMING MILK

## 3.1 Step 1

Take your steaming pitcher from the fridge. Ensure there is enough milk in the pitcher. The amount of milk you need depends on both how large the order is and how busy the coffee bar is at that particular time. If, for example, there is only one order for a specialty coffee but there are another ten people in line waiting to place orders, it would be prudent to measure out more milk so that you are prepared for the upcoming orders. If you are only steaming milk and not foaming it, you can fill the pitcher as much as three-quarters full. This will give you a lot more milk to work with.

You can always presteam the milk, put the pitchers back in the fridge, and give a quick shot of steam to bring the milk back up to a hot temperature (if necessary) for the next customer.

## 3.2 Step 2

Make sure the steaming wands are clean and the jets cleared *before* putting them inside the pitcher of milk. To clean the steam jets, turn the steam on for a second to clear out any residue left inside the four little holes. Wipe the outside of the wand with a cloth kept solely for that purpose.

## 3.3 Step 3

Place the wand in the pitcher, well below the surface of the milk, and turn the steam on full blast. It is very important that the steam is turned to its full capacity; otherwise you draw out the time it takes to heat the milk, degrading customer service. It is also very difficult to foam milk if there is not ample steam pressure to mix the air with the milk.

---

### CAPPUCCINO

(Use 12-ounce cup)

Put one pull of espresso grounds into the one-spout handle. Push the one-cup button on the espresso machine. Foam milk to a temperature of 160°F/71°C. Pour espresso into cup. Fill cup two-thirds full with steamed milk. Spoon milk foam on top (above cup line if order is to stay; at cup line if it is to go, so customers can put a lid on the cup without making a mess). Sprinkle with customer's choice of topping.

### FOR MEDIUM AND LARGE CAPPUCCINO:

Use 16- or 20-ounce cup. Put two pulls of espresso grounds into the two-spout handle (and another single pull in an additional wand if making a large) and push related buttons. Continue as above.

---

## 3.4 Step 4

As you steam, you will notice that there is a change in the sound of the steaming. This change in pitch is because the molecules of the milk move around faster as they heat (remember grade 8 science class?). If, however, you hear a high pitched squealing, you probably have the wand too far into the pitcher so that it is touching the bottom. This places the steam into direct contact with the metal of the pitcher, creating that loud, high pitched sound.

As you steam, do not move the pitcher up and down. As long as the wand is below the surface of the milk, moving the pitcher up and down isn't going to do anything to make the milk steam faster. If anything, such a movement slows down the steaming process, because as you move the pitcher down (possibly so far that the wand comes out of the milk), the steam mixes with air and creates foam.

## 3.5 Step 5

Heat the milk to 170°F/76°C. Use a milk thermometer to test the temperature. (A milk thermometer has a clip that attaches to the side of the pitcher, holding the thermometer in the milk during steaming.)

**Tip:** If you're busy, sit the pitcher on the tray of the espresso machine and let it steam on its own. This allows you to use your hands for other things, such as making espresso. One word of caution, though: Keep a close eye on the milk or it will scald. Scalding occurs at approximately 200°F/93°C. Scalding the milk creates foul-smelling and foul-tasting specialty coffee products. If you scald the milk, you will have to throw it away and start over again.

Keep your ears open, too. As the milk gets close to being ready, it will sound like it is about to take off (like an airplane). When you're experienced at steaming milk, you'll be able to know the temperature of the milk just by listening to it. As soon as the temperature reaches 160°F/71°C, pick up the milk and get ready to turn off the steam.

## 3.6 Step 6

Turn the steam off, remove the pitcher, and clean the steaming wand. A quick blast with a cloth around the wand will do this — essential to prevent clogging.

# 4. SIX STEPS TO FOAMING MILK

## 4.1 Step 1

Take the steaming pitcher from the fridge. The type of steaming pitcher you use is important: bell-shaped pitchers foam better than straight-sided pitchers. If you have prefoamed your milk, you will only need to reheat it up to 170°F/76°C. If you have not prefoamed, do the following:

Feel the side of the pitcher to determine if the milk is cold. If it is, add as much cold milk as you will need. If the milk is hot, put the pitcher back in the fridge and get a backup pitcher of cold milk. This is an important step because milk will not foam if it is hot. (If you need only hot milk rather than foamed, for a latte, for example, it doesn't matter whether you start with hot or cold milk, though the steaming time is reduced, of course, if you use hot.)

---

### CAFFE LATTE

(Use 12-ounce cup)

Put one pull of espresso grounds into the one-spout handle. Push the one-cup button on the espresso machine. Foam milk to a temperature of 160°F/71°C. Pour the espresso into a cup. Fill cup to seven-eighths full with steamed milk.

### FOR MEDIUM AND LARGE LATTE:

Use 16- or 20-ounce cup. Put two pulls of espresso grounds into the two-spout handle, and one extra pull in a one-spout handle for a large. Push related buttons and continue as above.

### CAFÉ AU LAIT:

Same as above, except use half regular brewed coffee and half steamed milk.

---

If all the backup pitchers have hot milk in them, pour one into another so that you are left with an empty pitcher in which to pour the cold milk.

When filling the pitcher with cold milk, keep in mind that foaming increases the volume of the milk three times, so fill the pitcher only one-third full. If you fill it much more than this, the milk will expand over the top of the pitcher. The milk also may not reach the high temperature it needs to, so you will need to pour the excess into another container before you can finish foaming in the first container.

Because you fill the container only one-third full, if you have an order for four large cappuccinos, for example, you will need to use three — possibly four — pitchers to get enough foam. Be prepared and have plenty of backup pitchers.

## 4.2 Step 2

Make sure the steaming wands are clean and the jets cleared *before* putting them inside the pitcher of milk. To clean the steam jets, turn the steam on for a second to clear out any residue left inside the four little holes.

## 4.3 Step 3

Place the steaming wand into the pitcher, well below the surface of the milk, and turn on the steam full blast. Quickly move the pitcher slightly up and down, keeping the wand just under the surface of the milk. This is critical to foaming the milk because, unlike steaming milk, to foam you must mix the air with the milk in order to create the bubbles.

### CAFFE MOCHA

(Use 12-ounce cup)

Put one pull of espresso grounds into the one-spout handle. Push the one-cup button on the espresso machine. Pour enough chocolate syrup to coat the bottom of the cup. Foam milk to a temperature of 160°F/71°C. Pour the espresso into the cup on top of the syrup. Fill cup to seven-eighths full with steamed milk. Top with freshly made whipped cream, and sprinkle with fresh grated Belgian chocolate.

### FOR MEDIUM AND LARGE CAFFE MOCHA:

Use 16- or 20-ounce cup. Put two pulls of espresso grounds into the two-spout handle (three pulls for a large) and push the two-cup button. Continue as above.

**Special tip:** Use hot-chocolate syrup instead of regular chocolate syrup; your taste buds will thank you.

## 4.4 Step 4

As you foam, you should be listening to the sound — pst, pst, pst — as the milk mixes with the air. Do not move the pitcher up and down very much or you will create foam while the wand is up but not while the wand is down. You will be wasting your foam potential for half the time you are steaming the milk. Instead, gradually move the pitcher up to match the increasing volume of the milk while still keeping the wand at the surface of the milk.

While you are doing this, watch the milk foam and examine the bubbles. If the bubbles are big and pop quickly, the steaming wand is too far out of the milk. If the bubbles are small and uniform, you are doing well. If you are getting no bubbles, your wand is probably in too far or you have started with milk that is too warm to foam.

## 4.5 Step 5

Heat the milk to 170°F/76°C, using a milk steaming thermometer to monitor the temperature.

## 4.6 Step 6

Turn the steam off, remove the pitcher, and clean the steaming wand.

---

**THE ULTIMATE FOAM TEST**

Take a scoop of foam out of the pitcher with a spoon after it has sat for 10–20 seconds. Hold the spoon upside down. If the foam sticks, it passes. If it falls, it fails.

---

# 5. SPECIALTY COFFEE MENU ITEMS

We recommend that all to-stay specialty coffees be served in glasses or cups on a small plate with the appropriate sized spoon, topped with either vanilla, freshly shaved Belgian chocolate, cinnamon, or nutmeg. All specialty coffees should be made available in the same three sizes as the gourmet coffees: small, medium, and large. The most common drinks are —

- **Cappuccino.** A strong shot or shots of espresso in a cup filled two-thirds full with steamed milk and then topped with foamed milk to approximately one inch above the rim.
- **Latte.** A strong shot or shots of espresso in a cup filled to half an inch below the cup rim with steamed milk and then highlighted by a spoonful of foamed milk on top.
- **Café au lait.** A 50/50 blend of brewed coffee and steamed milk.
- **Mocha.** A strong shot or shots of espresso in a cup, mixed with chocolate syrup. The cup is filled to half an inch below the cup rim with steamed milk, then highlighted with a generous topping of whipped cream.
- **Hot chocolate.** Made the same way as a mocha, minus the espresso.
- **Steamed milks.** A shot or shots of flavoring syrup in a cup, filled to half an inch below the cup rim with steamed milk, and then topped with a spoonful of foamed milk.

When assembling specialty coffees, use the following procedure.

(a) Have a glass or cup ready (with spoon if the order is to stay).

(b) Steam or foam the milk.

(c) Set the milk aside.

(d) Brew the espresso and pour into a glass or cup (or brew straight into a glass or cup if the order is to stay).

(e) Prepare the drink according to recipe requirements.

A word on toppings: Toppings should be applied by the person working at the specialty coffee station. Toppings should be treated as a treat and should be done as "the final touch to a masterpiece" by the staff member — not the customer. Staff should always ask customers which topping they want (ask them when they are up at the counter; don't shout the question across the coffee bar). Customers then get to watch as you carefully sprinkle their favorite topping on their order — a great way to build up anticipation!

### FLAVORED LATTE

(Use 12-ounce cup)

Put one pull of espresso grounds into the one-spout handle. Push the one-cup button on the espresso machine. Foam milk to a temperature of 160°F/71°C. Pour the espresso into a cup, along with 0.5 ounce of flavored syrup. Fill the cup seven-eighths full with steamed milk. Sprinkle with customer's choice of topping.

### FOR MEDIUM AND LARGE FLAVORED LATTE:

Use 16- or 20-ounce cup. Put two pulls of espresso grounds into the two-spout handle (three pulls for a large) and push the two-cup button. Proceed as above, using 1 ounce of flavored syrup for a medium, and 1.5 ounces for a large.

---

**TRAINING TIP**

When training staff, allow all staff members to make each of the drinks your coffee bar offers. Make sure they know which type of cup to use with which drink and for which size.

---

## 5.1 Iced coffee beverages

Iced coffee beverages are no longer just for summer. Iced coffee — ranging from simple cold coffee shaken with ice cubes to elaborate, blended concoctions with flavoring syrups, ice cream, and whipped cream — is popular all year round. In fact, in Canada, the popularity of iced coffee has doubled in the past five years.

Brew the coffee you'll need ahead of time and cool it for use in the drinks. (Note: Cool the coffee to room temperature before putting it in the refrigerator — sudden changes of temperature will shatter glass containers.) Some cafés add flavor by using ice cubes made of coffee instead of water — this prevents the flavor from being diluted as the customer enjoys the beverage.

If you are planning to offer blended beverages, you will need a blender. Otherwise, you can mix ice coffee in a cocktail shakers — which can make for a dramatic experience for your customer watching his or her drink being made.

There are many combinations of ingredients you can use to create different iced coffees, but basic technique remains the same: combine your coffee, ice, milk, and flavorings in the blender or shaker, agitate, and pour into a clear take-out cup or glass. If you are using a shaker, strain the mixture into a cup filled with ice cubes or shaved ice. Add any garnishes or extras such as whipped cream or chocolate shavings (use your imagination!), and serve with a straw.

If you are adding sugar to your iced coffee beverages, remember that sugar does not dissolve in cold liquids. Use a sugar syrup, or dissolve sugar in a small amount of hot coffee before adding it to the beverage.

For more information, ask your supplier about flavorings and recipes for iced coffee.

## SPECIAL NON-COFFEE DRINKS

### HOT CHOCOLATE

(Use 12-, 16-, or 20-ounce cup)

Squirt 1 ounce (1.5 ounce for a 16-ounce cup; 2 ounces for a 20-ounce cup) chocolate syrup around inside of cup with enough to cover the cup bottom. Foam the milk to a temperature of 160°F/71°C. Fill the cup seven-eighths full with milk. Stir. The mixture should be a medium-brown chocolate color. Top with freshly made whipped cream, and sprinkle with chocolate.

### FLAVORED MILK

(Use 12-, 16-, or 20-ounce cup)

Pour 1 ounce of syrup (1.5 ounce for a 16-ounce cup; 2 ounces for a 20-ounce cup) into the cup. Foam the milk to a temperature of 160°F/71°C. Fill the cup seven-eighths full with milk. Top with foam and topping of customer's choice.

# COMMITMENT BOX

I, _____ , commit to ensuring that all my staff are properly trained in the art of foaming milk and follow my recipes for specialty coffees.

_____          _____
*(your signature)*                    *(today's date)*

# 13
## TEA

Far in the dreamy East there grows a plant whose native home is the Sun's Cousin's garden.

— HENRIK IBSEN

## 1. THE CONTEMPLATIVE BEVERAGE

As we sit sipping a Moroccan mint herbal tea, we try to think of the best way to describe this very contemplative product. Ten minutes later we are still thinking — about the early British explorers and their struggle to get tea from the Chinese and Portuguese in Macao. We realize that our mental wanderings are typical of the state of mind that great teas induce. Very different from coffee. Not better or worse, just different.

And it is this difference that highlights the advantage of selling teas as a complement to your coffees.

No one chapter could ever do this subject justice, so we'll address the key aspects that relate to the business of selling and brewing fine teas.

## 2. A BRIEF HISTORY OF TEA

Legends shroud the origins of tea. The most interesting legend tells of a Buddhist monk who fell asleep in the middle of a nine-year meditation. On awakening, he was so upset that he slashed his eyelids, threw them to the ground, and from this grew the first tea plant, called "awakening."

Another legend tells of a Chinese emperor who was said to boil all his drinking water. One day the wind blew several leaves into his pot of water. The aroma and subsequent drink were tasty, so this emperor decided to have his water always steeped with leaves. We prefer the second explanation — it's a lot less painful.

Whatever its origin, tea has been known and used for more than a thousand years. Known as "chai" in India, Russia, and central Asia, and modified from "tu" to "te" by the Fijians, this plant is now known as "tea" in the West.

Herbal teas are mentioned as far back as the days of Plato and Aristotle in ancient Greece. Herbal teas are not a true tea, but a collection of various herbs, roots, berries, seeds, and flower buds. Ancient Romans took herb farming quite seriously and brewed herb teas with water and vinegar.

After the Boston Tea Party, true teas were not socially acceptable in the American colonies, so a series of "Liberty Teas" were created from various American herbs. Today herbal and regular teas can both be served with no fear of mass revolt.

# 3. GROWING TEA

The tea plant (*Camellia sinensis*) is a flowering evergreen. The ideal climate for this plant is relatively warm with a lot of rainfall distributed fairly evenly through the growing season. Tea is grown with equal success in open fields and on terraced hillsides. The major tea-growing regions in the world are India, Sri Lanka (Ceylon), Japan, China, Taiwan (Formosa), and Indonesia (Java, Sumatra). The wetter the climate, the more new growth or "flushes" for picking there will be. The cooler the climate, often the finer the tea — but in less quantity.

Tea is best grown under shady trees, as direct sun can damage the gentle leaves. Constant pruning and picking prevent the tea bush from becoming a full tree. Most harvesting is done by hand, by picking the two tiny leaves from the ends of each twig.

## 3.1 Fair trade tea and herbal tea

Fair trade tea is a new and growing segment of the tea market. The principles behind fair trade tea are the same as those behind fair trade coffee:

- Fair prices paid to farmers and co-operatives
- Safe working conditions and good wages for plantation workers
- Environmentally friendly growing practices, such as not using harmful chemicals on crops

In addition, importers of fair trade tea pay premiums to tea growers, and the money helps build housing and schools for workers.

Fair trade teas and herbal teas, including rooibos, are available in North America through over 70 tea brands and importers. You can find them through the Trans Fair USA website at www.transfairusa.org/content/certification/tea_program.php.

# 4. TYPES OF TEAS

The basic difference between prepared or finished teas is in the way they are processed. The three main types of tea — black, oolong, and green — are the result of three different methods of processing and are determined by whether the tea has been fermented, and if so, to what extent. (A fourth type, white tea, is rare but becoming popular.) Many tea leaves can be processed by each method. Generally, though, a given plant is processed only one or two ways.

## 4.1 Green

This is the only unfermented tea. The leaves are fired immediately after picking by steaming, hand or machine rolling, or heat-drying. These leaves are graded by leaf age and style.

Matcha is a high-grade green tea that is sold in powdered form. The leaves of the tea plants are covered several weeks before harvesting to deepen the color of the leaves. After harvesting, the leaves are laid out flat to dry and then ground to a fine powder. Matcha is often used as a catch-all term for green tea, but the real thing is the tea served in Japan's famous tea ceremony — serving genuine matcha requires some special techniques and equipment. More likely you will be offering "matcha lattes" or "green tea frappuccinos" — drinks that echo espresso-based beverages. These mixed drinks will not require such a high grade of tea.

## 4.2 Oolong

The oolong method involves starting a fermentation process on the leaves. Partway through, this process is stopped by firing the leaves. Oolong teas are fragrant and distinct in taste. They are graded by quality.

## 4.3 Black

The most common type of tea consumed in the world, black tea is fermented completely and then fired. The leaves are then sifted and sorted by the various grading methods, including size, age, and leaf style. Black teas are actually called red teas in China because the brew is a deep reddish color.

## 4.4 White

White tea comes from the same plant as green and black teas, but is made from immature leaves that have been picked before the plant's buds open. The silvery fuzz that covers the buds gives the tea its name, and the ratio of buds to leaves in the final product denotes the tea's quality. White tea is rarer and more expensive than other teas, but it is also starting to appear in bagged form. Fans of white tea praise its delicate flavor and lack of aftertaste.

## 5. HERBAL TEA

Herbal tea is a term that covers any tea that is not made from the leaves of the *Camellia sinensis* plant. Also known as tisanes, herbal teas are composed of infinite combinations of dried leaves, seeds, roots, and flowers. They can be made with any plant that contains an element of appealing flavor, including flowers, herbs, and fruit.

Herbal teas are naturally caffeine free, so they appeal to health-conscious customers. Some classic herbal teas include chamomile, peppermint, blackcurrant, and lemon teas. If you choose to offer herbal teas in your coffee bar, you may wish to seek out one of the many exotic combinations that are widely available in loose or bagged form.

## 5.1 Rooibos tea

Rooibos tea is native to South Africa. Rooibos means "red bush" in Afrikaans, the common name of the *Asphlathus linearis* plant from which the tea is made. (The leaves of the bush are actually green, but they turn red after being fermented.) Rooibos tea is red and tastes sweet and slightly nutty. Long a favorite tea in South Africa, it has become popular around the world for its healthy reputation. Rooibos tea is caffeine free, low in tannins, and rich in minerals.

# 6. BUBBLE TEA

According to legend, bubble tea was invented in the early 1980s by a vendor at a Taiwanese night market. The drink — a blend of hot or iced tea, milk, sweetener, flavoring, and tapioca pearls ("boba" or "bubbles") — spread like wildfire through Asia's tea-loving countries. Bubble tea shops are now found in towns and cities throughout the world. Bubble tea is more than a trend: it's here to stay.

Whether you decide to add bubble tea to your coffee bar's menu or to specialize in bubble tea, making the drink requires little special equipment (although you may decide to invest in an automatic cup sealer and/or a shaking machine). You will need a hot plate in order to cook the tapioca pearls, a cocktail shaker or blender to mix the other ingredients, and plastic cups with thick straws (at least ½" in diameter) to serve the bubble tea in. You might also choose no-cook alternatives to tapioca balls, such as coconut jelly, which comes in ready-to-use cubes. There are many suppliers of bubble tea ingredients and supplies in the United States and Canada; just Google "Bubble Tea" for a list or ask your current coffee and tea supplier.

Bubble tea comes in an astonishing range of flavors. There are two basic varieties however — sweet and creamy, and sour and fruity. Sweet and creamy flavors are usually based on a black tea, and sour and fruity flavors (such as mango or lychee) are usually based on green tea. Some flavors of bubble tea do not require tea at all; their flavor comes from the use of flavored powders or syrups.

Bubble tea is not difficult to make, and it's a fun drink with lots of appeal among children, teenagers, and young adults. It can be priced about the same as a premium espresso drink, so if you think your customers will like bubble tea, it could be a very profitable product for you.

# 7. MARKET POTENTIAL

The second-most consumed beverage in the world (after water), and one of the top dollar-volume beverages (second behind coffee), tea has been a major commodity since before the Boston Tea Party. The primary consuming nations are the United Kingdom, the United States, Canada, and Australia.

While overall consumption has grown steadily, tea still represents less than 10 percent of a gourmet coffee bar's overall sales. The best way to profit from tea is to carry a select range of high quality teas not available at your local grocery store. Tea consumption varies dramatically by region across North America. Don't assume that tea will sell well in your area — do some research.

As with coffee, there is a huge range of quality tea products available. Take the time to find a reputable wholesaler that knows what it is talking about.

# 8. TEA "BRANDS"

Teas usually carry a double name: a place name (the country or region where the tea was grown) and a grading or processing method. Table 2 lists some common tea varieties. All teas vary in quality and cupping characteristics, so always use taste as your final method of comparing teas.

In addition to all the varieties listed in Table 2, there are numerous private label tea blends, including common blends such as English Breakfast and Earl Grey. Each of

## TABLE 2
# TEA NAMES

| COUNTRY | MARKET NAME | GRADINGS | | |
|---|---|---|---|---|
| | | **Black** | **Oolong** | **Green** |
| Sri Lanka | Ceylons<br>　　High-grown<br>　　Medium-grown<br>　　Low-grown | Orange Pekoe<br>Broken Orange Pekoe<br>Pekoe<br>Broken Pekoe<br>Pekoe Souchong<br>Souchong<br>Fannings<br>Dust | | |
| India | Assams<br>Cachars<br>Sylhets<br>Dooars<br>Terais<br>Darjeeling<br>Tranvancores<br>Kanan Devans | Orange Pekoe<br>Broken Orange Pekoe<br>Pekoe<br>Broken Pekoe<br>Pekoe Souchong<br>Souchong<br>Fannings<br>Dust | | Fine Young<br>Hyson<br>Young Hyson<br>Hyson No. 1<br>Twankay<br>Sowmee<br>Fannings<br>Dust |
| China | North China Congous<br>South China Congous<br><br>Country Greens<br>　　Pingsueys<br>　　Hoochows | Flowery Pekoe<br>Orange Pekoe<br>Pekoe<br>Souchong | | Gunpowder<br>Imperial<br>Young Hyson<br>Hyson Skin<br>Twankay<br>Dust |
| Japan | Japans | | | Extra Choicest<br>Choicest<br>Choice<br>Finest<br>Fine<br>Good Medium<br>Good Common<br>Nibs<br>Dust<br>Fannings |

TABLE 2 — CONTINUED

| COUNTRY | MARKET NAME | GRADINGS Black | Oolong | Green |
|---|---|---|---|---|
| Indonesia | Javas<br>Sumatras | Flowery Orange Pekoe<br>Orange Pekoe<br>Broken Orange Pekoe<br>Pekoe<br>Broken Pekoe,<br>   No. 1 and No. 2<br>Pekoe Souchong<br>Souchong<br>Broken Tea<br>Dust<br>Bohea | | |
| Taiwan<br>(Formosa) | Formosa Oolongs | | Choice<br>Fine to Choice<br>Finest<br>Fine to Finest<br>Fine Up<br>On Fine<br>Superior to Fine<br>Superior Up<br>Fully Superior<br>Superior<br>On Superior<br>Good to Superior<br>Good Up<br>Fully Good<br>Good<br>On Good<br>Standard | |

these blends varies greatly, depending on the teas used to create them. Many mass market teas contain flavor crystals and compounds, so beware.

# 9. FIVE KEYS TO GREAT TEA

There are five key elements you must take into account if you wish to brew great tea: water quality, temperature of the water, amount of dry leaf, steeping time, and, of course, the quality of the tea leaf itself. Let's briefly look at each.

## 9.1 Water

The quality of water is crucial to tea. Always use filtered or dechlorinated water. Natural spring water (with minerals) will allow for the best flavor. According to the American Tea Masters Association, the ideal pH level is an alkaline pH of 7.9. You will need a good commercial filter for the teas you make in your coffee bar. (Recommend to your customers brewing the tea at home that they use a water filter such as the Brita system to obtain this pH level.)

## 9.2 Temperature of water

For most teas, water should be just about to boil (212°F/100°C) or just off the boil. If water is boiled too many times it will lose oxygen, and tea made from it will be flat and tasteless. Green tea is often better made with water that is at a slightly lower temperature. You can use boiling water for herbal teas. In fact, seeds or roots will need to be simmered on a stove for 10 to 20 minutes to release their full flavor and aroma.

## 9.3 Amount of dry leaf

One teaspoon of tea per person and one for the pot is the standard measurement of dry leaf tea, though the amount needed for each particular tea will vary. You can easily measure the number of teaspoons if you are using an infuser.

Experiment with loose teas to find the best combination, then rigorously enforce that amount. This can be a challenge with staff — especially those well-meaning but ill-informed staff members who think "if a little is good, then a lot must be better." Watch for these tea-abusers.

Several of the better tea wholesalers package their loose teas in cloth tea bags. This allows for proper expansion of the leaf and ease of fast measurement.

Be sure to roll the leaves of herbal teas just before steeping, and crush nuts and seeds. This will allow even more flavor to be released.

## 9.4 Steeping time

Practice, practice, practice. Nowhere is this more important than steeping time. Generally three to four minutes is good. Some teas, however, need six or seven minutes, and some will be far too strong after only three minutes. Read about the specific teas, ask your wholesaler questions, and taste for yourself.

## 9.5 The quality of the tea

The actual tea leaf is important. Take the time and care to buy quality teas. Your customers will appreciate it. And keep in mind that, with tea, you do get what you pay for. So if one wholesaler has a "great" Earl Grey for 55 percent less than your regular wholesaler, ask yourself why.

# 10. CUPPING TEA

Cupping tea, known as tea tasting, is quite an art. It is often the exclusive domain of expert buyers, blenders, and government officials, though it is possible to do your own tasting sessions. When you open these sessions to your customers, it can inspire incredible loyalty.

Tea is judged on three things: appearance and smell of the dried leaf, color and odor of a weak infusion, and the flavor characteristics of the drinking infusion.

## 10.1 Tea tasting terms

Before we discuss the three stages of cupping tea, here are some examples of the more common terms used during cupping.

(a) **Aroma.** Also known as fragrance, it is actually the odor of both the infused leaf and the tea liquor itself. Most analogies are to flowery essences or fruits.

(b) **Bitter.** An unpleasant biting taste, frequently resulting from over-steeping or allowing teas to remain too long in the liquor.

(c) **Body.** The viscosity or the strength of the liquor combined with its weight on the tongue; body may be "'full," "light," etc.

(d) **Bright.** A sparkling liquor characteristic of well-manufactured teas.

(e) **Coarse.** A harsh taste; quite undesirable.

(f) **Complex.** The harmonious melange of flavors characteristic of the very finest teas.

(g) **Earthy.** A flavor which can be either a natural attribute from the region where the tea is grown or the result of storage in too damp an area.

(h) **Harsh.** A very rough-tasting under-withered tea.

(i) **Orange Pekoe.** Not a type of tea but rather the larger of the two leaves of a tea plant; the orange refers to the orange or golden color of the leaf when plucked.

(j) **Peak.** The high point of the tasting experience when, after the liquor enters the mouth, its body, flavor, and astringency make themselves fully felt. Greens and oolongs do not peak, but stand immediately and fully revealed.

(k) **Stewed.** Oversteeped tea leaves that have turned bitter.

(l) **Tarry.** An aroma of smokiness associated with Lapsang Souchang or some Russian Caravan-style teas; the scent derives from being smoked over wood or charcoal. (If it smells like rubber, do not buy it.)

(m) **Tip.** Literally the tip of the youngest leaves, which is a true sign of good picking.

(n) **Well-twisted.** The fully withered leaf of whole-leaf grades which is tightly rolled length-wise.

## 10.2 Appearance and smell of the dried leaf

First examine the dried leaf. Black tea leaf should be dark (blackish-brown) and well twisted, indicating a good wither (brown, flaky leaf is a sign of a poor wither). An open, flat leaf infuses quickly; a closely twisted leaf takes longer to infuse and will give a better second cup.

In general, the leaf should be small, hard, well rolled, and uniform in appearance. The presence of tips, or bud leaf, is not always an indication of quality; tippy tea should be golden, long, and well twisted. Squeeze the dry leaf to test for the resilience that characterizes young tea.

(The appearance and smell of the leaf are not critical determining factors for the cup quality of oolong and green teas.)

## 10.3 Color and odor of a weak infusion

Next examine a weak infusion of tea. If black or oolong tea has not been fermented long enough, the infusion will be conspicuously bright in color and the leaf will have a green tint. A dark green infusion indicates insufficient withering and overfermentation. An infused leaf with a green-yellow tint indicates pungency; a rich golden leaf, quality; a reddish leaf, full, rich liquor; a dark leaf, low-grade common tea.

A green tea leaf that has a clear green-yellow or green-golden color in a weak infusion is a young, early-picked leaf. A dull, lifeless dark yellow color denotes old or low-grade tea. The lighter the liquor, the younger the leaf and the better the tea.

Smell the weak infusion to get some indication of the character of the tea and to detect possible burning during firing.

## 10.4 Flavor characteristics of the drinking infusion

The final step is to taste the flavor of the tea infusion. What you seek is a tea with marked character, distinctive flavor, and aroma — a tea that will be useful for blending.

Perfect black tea will be full-, rich-, and thick-looking in the cup, rich in color, with a bright sparkling appearance immediately after pouring.

Oolong teas will turn cloudy or "cream down" as they cool. The finest green teas will be light in the cup, mellow, sweetish, and flowery.

## 11. SERVING TEA

The staff member at the gourmet coffee station will likely be put in charge of preparing tea as well as gourmet coffee orders. Here are some serving tips:

- Fill the teapot with hot water from a hot water dispenser.

- Serve teapot on a doilied plate with a spoon and napkin on the side. The preheated teacup or mug should be on a separate plate.

- Place the tea bag or infuser either in the pot or on the plate holding the teapot. Tea drinkers can be a fussy lot: most have a very strong opinion on where they like their bag to be, so ask customers what they prefer.

- Give customers their order and tell them where the honey (a must-have condiment for serious tea drinkers) is as well as the location of the cream and sugar.

## 12. SELLING TEA TO YOUR CUSTOMERS

This process is the same as selling coffee, so review and adapt the earlier information. Your tea wholesaler can help you decide which teas to carry.

Remember that heat, air, and direct sunlight degrade tea. Glass jars may be great visual merchandisers, but they will definitely hurt your long-term sales if they don't keep the tea fresh.

Tea customers are slow to convert, but very loyal when they find tea they love. Have patience and you will be rewarded.

## 13. TEAHOUSES — TO BUILD OR NOT TO BUILD

Should you build a dedicated teahouse or simply have a selection of teas in your coffeehouse? Unlike many coffee bar customers, teahouse customers want to linger. They occupy a given space longer, with less dollars per chair. This means once you build your volume to large levels, you will not have enough seats to sustain long-term profit.

"Okay," you say. "I want to build a teahouse despite these warnings. What do I do to minimize my risk?" Make sure you select your location well. Make sure you market aggressively, using the methods we recommend in this book. And most of all, make sure you become so passionate about tea that you could write your own book.

# COMMITMENT BOX

I, _____ , commit to
ensuring that each of my staff are properly trained
in the art of brewing and serving tea.

_____          _____
(your signature)                 (today's date)

# PART 3
## OPERATIONS

# 14

# THE MONEY EXCHANGE STATION

When riches begin to come they come so quickly, in such great abundance, that one wonders where they have been hiding during all those lean years.

— NAPOLEON HILL

## 1. THE MONEY EXCHANGE STATION — WHERE IT ALL HAPPENS

As we mentioned earlier, the staff member assigned to the money exchange station is responsible for taking and suggesting orders and accepting money in exchange for the products he or she is serving. While all staff members are responsible for greeting customers, depending on the layout of the coffee bar this duty may fall mainly on the shoulders of the person at the till.

The person at this station will also be responsible for maintaining the till.

## 2. THE TILL: POLICIES AND PROCEDURES

### 2.1 Purpose of the till

The major purpose of the till — whether you have chosen to use a cash register or a computer software program — is to track coffee bar sales. Depending on how sophisticated your till system is, you may also be able to obtain reports for the sales made by each individual staff member, sales made in each department (e.g., coffees, specialty coffees, and baked goods), sales made during certain periods of the day, and average checks and customer or invoice counts.

You should also be able to track the success of promotions and coupons you receive and the amount of "add-on sales" for each of these. We recommend using software that can actually accumulate a history so that at the end of the month you print off a summarized report of the "free stuff sales" for the value of the items you supplied at no cost plus the add-on sales totals.

You will also want a system that records your customers' coffee bean-buying histories so that you can provide better service and increase your retail bean volume.

Despite massive leaps in software, a full system is still fairly expensive, and we know many coffee bar owners start with a basic cash register from Costco. As a result we will focus on how things work from a very basic level. However, we strongly encourage you to get good software as it will make your life that much easier.

## 2.2 Till policies

We recommend that you adopt certain till policies for both security reasons and good customer service.

Keep the till drawer closed at all times except when making change. Tills are not to be used for personal purposes such as making change or cashing checks.

If a customer forgets to take his or her change, give the money to the customer if he or she is still inside the coffee bar. If the customer has already left, keep the money in a sealed envelope with the date, signature of staff involved, and a description of the customer as best remembered. The envelope should then remain in your coffee bar for at least one week, to give the customer a chance to reclaim it. At the end of the one week period, the amount should be

added to your daily cash sheet total and deposited with that day's deposit or donated to a charity such as Coffee Kids. If small change (under one dollar) is left at the counter, put it into the donation container.

## 2.3 Keeping the till in order

Here are some tips for keeping the till in order:

- Keep a float of $300 to $400. The amount should be an even number that is easy for staff to remember and sufficient so that you don't run out of change during the day.

- Keep lots of small bills for backup.

- Keep bills facing one way so that you don't have to sort them all at the end of the day.

- Put dirty, torn bills at the bottom of the pile so that customers do not get them.

- Put large bills under the cash drawer so that they are less likely to be stolen or lost.

- Put checks under the cash drawer so that they are out of the way of the bills.

- Keep a backup float of at least one to five rolls of coins per denomination that you can use if you run out of the loose coins in the cash drawer. You want to serve customers, not inconvenience them by running out of quarters or dimes.

## 2.4 Refunding

We recommend you adopt the policy of offering a customer his or her money back if any of the following occur:

(a) An order is not filled efficiently (e.g., you just ran out of prep to make a freshly squeezed juice and the customer had to wait while you cut up oranges).

(b) You forget to prepare an order (when this mistake is pointed out, prepare the order and then offer it "on the house").

(c) The customer receives a product of inferior quality for any reason.

## 2.5 Payouts

Some coffee bars choose not to have a separate petty cash fund, but pay minor expenses out of the cash register. If you do payouts from the till, you must record and track the dollars spent. Depending on your coffee bar's policy, payout privileges may be restricted to owners and managers.

We recommend the following payout policies:

(a) Have all payouts approved by yourself or the manager (unless neither are available and it's an emergency, e.g., running out of milk).

(b) Set budgets for your payout categories.

(c) Write down on a till receipt the amount of money taken and why, along with the initials of the staff member receiving the money.

(d) Once the item has been purchased, staple the receipt to the till receipt and clearly mark which category the purchase was made for. These will then be totaled at the end of the month and added to your profit/loss statement. Categories include:

- Food and paper
- Maintenance and repair
- Casual labor
- Advertising
- Office supplies
- Promotion

Circle the receipt total and underline the tax amount so they are easier to record at the end of the day.

(e) Put stapled receipts out of the way under the cash drawer and ensure that the change from the original amount of money you took has been returned to the till.

# 3. ELEVEN STEPS TO CUSTOMER SERVICE AT THE COUNTER THAT WILL WOW! YOUR CUSTOMERS

## 3.1 Greet your customer

The art of greeting customers has been mastered by the Japanese, who have taken it to a new level. If you have ever been to Japan, you will know that as soon as you walk into any restaurant, every single staff member looks at you and loudly says "Welcome to our place." This happens every time, everywhere. And it's great!

Model your greeting procedure after this Japanese tradition by recognizing your customers in the same way every time they walk into your coffee bar. Use an honored guest greeting procedure to help set you apart from your competitors and make your customers' experience in your coffee bar stand out in their minds.

Acknowledge customers no matter how busy you are. As well as a verbal greeting, try to make eye contact with your customers and, most importantly, smile.

## 3.2 Find out if the customer is a first-time customer

This step is so important, we cannot emphasize it enough. If you consistently find out whether a customer has been to your coffee bar before, you will be in an excellent position to better meet the needs of the customer.

What do we mean by this? Let's look at an example:

*Staff member, while smiling:* "Welcome to The Coffee Bar! Is this your first time here?"

*Customer:* "Yes it is."

*Staff member, enthusiastically:* "Great! I'm glad you stopped by. Here are our baked goods (pointing to display case), our specialty coffees are described here (pointing to menu board), and we have some excellent coffees on tap that we roasted right here this morning (pointing to daily roasts sign). Do you have an idea of what you might want to try today?"

If you know that the customer is a first-time customer, you are able to tell him or her about the unique features of your coffee bar and expose the customer to products and services he or she may be interested in.

We have had store owners complain to us that using this question over and over again is boring; it creates robotic staff; customers don't like hearing it every time they enter the coffee bar; and it is difficult to enforce its use by staff. Let's look at each of these objections.

(a) *"It's boring asking the same question all the time."* Let us ask you this — is making more money boring?

(b) *"Creates robotic staff."* Does this mean that staff who say, "Can I help you?" over and over again are not robotic? We designed this question to allow staff the flexibility of focusing on different product lines, unique features of the coffee bar, and daily promotions.

(c) *"Customers don't like hearing this question every time they enter the coffee bar."* What customers don't like is being told the same things about your coffee bar over and over again. By asking this question you ensure customers do not hear the same thing over and over again. If you have done a good job choosing long-term staff, they will get to know who has been in before and who has not, so they won't ask the regulars this question. You will begin to hear your staff say things like, "I don't remember seeing you before, is this your first visit to The Coffee Bar?"

(d) *"It's difficult to enforce with staff."* Our policy was simple: either our staff asked the question or they didn't work for us. There is no mystery here. This question, in our opinion, is so important to the success of your business that not asking it costs you money. And you don't hire staff to cost you money; you hire them to help you make money!

### 3.2a Script tips

Ask the question from the moment you open your coffee bar. While customers on the first day will be new, you will be surprised at how many people become "regulars" almost immediately. You also want to get your staff into the routine of asking the question as part of the service they give.

As well as giving first-time customers a tour of the major products in your coffee bar, you and your staff will want to pick up on customers' body language to help determine which script to use. For example, someone looking at the baked goods is probably not interested in your coffee home delivery service. He or she is probably interested in the kinds of muffins you have, and in the information that they are baked fresh in your coffee bar every day and are low in cholesterol and saturated fats.

If in-store roasting is what your concept is all about, make sure that, at the least, all new customers learn that you custom roast individual pounds of beans for the customer to take home hot out of the roaster and that your coffees are all certified organic (or at least grown sustainably).

Make sure you don't overwhelm customers with too much information. Be perceptive and flexible especially when you have a long lineup.

Watch for signs that a customer has been to the coffee bar before. If he or she walks confidently up to the counter and hands you his or her preferred-customer card (see Chapter 16) — you can bet this customer has been in before. You will need to be flexible and deal with these customers differently than you would those who wander aimlessly in and stare confusedly at the menu board. Mentioning daily specials is an excellent script for customers who have been in the coffee bar before.

Watch for signs of how customers are feeling. If it is 6 a.m. and they come groggily in and mumble something about a coffee, you may not want to enthusiastically ask if they have been in before and if they want to try a mocha, double espresso con panna, or a vanilla latte.

Watch how customers behave. Do they look confused? Are they looking around the coffee bar in search of something? There is nothing wrong with starting out a conversation by commenting on this, for example, "You look as though you are looking for someone — are you supposed to be meeting someone here?" or "You look puzzled by something — can I help you at all?"

Then watch how your customers respond to you — are they friendly and responsive or do they glare at you with a "leave me alone until I decide look"? Don't let unhappy or unresponsive customers affect your positive state of mind. There is an adage that whoever is more committed to his or her state of mind, wins. If you are more committed to being happy and enthusiastic and delivering top-notch customer service, you will win over the customer who is a grouch. Sometimes a staff member can break a customer out of an unhappy state by asking him or her a question such as, "So, what has been your biggest success so far today?"

## 3.3 Ask great questions

Asking questions — great questions — helps you determine what customers want so that you are in a better position to meet their needs. In addition to finding out whether customers are new or not, you may want to find out what they feel like having today, what they see that interests them, or what sounds good to them. The following scripts may give you some ideas for questions to ask your customers.

### 3.3a First-time customers

*Staff member, while smiling:* "Welcome to the Coffee Bar! Is this your first time here?"

*Customer:* "Yes it is."

*Staff member, enthusiastically:* "Great! Welcome. Our coffees are all certified organic and we do our own roasting right there (pointing to the roaster). You can take home coffee hot out of the roaster in about the time it takes you to drink your latte. Could I get you some?"

or:

*Staff member, enthusiastically:* "Great! Welcome. We have freshly squeezed juices and ice cream in addition to our coffee that we roast right here in the coffee bar. We also have some great muffins that just came out of the oven. Would you like to try one?"

### 3.3b Repeat customers

*Staff member, while smiling:* "Welcome to the Coffee Bar! Is this your first time here?"

*Customer:* "No, I was in yesterday (or last week, or this morning)."

*Staff member, enthusiastically:* "Great! Welcome back. Did you see our daily special? We're offering a complimentary flavor in any latte today."

or:

*Staff member, enthusiastically:* "Great! Welcome back. Can I tempt you with one of our cookies? They just came out of the oven."

or:

*Staff member, enthusiastically:* "Great! Welcome back. What did you have last time you were here? Would you like to have that again or would you like to try something a little different today?"

or (for customers who "come in all the time" and who seem unsure of what they want):

*Staff member, enthusiastically:* "Great! What do you feel like today — something hot, something cold? I could make you an iced latte if you like."

## 3.4 Take the order

A classic mistake that coffee bar owners and staff make is to take an order in the wrong place in the coffee bar. Orders must always be taken at the till. Again, this may seem like a little thing, but if you do not ring orders in at the till, you can create complete chaos in your coffee bar in a very short period of time, particularly if you do not have different staff members assigned to the money exchange station and the coffee making stations.

What happens is this: a customer walks in and you, at the specialty coffee station, for example, greet the customer, ask some questions, then take the order. You walk to the till to ring in the order. In the meantime, another customer walks in. He has been to the coffee bar before, so he goes directly to the till. But you walk away from the till because you are serving a customer at the specialty coffee station. The second customer is left standing there, waiting.

A customer who has never been to your coffee bar before walks in. She sees one customer standing at the till and one at the specialty coffee station where you are, so she goes and stands behind the customer at the specialty coffee station. You take your first customer's money and walk back to the till. The second customer is still there, waiting and watching you get your exercise. You walk back to your first customer with her change.

Now a fourth customer walks in and stands behind the third customer at the specialty coffee station because it's starting to look like a formal lineup. But then you confuse them all by walking down to serve customer 2 who is still standing, waiting at the till. Now customers 3 and 4 are wondering what's going on, especially as customer 5 walks in and stands behind customer 2.

Unless you are really good at remembering exactly who walked in when, you have a mess on your hands. Customers must decide among themselves who was there first, and you end up running back and forth from one place to another, looking, feeling, and being very disorganized and inefficient.

Don't laugh. We've seen this happen all too often.

Make sure you take orders at the till. If a customer is standing at a different station in the coffee bar, call them over, saying something like, "Come on over here — I can serve you better from here." And wave them down to the till. An "Order Here" sign hanging over the money exchange station also works well.

Remember that you can't point to cup sizes, show the customer the "Daily Roasts"

sign, or ring in the order if he or she is at the other end of the coffee bar.

### 3.4a Tips for taking orders

(a) **Gourmet and specialty coffees:** You must find out three things:

- Whether the coffee is to go or stay
- Which daily roast is required
- What size the customer wants

(b) **Baked goods:** If customers order baked goods, ask if they want any accompaniments (e.g., butter or jam). Make sure you serve any baked goods with a knife or fork (as required) so that customers are not forced to use their hands to break apart a muffin.

(c) **Custom roasted coffee to go:** Ask the roast master to help the customer.

(d) **Tea:** As well as finding out whether the order is to stay or go, you must also find out if customers want their tea bag on the side or directly in the pot.

## 3.5 Take the sale one step further — suggestive sell

Once you have greeted the customer, found out if the customer is a first-timer or not, and asked some questions to better fulfill his or her needs, your next step is to increase the amount of money the customer spends in your coffee bar by making a suggestion or recommendation. This is helpful to the customer because it points out a product or service you have to offer that may meet a need the customer has. See Chapter 16 for more on suggestive selling.

## TIPS FOR SERVING BAKED GOODS

- If the item is to go, place it in a brown paper lunch bag with a napkin folded in half and placed inside the bag. (Put the napkin on the side if the item is sticky and will dirty it.)

- Bags should be opened using tongs, not fingers.

- If the customer is going to eat at the coffee bar, place the item on a clean plate with a napkin folded in half on the side. Don't put food items directly on top of the napkin. This makes the napkin difficult to get out and dirties the napkin.

- Microwave the product if requested. Put cutlery and condiments on the plate after microwaving.

- If the item is to be eaten in and requires a knife or fork, place the cutlery on top of the napkin on the plate.

- Place any condiments on the side.

## 3.6 Ring in the order

Make sure that the order is rung in and the total amount clearly stated to the customer before an order is assembled. It is more efficient for customers to get their money out while you are stamping their preferred-customer cards, and this will also help prevent customers from following you or the staff member as the order is prepared (this could create confusion as to where the line-up is).

**Note:** If you have done a good job with your impulse merchandising displays at the counter, a customer who is waiting for an order may decide to buy something else. However, if your staff is following correct procedure, suggestive selling will have already occurred.

There are four steps to exchanging money:

(a) Clearly state the amount of the total order. ("That will be a total of $7.20, please.")

(b) When the customer hands you the money, call out the currency unit from which you are making change. ("Out of ten? $2.80 is your change.")

(c) Place the customer's money across the top of the cash drawer until the change is made. This is very important to avoid confusion over how much money was handed over. If there is any discrepancy over the amount of money given to you or the amount of change you have given, both you and your customer will be able to see the amount of money originally given to you.

(d) Put loose change in the customer's hand first, then the bills. Never put the bills and coins on the counter, forcing the customer to pick them up.

### 3.6a *Other forms of payment*

Plan to carry direct debit, Visa, and MasterCard at minimum — especially if you plan to carry large ticket items such as espresso machines or brewing equipment.

It's up to you whether you accept personal checks. We have, and have never had a problem. In fact we suggest not even asking for customer ID for the check. It will surprise them, and you'll stick out as a place that trusts people. In 20 years we've had one check go bad, and that was for less than $25.

Traveler's checks should be handled as paper money. Remember that companies that issue traveler's do checks require you to ask for identification before accepting the check.

## 3.7 Stamp the preferred-customer card

After the customer has paid, stamp his or her preferred-customer card. See Chapter 16 for a further discussion of preferred-customer cards.

## 3.8 Relay the order to the appropriate station

If the person at the till station is not the person who will be preparing the order, the order must be relayed to the appropriate station. Use a first-name system where the first name of the customer ordering is written on the order so that he or she can be called when the order is ready. This is a friendly, more personalized, less confusing method than yelling out "double latte" and having ten customers rush to the counter because they all ordered double lattes.

### 3.8a Relaying to the gourmet coffee station

This station rarely becomes backed up, since orders can be filled quickly. Orders to this station can usually be conveyed verbally.

### 3.8b Relaying to the specialty coffee station

This station can easily become backed up with orders; it is most efficient to convey orders through a written system. Write codes on the sides of the cups or check off the order on a sticky-note, which is then passed to the station. A more elaborate computer system will have either a remote printer or a remote video screen to view the orders on.

### 3.8c Relaying to the baked goods/food items prep station

How you relay orders to this station will depend on your coffee bar's traffic and staffing patterns. Orders can be relayed either verbally, in writing, or via a computerized system direct to the kitchen. Most coffee bars write the customer's name on the receipt and pass it to the staff member making the order, since most coffee bars don't have large kitchens.

## 3.9 Hand your customer the receipt

Present the receipt to the customer and mention any special promotion that is on the receipt. (See Chapter 16 for more details on bottom-of-receipt promotions.)

## 3.10 Ready and/or waiting

Explain to the customer where the order can be picked up. If possible, tell the customer the first name of the staff member who will be preparing the order: "Karen will have that ready for you right down there" (pointing to the specialty coffee station). Using the first names of staff makes them seem more familiar and friendly to the customer.

## 3.11 Thank the customer

The final step in the serving process is to thank the customer for visiting your coffee bar and ask that he or she come again.

## 4. SPECIAL REQUESTS

If a customer requests an item not on your menu, be as accommodating as you can and, if possible, create the item from what you have on hand or suggest a similar item.

If the request is for an item that you cannot replace, use this as an opportunity to promote the benefits of your coffee bar. For example, you might say, "The best place to have lunch is called _____ , just down the street. When you're done, pop back for a piece of cheesecake and a cup of organic coffee — and have your first coffee on us" (hand the customer a complimentary-coffee card).

## 5. LONG LINEUPS

Most customers will not resent standing in line if they have been greeted on entering the coffee bar and if they feel as though they are making progress through the line-up. When a line slows down or comes to a complete standstill, customers become understandably impatient. If you see a customer who is obviously impatient (e.g., peering past the line to find out what is going on, looking at his or her watch), acknowledging that customer's presence is often enough to settle him or her down. If the customer sees that you and your staff are working as quickly as possible, he or she will likely feel that everything possible is being done.

## COMMITMENT BOX

I, _____ , commit to using the 11 steps to fabulous customer service to WOW! my customers.

_____            _____
(your signature)                                      (today's date)

# 15

# HOW TO MANAGE A SUCCESSFUL COFFEE BAR BUSINESS

Obstacles will look large or small to you according to whether you are large or small.

— ORISON SWETT MARDEN

## 1. BUSINESS MANAGEMENT

You will need good management skills for nearly every aspect of your coffee business, from staff and managers (employee management) to the products you serve your customers (product management). As well as managing the coffee bar itself, you will also need to learn to manage the financial aspects of your business.

### 1.1 Daily

Daily management encompasses day-to-day activities such as opening and closing the coffee bar. Checklists 4 and 5 list the tasks to be done each day at opening and closing.

### 1.2 Weekly

As well as completing the weekly summary sheets (see section **4.3**) and spending time on your marketing plan (see Chapter 16, section **7.**), take time each week to plan the next seven days. This is the ideal time frame to keep up to date on your business.

### 1.3 Monthly

As well as completing your monthly profit and loss statements and reviewing your marketing plan, take time each month to review your progress toward your goals.

### 1.4 Annually

If you wait to apply your business management strategies annually, it is too late to make a difference (other than for tax purposes). Take action now!

# 2. EMPLOYEE MANAGEMENT

## 2.1 Staff perks

Different staff will be motivated by different things. Some of the perks you can offer your staff include medical/dental plans, flexible hours, and time off. Detailed surveys have shown that money is not the best motivator for staff. In fact, most surveys show that recognition for work done and travel rewards are far more powerful motivators.

## 2.2 Breaks, shifts, and scheduling

You will want to follow your area's employment standards when you set the length of employee breaks and shifts, and when you are scheduling shifts. Generally, you will want a 15-minute break for shifts of 5 hours, and at least a 30-minute break for longer shifts. (Please note that only owners are permitted to work 17 hours in a row without a break!) Schedule breaks during slow times or when there is ample coverage by other staff.

Scheduling is a function of your coffee bar's hours, your sales figures, staff productivity, past results, and future predictions. The rule of thumb is to overschedule rather than underschedule, especially in the early stages of your business. For example, it is better to have two staff on, even when your sales indicate only one is necessary. Why do this?

First, because when you are a new coffee bar, establishing a reputation for excellent service is of paramount importance.

Second, your sales cannot grow past a certain point when you have a limited number of staff. Therefore, it is better to go out and market your coffee bar to create the business rather than cut staff.

Third, if the focus of your coffee bar is the beans and the roasting, and you have a limited number of staff on shift, they will be unable to service this area well. This will result in loss of bean sales — and bean sales are what will form the foundation on which to build your coffee bar's sales.

Because the staff's state of mind is so important to the type of atmosphere you create in your coffee bar and the service the customer receives, you should try to keep the staff as happy as possible. This means working your coffee bar's schedule around that of your staff's. For example, Cindy may have baseball Tuesday nights and Peter has acting classes on Thursdays. Scheduling around their hours will result in staff who are more motivated to work well for you.

You will also likely have part-timers who are still in school. Make sure you allow them enough time for homework. Although you are not there to tell them how much time they need for school, do be considerate of the fact that they will have to dedicate a certain amount of time for their education.

You may also have staff that want as many hours as they can get. Again, these are tricky situations. If you give the people too many hours, they get burnt out, their school work suffers (if they are students), and they are ineffective as staff. However, if you don't give them enough hours, they will likely get another job and you lose a hard worker.

Check with your local government office to see how long in advance you are required to give staff their schedule before their shifts. In some jurisdictions it's as much as two weeks in advance.

# OPENING CHECKLIST

**SECURITY CHECK**
- ❑ Check for broken windows, unlocked doors, etc.
- ❑ Check doors for tampering before unlocking.

**LIGHTS AND POWER**
- ❑ Turn lights and power on.
- ❑ Check for burned-out light bulbs.
- ❑ Turn on equipment.

**TABLES AND CHAIRS**
- ❑ Ensure that tables and chairs are in order.
- ❑ Ensure that seating area is neat, tidy, and clean.

**CASH REGISTER**
- ❑ Unlock safe and take out float.
- ❑ Turn till on.
- ❑ Re-count float.
- ❑ Put float in cash drawer.

**LAST NIGHT'S CASH**
- ❑ Check accuracy of last night's deposit.
- ❑ Check cash sheet's plus/minus figures.

**DISHES**
- ❑ Ensure that dishes are clean and placed in their ready-to-use places in the coffee bar.

**COUNTERS AND CUPBOARDS**
- ❑ Ensure that all serving areas, counters, and cupboards are clean.

**COFFEE CARAFES**
- ❑ Ensure that carafes are clean.
- ❑ Prewarm coffee carafes using steaming jet on espresso machine.

**COFFEE GRINDERS**
- ❑ Grind coffees as required for brewing.

**BREWING SYSTEM**
- ❑ Ensure that brewing system is clean.
- ❑ Begin to brew coffees for your daily roasts.

**ESPRESSO GRINDER**
- ❑ Grind just enough espresso for the first few customers.

**ESPRESSO MACHINE**
- ❑ Ensure that group handles are in place.
- ❑ Run hot water through group handles to heat them and clear out any cleaning residue from night before.
- ❑ Run steam through each of the steaming wands to ensure they are free of milk particles inside.

**HOT WATER DISPENSER**
- ❑ Ensure that hot water dispenser is clean, filled, and turned on.

**STEAMING PITCHERS/MILK**
- ❑ Ensure that steaming pitchers are clean.
- ❑ Put milk into steaming pitchers so you're ready to go for the first customer.
- ❑ Check milk supplies to make sure you have enough to get you through the day.

**CREAM AND SUGAR STATION**
- ❑ Ensure that cream and milk thermoses are clean and were properly sanitized overnight.
- ❑ Put cream and milk into thermoses.
- ❑ Double-check to make sure cream and sugar station is clean and well stocked with napkins, sugars, honey, and stir sticks.

**TOPPING SHAKERS**
- ❑ Ensure that the chocolate syrup container and the topping shakers have been cleaned and refilled.

**FLAVORING SYRUPS**
- ❑ Ensure that flavoring syrup bottles are clean and there is enough syrup for the day.

**GREEN BEANS**
- ❑ Check green bean supplies.

**BAKED GOODS/FOOD ITEMS**

❏ Begin baking, if necessary.

❏ Prepare any food items as required for the day.

❏ Put food items into proper displays.

❏ Ensure that plates are clean in display cases.

**JUICE PREP**

❏ Prepare fruits and vegetables for juicing for the day.

**ROASTER**

❏ Turn on the roaster.

**CHECK ROASTED COFFEE SUPPLY**

❏ Confirm you have enough for the day.

**SPECIALS BOARD**

❏ Write the daily specials on board.

**MARKETING CALENDAR**

❏ Check marketing calendar for daily "to do's."

**STAFF SCHEDULE**

❏ Check to see who is coming in, and when.

**SERVICE**

❏ Should customers enter the coffee bar prior to opening, attempt to serve them as best as possible. If an item is not ready, ask if they would like to wait and suggest an alternative. Give customers an option.

Scheduling is always a bit of a balancing act. Below are a number of additional tips that may help you in your scheduling efforts:

- Schedule "stars" or leaders with followers (although ideally, all your staff will be "stars"). In this way, the person who likes responsibility is happy, the person who likes to just follow along is also happy, and you can comfortably leave your coffee bar in the hands of someone in whose abilities you are confident.

- Employment standards bulletins are available from many state or provincial government labor or employment agencies. These bulletins cover issues such as complaints, annual vacation pay, and maternity leave.

- Be creative in your scheduling. For example, if you have only one eight-hour shift to give to two staff who both want more hours, split the shift in half and give them each four hours.

- Be fair in your scheduling.

- Ask staff to write requests for time off at the bottom of the schedule or to notify the manager.

- Show staff how payroll works, as well as why and how their deductions work. Payroll slips must accompany every check for the staff's records.

## 2.3 Common scheduling challenges and how to overcome them

### 2.3a Challenge 1: Figuring out how many people you need in what hours

You will need to examine your traffic patterns and sales-per-person-hour (SPPH) goals. Staff productivity can be increased by putting a suggestive selling program in place inside the coffee bar or by going out and marketing the coffee bar.

# CHECKLIST 5
# CLOSING CHECKLIST

**PERISHABLES**

❏ Cover perishables and store properly overnight (in fridge, freezer, or airtight container).

**ESPRESSO MACHINE**

❏ Remove group handle screens. Clean screens and inside group heads with scrubbing pads. Put back on espresso machine and clear with water.

❏ Use bristle brush to clean water jet grates.

❏ Remove tray and clean with soap and water.

❏ Use vinegar or baking soda to clear water drain.

❏ Clear milk jets.

❏ Remove all traces of milk.

❏ Wipe down switches.

❏ Polish.

**ESPRESSO GRINDER**

❏ Let espresso run out so that espresso is ground fresh in the morning and is not losing flavor overnight by being exposed to air.

❏ Clean outside of grinder.

❏ Wash bean storage hopper if necessary and refill with roasted beans (should be done at least weekly).

**COFFEE GRINDERS**

❏ Clean and free of all coffee grounds and any flavor residue.

❏ Wipe outside of grinder.

**HOT WATER DISPENSER**

❏ Fill for next day.

**COFFEE CARAFES**

❏ Empty coffee.

❏ Soak with cleaning solution or baking soda if glass is discolored inside.

❏ At a minimum, clean all carafes weekly.

❏ Wipe the outsides of carafes.

**CARAFE STANDS**

❏ Wash inside parts with hot soapy water.

❏ Wipe stands.

**BREWING SYSTEM**

❏ Wipe off the machine.

**STEAMING PITCHERS**

❏ Throw out old milk in steaming pitchers.

❏ Ensure that pitchers are clean.

❏ Use scrubbing pads if necessary (on inside only; they may scratch the outside).

❏ Use dishwasher to properly sterilize the pitchers.

❏ Put in the fridge so they are easily accessible and cold to start off the next morning.

**CREAM AND SUGAR STATION**

❏ Top up condiments for next day, including napkins, sugars, honey, and stir sticks.

❏ Clean, sterilize, and refrigerate milk and cream bottles.

**TOPPING SHAKERS**

❏ Wipe the topping shakers clean.

❏ Wash out shakers at least once weekly.

❏ Put topping shakers on a plate and cover.

❏ Wash chocolate grater.

❏ Wipe clean the chocolate squirt bottle.

**REFRIGERATORS**

❏ Wipe with light soap and water.

❏ Ensure that it is fully stocked, with oldest goods toward the front.

**DISHES AND SINK AREA**

❏ Clean, sterilize, and put away all dishes.

❏ Clean sink and drains.

**COUNTERS AND CUPBOARDS**

❏ Completely wipe and clean counters and cupboards.

**FLOOR**

❑ Sweep everywhere (under tables, oven, fridges, etc.).

❑ Mop entire floor with sanitizing solution.

**TOASTER AND PREP AREAS**

❑ Clean these areas.

**MICROWAVE**

❑ Wipe inside and out.

**GARBAGE CANS**

❑ Wash inside and out.

**MILK DISPENSER**

❑ Make sure it's clean and free of ice.

**SPECIALS BOARD**

❑ Erase the day's specials.

**OUTSIDE SIGNAGE**

❑ Bring banners and sidewalk signs in from outside.

**TABLES**

❑ Bring tables in from outside.

❑ Clean the tables, being sure to wipe bases and check for gum and other stickies underneath.

**SHELVES AND BEAN DISPLAY**

❑ Wipe free of dust, dirt, and stray coffee beans.

**BEANS AND SAMPLE PACKS**

❑ Ensure that there are enough beans for next morning.

❑ Make sample packs (ground) for the next day (at least five of each if there are enough beans left over). Neatly label them and place on counter for next day's staff to hand out.

❑ Pack leftover beans in one-way valve bags. Label and date the bags.

**DISPLAY CASES**

❑ Shine glass and wipe inside free of any food particles.

❑ Exchange the plates that goods are on for clean ones.

❑ Wrap and store any perishables as necessary.

**ROASTER**

❑ See manufacturer's recommended daily maintenance manual.

**CASHING OUT**

❑ Cash out, fill out cash sheet.

❑ Lock money in secure spot.

**TELEPHONE**

❑ Ensure answering machine is on.

**ELECTRICAL**

❑ Ensure that lights are off.

❑ Turn off any other power that is safe and/or recommended by manufacturer to do so.

**SECURITY**

❑ Ensure that coffee bar is locked. Double-check doors are locked.

❑ Leave security light on.

❑ Turn alarm on.

### 2.3b Challenge 2: Figuring out which people to schedule

Remember that you will always want at least one person behind the counter and, if you are roasting in-store, one PR person as the roast master, working with your customers out in front. You will want to schedule a strong staffperson in each of these areas, taking into consideration their levels of experience. Don't schedule two new staff members together, for example. And also keep in mind personality mixes and how well staff work together.

### 2.3c Challenge 3: Accommodating staff who want to switch shifts

Establish a rule that staff wishing to switch shifts with other staff make arrangements on their own. This saves you from having to spend Friday afternoon rounding up someone to cover a shift on Friday night. If you don't establish this rule, expect to do a lot of shifts on your own.

### 2.3d Challenge 4: Not enough hours to go around

If there are not enough hours for all your staff, ask yourself if this is a permanent situation or not. If you expect the shortage of hours to continue indefinitely, you need to consider letting someone go. We have always found it best to be up front with staff members about any change in hours. Let them know why the change is taking place.

### 2.3e Challenge 5: Too many hours and not enough staff

If your current staff mix can't handle the hours, hire more staff or cover some of the hours yourself.

## 2.4 How to hold staff meetings

Check your government's employment standards for guidelines dealing with pay requirements for staff meetings. Generally, if you require attendance at these meetings you must pay your staff for their time; if the meetings are voluntary, you need not. Try to hold the meetings either after or before operating hours, or during a quiet time of the day. It is often very difficult to meet everyone's schedule, but try the best you can and let the majority rule.

Sample 8 is a sample manager's meeting form. Design your own and use it to keep the meeting on track and as a record of what was decided at the meeting (and who was assigned to do it). Here are some other tips for holding staff meetings:

- Keep your staff meetings positive, upbeat, and fun.

- Encourage feedback from your staff.

- Keep the meetings short. Respect the time your staff are taking out of their nonwork schedules. Many will have family, school, or social obligations. As well, the staff's focus and attention will start to wane after about an hour.

- Explain the format of the meeting to your staff, including how long it will take and what topics you'll be covering. Make sure to include a section when your staff can raise issues if they wish. Handing out an agenda can help the staff stay focused and help create a sense of team work.

- Try not to be accusatory or to pinpoint one staff member for any challenges occurring in your business.

# MANAGER'S MEETING FORM

Date: _____ Store: _____

Purpose of meeting: _____

TOPIC                         ACTION

_____      _____      Who _____

_____      _____      Who _____

_____      _____      Who _____

_____      _____      Who _____

_____      _____      Who _____

_____      _____      Who _____

_____      _____      Who _____

_____      _____      Who _____

_____      _____      Who _____

_____      _____      Who _____

_____      _____      Who _____

_____      _____      Who _____

_____      _____      Who _____

_____      _____      Who _____

_____      _____      Who _____

_____      _____      Who _____

Next meeting scheduled for: _____

- Create a sense of team work. How? By informing staff of what's going on, including them in decisions, asking for their ideas, setting common goals.

## 2.5 Pay periods, raises, bonuses, and profit sharing

As a general rule, your staff should be paid above-average wages in order to attract the quality of people vital to the success of your operation. We recommend paying your staff about 20 percent above the going rate, moving up to 25 percent above when staff are well trained. Because you invest so much in your staff during the training stage, paying above-average wages will help keep the staff in the long term, thus helping to offset the training investment you make in them. While deductions can be estimated at 8 percent of total wage cost, check with the appropriate government agency for specific figures.

Raises should be given at regular intervals throughout the year with performance reviews being conducted every three to six months (see section **2.6** below).

Wages and raises will likely vary for part-time and full-time staff. We recommend the following:

(a) **Part-time staff.** Part-time staff should begin at a wage $1 per hour above minimum wage. After staff have learned their jobs (approximately two to three weeks), this should be increased by 50¢.

(b) **Full-time staff.** Full-time staff should begin at a wage $1.50 per hour above minimum wage. After the one-week trial period is complete, this should be increased by 50¢.

(c) **Assistant managers and managers.** The salary for assistant managers and managers varies, depending on where in the country you are and on the cost of living. Find out what the industry standard is to get a ballpark figure. As additional responsibilities are added and as the assistant manager or manager shows the ability to positively affect coffee bar profits, the salary should be raised.

Bonuses and profit sharing can be effective tools to motivate and inspire staff and management, so give this some consideration. Generally, staff bonuses should be linked to sales, and management's bonuses to overall profit, since each group has direct control over those respective areas.

## 2.6 Performance reviews

As mentioned in Chapter 7, you should hold staff performance reviews every three or six months. We find that every three months is the best length of time as it lets you ensure your training systems are on track (the amount of wage increases would be half of the increase available for a six month review, so there is no additional cost). There are five possible outcomes of a review:

(a) **On probation.** You may want to put a staff member on probation if his or her performance has slipped significantly and if he or she is not meeting the needs of the customers.

(b) **No raise.** You would not give a staff member a raise if there has been no improvement in his or her performance of the duties and responsibilities involved in his or her job.

(c) **Small raise.** A small raise would be about 25¢ per hour, given for a small improvement in the staff member's performance on the job.

(d) **Medium raise.** A medium raise would be about 50¢ per hour, given for a good improvement in the staff member's overall performance.

(e) **Large raise.** A large raise would be about 80¢ per hour, given for outstanding improvement in the staff member's performance since his or her last review.

The key to a system like this is to clearly define the review system, teach what is required to achieve each level, and then consistently complete the reviews. This system is used effectively by McDonald's worldwide to help motivate enthusiastic service staff every day.

# 3. PRODUCT MANAGEMENT
## 3.1 Proper product management

Product management involves using funds to acquire quality inventory that can be sold for a maximum profit. It may sound simple enough, but accomplishing the task requires considerable skill. From ordering raw materials to security, storage, and preparation, to processing and assembling, to the maintenance of critical equipment, you will continually need to monitor and adjust your product management in order to yield the greatest return on your dollar.

Because inventory has a cash value, products must be purchased wisely, turned over quickly on a first-in, first-out basis, and repurchased in a way that ensures sufficient quality and quantity while tying up the least amount of cash possible. How well your funds are invested and used has a direct bearing on the profit margins and cash flow of your location. In the coffee business, where sales can fluctuate and the quality of some raw materials (such as produce) can vary, continual monitoring is essential.

The process of ordering products is determined by two major factors: usage (which is a function of sales), and frequency of delivery (which is a function of availability). A balance must be struck between these two factors. You must also be concerned, once these products are procured, with security and proper storage. If you misjudge in these areas, you can end up with not enough stock or too much, resulting in waste and product losses.

### 3.1a Maintaining efficient inventory levels

The key to maintaining efficient inventory levels is accurate ordering. To do this, you must determine the inventory levels of the products you need to operate your business, along with an estimate of how much of each product is needed for your next sales cycle. For example, if you have 20 quarts (19 liters) of milk currently on hand and you go through approximately 100 quarts (95 liters) per week, you will want to order about 90 quarts (85 liters) for that week.

When determining inventory levels, keep in mind that all products must remain fresh. The following example illustrates the importance of this: A customer comes in every day and buys a muffin and a coffee on his or her way to work. A $1.50 purchase each weekday for one year translates into almost $400. If the muffins are not fresh and the customer stops buying the muffin, you will lose that income. What if this happens with a few other customers? You can see how quickly a stale item can translate into lost sales.

The quantity of inventory needed can and does change week to week and is affected by things such as holidays, weather, special events, and the marketing strategies that you plan to implement during that sales cycle. Once your coffee bar has been up and running for some time, you will be able to project with reasonable accuracy and make adjustments if necessary along the way.

To ensure accuracy in your ordering efforts, you must keep accurate records. We recommend you use inventory order forms that allow you to track usage and ordering, as well as letting you verify the amounts actually received at delivery. Sample 9 is a sample inventory order form.

Organize these forms in a binder along with a complete listing of every product you need, grouped according to product type, supplier, and delivery frequency. Also keep a list in the front of the binder with the names and phone numbers of all your suppliers, along with order and delivery days so you don't miss placing an order. If you are using a computer system, you can graph the figures from your inventory order forms to get a visual picture of the product trends in your business.

To determine what needs to be ordered in what quantities, a physical count must first be done. Determine the amount used by adding the on-hand and received levels from the previous order cycle and subtract this cycle's on-hand counts. Once usage has been determined, subtract the amount currently in stock and order in the difference with a 15 percent extra safety margin (you will want to be especially sure of including a safety margin in the early stages of your business).

By using this approach to purchase all products, you can easily keep the inventory at a level that will provide sufficient quantities and maintain the quality of all items, especially perishables.

Because produce comes from many sources throughout the year, dramatic fluctuations occur in pricing, sizing, and quality. It is important to specify the grades of produce required and obtain regular price quotes from several reputable suppliers. (We recommend Number 1 or Grade A quality.) You will want to ensure that you are regularly updating your inventory order sheets for the latest price changes.

### 3.1b Managing your inventory

Maintaining appropriate inventory levels reduces the amount of cash tied up and the amount of leased space needed to store goods. It also makes stock taking much easier and more accurate, which is critically important when calculating the cost of goods and establishing on-hand levels for the placing of orders. Further, keeping inventory as low as possible makes theft easier to spot.

If you keep all storage areas organized and indicate clearly where each product goes, you will be better able to manage your inventory by making it easy to use and keep track of stock and by making sure the same products are not stored in several locations.

Once you have a track record for both food inventory and food sales over a certain period, you can calculate your "food cost." This term describes your inventory as a percentage of your sales. If you know your food cost, you know how much inventory you need on hand to fill your anticipated sales for the month. Most food establishments work with a 30 percent to 35 percent food

# SAMPLE 9
# INVENTORY ORDER SHEET

**MONTH:** November

**SUPPLIER:** Henry's Wholesale Co.

*Notes:*
Order every Wednesday, delivered next day by 10 a.m. or earlier

| ITEM | AMOUNT | DAY: 1 Ordered | 2 Received | Ordered | Received | Ordered | Received | Ordered | Received | Ordered | Received | Ordered | Received |
|---|---|---|---|---|---|---|---|---|---|---|---|---|---|
| **Dairy** | | | | | | | | | | | | | |
| 2% milk | jug | 22 | ✓ | | | | | | | | | | |
| cream | carton | 16 | ✓ | | | | | | | | | | |
| skim milk | jug | 10 | ✓ | | | | | | | | | | |
| **Condiments** | | | | | | | | | | | | | |
| butter pats | 1,000/box | 1 | ✓ | | | | | | | | | | |
| jam portions | 500/box | n/a | – | | | | | | | | | | |
| **Sugar** | | | | | | | | | | | | | |
| bulk sugar | 5 lb bag | n/a | – | | | | | | | | | | |
| sugar packets | 1,000/box | 1 | ✓ | | | | | | | | | | |
| bulk brown sugar | 1 lb bag | n/a | – | | | | | | | | | | |
| brown sugar packets | 1,000/box | n/a | – | | | | | | | | | | |
| sugar substitute | 2,000/bag | n/a | – | | | | | | | | | | |

cost. Monthly variations above or below this percentage will indicate that the ordering procedures have gone awry, that inventory has become unbalanced (with excessive or insufficient levels of use of certain products), or that an inventory miscount has occurred.

To determine your food cost, subtract the total value of inventory you had left in your coffee bar at the end of the month from the total value of inventory you had at the beginning of the month, plus any inventory purchases you made during that month.

For example, say you had $2,000 worth of food inventory in your coffee bar at the beginning of January. You then purchased $2,500 worth of beans, $750 worth of dry goods, and $1,500 worth of dairy and produce. Your total inventory is $6,750. If you have $2,300 worth of stock in your coffee bar at the end of January, your food cost for the month was $4,450.

If you had $15,000 worth of sales for the month, this would mean that your food cost was 29.7 percent. Depending on how much wholesale business you are doing, this is likely a good percentage.

What would happen, though, if you discovered that your food cost was 50 percent? This would mean that for every $1 you make, 50¢ of that dollar is going toward the food cost of that sale (e.g., the milk, cream, and sugar.) You then have 50¢ from which to operate your business and hopefully make a profit. As we mentioned before, most food establishments work with a 30 percent to 35 percent food cost. Finding out that you are up around 50 percent should give you strong warning signals that maybe you aren't operating your business with as much control as you should.

Use your food cost percentage when you establish your pricing, too. If an item costs you $1.25, you should, on average (using a food cost percentage of 33 percent), be selling that item for $3.75. Be sure to include paper products needed for that item — e.g., napkins, straws, and lids — when calculating the cost of the item.

Controlling food cost is a delicate balance between giving customers good value for their money and leaving enough profit at the end of the day for you to make a living. Keep in mind, though, that if you don't have any customers, there won't be any chance for profit.

## 3.2 Product preparation

The amount of product preparation you do depends on how many food items you carry in your coffee bar. Because you are dealing with ready-made items rather than made-to-order items, you will need to control the preparation of food items on a daily basis. The skill with which you establish procedures for product preparation and assign your staff to each task has a direct impact on both your food costs and the quality of

| CALCULATING FOOD COST | |
|---|---|
| Opening inventory | $ 2,000 |
| Purchases | 2,500 |
| | 750 |
| | 1,500 |
| | 6,750 |
| Less closing inventory | 2,300 |
| Food cost for month | $ 4,450 |
| Sales | $15,000 |
| Food cost (as a percentage of sales) | 29.7% |

products you serve to your customers. Lack of planning can result in waste, spoilage, and possible shortages.

### 3.2a How to determine preparation levels

Preparation levels vary from day to day in direct relationship to your anticipated sales and must be carefully calculated to provide appropriate supply and reduce wastage.

Anticipated prep levels should be determined at the beginning of each day by first recording on a daily prep sheet (shown in Sample 10) the on-hand amounts of all prepped items carried over from the previous day (if any). At the same time as this count is being done, the quality of each item should be checked and any items of poor quality discarded, noted for follow-up, and recorded as waste.

The next step is to pinpoint, based on past preparation records and anticipated sales for the day, the amount of each item that will be needed to provide an adequate supply. The difference between the quantities of each item needed and the amount on hand constitutes the quantities that need to be prepped that day. The quantities needed should then be recorded on your daily prep sheet.

At this point, you will need to organize the production schedule for the day so that all materials to be prepped are assigned to the appropriate staff and processed in order of priority and in such a way as to maximize the productivity of staff on all shifts. It is not necessary that all production be done by the same staff member (e.g., the staff member assigned to the food items prep station), but the process must be planned so that you are operating with maximum efficiency.

## 4. FINANCIAL MANAGEMENT

### 4.1 Computers versus cash registers

When you are considering whether to purchase a cash register or a computer system, consider the following.

Computers have many advantages. For instance, you can access records from your home or on another computer system through a modem. Computers also allow you to generate reports that you are not able to on a cash register.

However, the initial cost of purchasing a computer is often beyond the budget of first-time coffee bar owners. As well, depending on the software, computers may not be as fast as a cash register if, for example, multiple key strokes are required in making a sale. On balance, we recommend them.

### 4.2 Daily record keeping

You will need some kind of cash recording system to use on a daily basis to compare the sales that were recorded coming in to the coffee bar to the money you actually have in the till. Sample 11 shows a daily cash sheet you can use to keep track of your daily sales.

You will want to fill in the comment line on the daily cash sheet if there was anything different or unique about the day. When you look back at these sheets in the weeks or months to come, anything that will help explain the day's sales will be helpful.

You will also want to record the number of invoices you had that day, the average check (if your cash register or computer does not automatically provide you with

# DAILY PREP SHEET

MONTH: September     DAY: _____

| Morning Prep | | ITEM | 1st Anticipated | On hand | Discarded | Needed | Initials | 2nd Anticipated | On hand | Discarded | Needed | Initials |
|---|---|---|---|---|---|---|---|---|---|---|---|---|
| Muffins | | blueberry bran | 24 | 10 | 2 | 16 | IE | 30 | 0 | 0 | 30 | IE |
| | | cranberry oatmeal | 24 | 0 | 0 | 24 | IE | 30 | 1 | 1 | 30 | IE |
| | | banana choc. chip | 12 | 2 | 1 | 11 | IE | | | | | |
| | | orange | 12 | 6 | 2 | 8 | IE | | | | | |
| Swirls | | cinnamon | 26 | 5 | 0 | 29 | IE | | | | | |
| | | fruit | 24 | 2 | 1 | 23 | IE | | | | | |

# SAMPLE 11
# DAILY CASH SHEET

Store location: _____   Completed by: _____
Date: _____   Weather: _____
Crew hours: _____   Manager hours: _____
Promo: _____   Comments: _____
Invoice count: _____   _____
Average check: _____   _____
Bean sales: _____   _____

**Money in cash drawer**

Cash

| | | | | | | |
|---|---|---|---|---|---|---|
| 0.01 | x | _____ | = | _____ | Cash | _____ (A) |
| 0.05 | x | _____ | = | _____ | Checks | _____ (B) |
| 0.10 | x | _____ | = | _____ | Credit cards | _____ (C) |
| 0.25 | x | _____ | = | _____ | Back-up float | _____ (D) |

Foreign currency (face)

| | | | | |
|---|---|---|---|---|
| 1 | x | _____ | = | _____ |
| 2 | x | _____ | = | _____ |

x exchange @ _____ %   =   _____ (E)

**Total A+B+C+D+E**   =   _____ (F)

| | | | | |
|---|---|---|---|---|
| 5 | x | _____ | = | _____ |

*Less:* Float   –   _____

| | | | | |
|---|---|---|---|---|
| 10 | x | _____ | = | _____ |

**Net Cash**   =   _____ (G)
(Total Deposit)

| | | | | |
|---|---|---|---|---|
| 20 | x | _____ | = | _____ |

*Add:* Charge to account   _____ (H)

| | | | | |
|---|---|---|---|---|
| 50 | x | _____ | = | _____ |
| 100 | x | _____ | = | _____ |

*Less:* Paid on account   _____ (I)

**Total Cash**   =   _____ (A)

| Paid out item | Category | Receipt total | Tax |
|---|---|---|---|
| _____ | _____ | _____ | _____ |
| _____ | _____ | _____ | _____ |
| _____ | _____ | _____ | _____ |
| _____ | _____ | _____ | _____ |
| | Total | _____ (J) | _____ |

**Total sales**
**(Sales cash count)**
**(G+H–I+J)**   =   _____ (K)

**Sales by tape**   =   _____ (L)
   *Less:* Federal tax/GST, if applicable
      *(rate: _____ %)*   –   _____
   *Less:* State/Prov. tax
      *(rate: _____ %)*   –   _____
**Net sales**   =   _____

**Cash difference**
**(K – L)**   =   _____ (Difference + or –)

this information, take your daily net sales and divide by the invoice count), and the dollar amount of your whole bean sales.

When you total the bills, coins, credit card remittances, and checks you have received, don't forget to include the back-up float in your count.

If your business accepts foreign currency, you will need to total the face value of those bills you have received and multiply by your store's exchange rate, and then add both figures to your total.

You will also want to keep track of your paid out items. List receipt items (e.g., milk, cleaning supplies). Then determine which category those items fall into. We use five:

   (a)  Food and paper (F&P) — e.g., milk

   (b)  Maintenance and repair (M&R) — e.g., light bulbs

   (c)  Office (Off) — e.g., pens

   (d)  Promotions (Pro) — e.g., flowers to give away with a latte

   (e)  Advertising (Adv) — e.g., a small ad insertion you pay cash for

By subtracting your sales by tape (the amount of gross sales recorded by your cash register system) from your sales cash count (all money items totaled), you will arrive at the cash difference, either a credit, a loss, or balanced.

## 4.3 Weekly record keeping

Keep your weekly records in the form of a weekly summary (see Sample 12). A weekly summary is a great tool for your coffee bar's manager to use. It forces him or her to set goals on a weekly basis and compare the actual figures to his or her goals. If you are absent from your business for any period, the weekly summary can form the basis of any communication you have with your coffee bar.

Your daily SPPH (sales per person hour) will be your sales divided by hours of labor. Forecast your sales and labor hours on a daily basis, and then calculate actual sales and labor hours. Calculate your weekly SPPH by dividing weekly sales by the week's total labor hours.

It is also useful to keep a record of the value of your employee food consumption, waste, and promotion. Calculate employee food consumption based on the retail value of the items. When tracking wastage, total the retail value of any items you had to discard during the week. For instance, add up the retail cost of the six bagels you had to throw away on Monday (otherwise they would be stale the next day), the two pieces of cheesecake on Tuesday, the four muffins on Wednesday, and so on. Weekly promotion totals reflect the retail value of any promotions, such as coupons or free coffees, you offered during that week.

Keeping track of these weekly totals will help you better calculate and control your food costs.

## 4.4 Monthly record keeping

We recommend that you do a complete inventory count at the end of every month, and prepare an income and expense statement. Many managers either forget to count their inventory at month end, or, once it is counted, don't bother calculating the value of it. If you don't know the value, you cannot determine how much stock is on hand relative to your sales to determine your food costs (go back to section **3.**). A monthly count also lets you see if there are inventory discrepancies.

## SAMPLE 12
# WEEKLY SUMMARY

From: __West side__            (location)

Date: __Nov 6__       Manager: __Marybeth__

Week ending: __Nov 5__       Weather: __Generally sunny__

Weekly totals:    Employee food consumption: $ _____

                 Waste: $ _____

              Promotion: $ _____

|  | Sales forecast | Sales actual | Comments |
|---|---|---|---|
| Monday | $1,600.00 | $1,400.00 | Hockey playoffs this week |
| Tuesday | 1,700.00 | 1,650.00 | |
| Wednesday | 1,900.00 | 2,390.00 | Big game on |
| Thursday | 1,900.00 | 2,010.00 | |
| Friday | 2,200.00 | 1,720.00 | |
| Saturday | 2,600.00 | 2,490.00 | |
| Sunday | 2,000.00 | 1,500.00 | |
| **Total sales** | **$13,900.00** | **$13,160.00** | |

|  | Avg. chk. forecast | Avg. chk. actual | Comments |
|---|---|---|---|
| For week | $4.80 | $4.62 | |

|  | Labor hours forecast | Labor hours actual | Comments |
|---|---|---|---|
| Monday | 51 | 51 | |
| Tuesday | 51 | 51 | |
| Wednesday | 51 | 51 | |
| Thursday | 54 | 56 | |
| Friday | 54 | 51 | |
| Saturday | 59 | 59 | |
| Sunday | 48 | 40 | |
| **Total hours** | **368** | **359** | |

|  | SPPH forecast | SPPH actual | Comments |
|---|---|---|---|
| Monday | $31.37 | $27.45 | |
| Tuesday | 33.33 | 32.35 | |
| Wednesday | 37.25 | 46.67 | |
| Thursday | 35.19 | 35.89 | |
| Friday | 40.74 | 33.73 | |
| Saturday | 44.07 | 62.20 | |
| Sunday | 41.67 | 37.50 | |
| **Average SPPH** | **$37.66** | **$39.40** | |

An income and expense statement allows you to compare your business costs month to month. Making these comparisons will show you what is happening financially in your business so you can adjust, if necessary. For example, an income and expense statement will show you if your food cost one month is 32 percent of food sales, but rises to 36 percent the next month.

You must be able to recognize fluctuations in your business in order to analyze them, and you must be able to analyze fluctuations in order to exert control over your profit; if you don't know where you stand, you won't be able to control where you are going. You will not know what your profit is, nor what your food or labor percentages are. Not knowing these percentages means you will have no way of analyzing trends in your business so that you can better plan in future and increase your profits. For example, if last year's Christmas-season labor cost percentage was double that of November's, you will want to cut down on staffing this Christmas season.

### 4.4a Preparing monthly records

Be sure to keep your start-up costs separate from your operating costs and your first order receipt separate from general inventory receipts. The former costs will be incurred when you are still feeling your way in the coffee business and while you are spending lots of money to get started, while operating and general inventory records will show the actual month-to-month costs of running your coffee bar.

Fill in an income and expense statement (see Sample 13) using the following method:

**Income**

(a) Add up the income your business brought in for the month (don't include sales tax in this count).

(b) Count all inventory in your coffee bar, calculate the value of each item, and total the value.

(c) Add up the inventory purchases you made during the month (don't include sales tax).

(d) Add to this figure the inventory you started with at the beginning of the month.

(e) Subtract from this figure the total value of the inventory you have on hand. This final figure will reflect your food cost.

(f) Calculate the food cost percentage by dividing the food cost figure into the sales figure.

**Expenses**

(a) Add all the expenses you incurred during the month, including:

- labor (including employer's contribution to payroll deductions submission)
- rent and CAM
- electricity and gas
- telephone
- office expenses
- advertising
- promotion
- maintenance and repair
- professional fees
- insurance
- franchise royalties (if applicable)

## SAMPLE 13
## MONTH-END INCOME AND EXPENSE STATEMENT

For the month of: _____

| | Revenue | Expenses | As % of sales | Tax 1 | Tax 2 |
|---|---|---|---|---|---|
| Sales (includes source donations) | $30,000.00 | | | | |
| *Less:* Cost of sales | | $10,000.00 | 33.3% | | |
| **GROSS INCOME** | **$20,000.00** | | | | |
| | | | | | |
| Labor | | $6,900.00 | 23.0% | | |
| Rent & CAM | | 3,125.00 | 10.4% | | |
| Electricity & gas | | 375.00 | 1.3% | | |
| Telephone | | 125.00 | 0.4% | | |
| Office expenses | | 75.00 | 0.3% | | |
| Advertising | | 1,200.00 | 4.0% | | |
| Promotion | | 1,200.00 | 4.0% | | |
| Maintenance & repair | | 150.00 | 0.5% | | |
| Professional fees | | 75.00 | 0.3% | | |
| Insurance | | 175.00 | 0.6% | | |
| Other | | | 0.0% | | |
| Other | | | 0.0% | | |
| Other | | | 0.0% | | |
| **TOTAL EXPENSES** | | **$13,400.00** | **44.7%** | | |
| | | | | | |
| Net income before cost of money | $6,600.00 | | | | |
| *Less:* Payment (e.g. bank financing) | | $900.00 | 3.0% | | |
| **TOTAL INCOME** | **$5,700.00** | | **19.0%** | | |

- permits and licenses (if applicable)
- signage or equipment leases (if applicable)

(b) Put the total amount in appropriate column.

(c) Separate taxes and put in appropriate column.

(d) Calculate the percentage points of each of your columns.

Now subtract the total expenses from the total income to get your net income before cost of money. If you have cost-of-money expenses, you will subtract this amount from your net income.

Separating cost-of-money expenses from other expenses is a good idea since it is a short-term expense (e.g., it will be paid off at some point in the business). Should you ever decide to sell the business, the prospective buyer may not have the same cost-of-money expense. By separating this expense, you will be able to show the prospective buyer income and expense statements that more accurately reflect the net income the business would generate with no cost-of-money expense.

### 4.4b Analyzing your monthly records

When analyzing your income and expense statement, analyze first your sales, then your costs, including your food costs.

Break down your monthly sales into a daily average. Then calculate your "average check" by taking your customer count and dividing that into sales. Track this monthly.

There are two types of costs that you will be analyzing in your business:

(a) Fixed expenses that don't change month to month, regardless of the volume of business created (e.g., rent)

(b) Variable expenses that are a function of the number of customers your coffee bar serves within the month (e.g., staff payroll and food cost)

Examine each cost separately, considering whether each percentage is appropriate or perhaps too high. Look for areas where you might reduce expenses. Sections **4.5** and **4.6** below discuss ways in which you can reduce both fixed and variable expenses.

## 4.5 Reducing expenses

While it is difficult to control fixed costs such as rent, other fixed costs can be reduced. Electricity costs, for example, can be reduced by installing energy-efficient lighting systems and turning unnecessary power sources off at night. (**Note:** Turning some equipment, such as a computer, on and off each morning and evening can actually use up more power, and be harder on the equipment, than leaving it on overnight.) The following is a list of some of the things you can do to better manage or reduce some of the fixed and variable expenses your business will incur:

(a) Labor
- Are you being effective in your scheduling efforts? Perhaps you can cover a couple of quiet hours in the coffee bar on your own.
- Analyze your labor cost on a sales-per-person-hour (SPPH) basis. Determine how many dollars (sales) are generated by one

hour of work by your staff. The most profitable operations have an average of about $40 to $50 SPPH. If your SPPH is significantly lower than this, examine ways to increase it, possibly by decreasing the number of staff shifts.

(b) Electricity

- Contact your local electricity company and ask for information on how you can reduce your electricity costs. Book a time for a representative to come to your coffee bar and give you ideas on how you can reduce your electricity costs (local electrical utilities in most regions will send out a representative to measure watts and voltages free of charge).

(c) Telephone

- Join a reduced-rate long-distance company, or use an online VoIP service with no long-distance charges. This way you can offer free calls for your customers.

- Make long-distance phone calls and faxes during nonpeak times.

- Record long-distance calls to determine where the bulk of your calls are going and for what purpose. Can you change or reduce your calling pattern in any way to reduce cost (for example, by doing more ordering online)?

(d) Office expenses

- Determine whether your purchases are necessary for the business.

- Purchase paper in bulk for printing and photocopying.

- Compare the cost of leasing a photocopier versus photocopying at your local print shop (leasing may save you money in the long term).

- Compare costs of printing versus photocopying (you may be better off printing forms in larger volume).

(e) Promotion and advertising

- When looking at reducing expenses, do not look here. Many businesses fail because they start to look for ways to cut corners and they often start cutting marketing. However, marketing is one of the best ways to make your business thrive.

- Shoot for a target of at least 8 percent of fixed expenses on total marketing (4 percent advertising and 4 percent promotions).

(f) Professional fees

- Reexamine dollars you are spending on professional fees — if fees are for a bookkeeping service, for example, you might want to look at incorporating this task into low-priority times during your day. See section **4.8** below for details on do-it-yourself computerized bookkeeping programs.

(g) Leases

- Reexamine the cost of purchasing any signage or equipment you are leasing. Will it save you money in the long term?

## 4.6 Reducing your food costs

There are numerous things you can do to control and reduce food costs. Most of them involve a little effort, but add up to a lot of savings.

For example, watch that your staff members do not get into the habit of filling cups right to the brim. While this may appear to be good value to the customer, it can actually be negative in two ways. First, a cup filled to the brim is easier for the customer to spill than one with a bit of space left at the top (and you will have to pay your staff to clean up the spills), and it doesn't leave a lot of room for the customer to add sugar, again increasing the chance of spills.

Second, that extra dash of milk really adds up. If you serve 100 specialty coffees in a day, an extra dash of milk in each cup adds up to 100 dashes of milk. That 100 dashes can add up to a jug or two of milk, and at $3 to $5 dollars a jug, that extra milk is costing you up to $10 dollars each day. That $10 a day is $300 dollars per month. Think back to the food cost example in section **3.** If you reduced it by $300, your food cost percentage would drop significantly.

To reduce your food costs, go through every product in your coffee bar. Examine it, measure it, weigh it. Portion it. Count it. Look at every product from the cream cheese that goes on a bagel to the chocolate you sprinkle on top of hot chocolates to the amount of cleaning products you are using. Do a cost analysis on everything in your coffee bar.

Explain cash and food handling procedures to your staff and stress the importance of correct inventory control and the methods used to check product usage. Explain areas of controllable waste, how food cost control procedures work, and why they are important.

You will be amazed at the dramatic differences a few changes can make. A cup of coffee, for example, costs only about seven cents if you are roasting coffee in-store. Now add the cost of a stir stick, napkin, cream, sugar, cup, and lid — you'll be surprised. Your 5 percent food cost can quickly jump to 30 percent. While this is part of being in business, you must be aware of the importance of food costs and how it influences your profits.

Your food costs will also be influenced by the weighted average of your product categories. For example, coffee generally has a much lower food cost than a piece of cheesecake. So, in the simplest of examples, if your product mix is 50 percent coffee at 10 percent food cost and 50 percent cheesecake at 50 percent food cost, your calculated overall food cost is 30 percent. Next month, if you sell 80 percent coffee and only 20 percent cheesecake, your food cost drops to 18 percent. This is not necessarily bad, it just changes your figures. As an owner, you must be aware of how changes in product purchases can change food cost. Monitoring the figures is always a good idea.

Your wholesale coffee business will have a direct influence on your food costs because the profit margins drop from 70 percent on retail to about 50 percent on wholesale — sometimes less if you are selling to a large account that has negotiated a bigger discount. For this reason, you may want to track your wholesale revenues separately from the retail side of your business to get a more accurate picture of your instore cash flow and food cost.

## 4.7 Annual record keeping

You will need to prepare annual business tax returns as well as personal tax returns.

## 4.8 Bookkeeping and accounting

Unless you want to pay a bookkeeper, use a computerized accounting system such as QuickBooks. This software allows you to track income and expenses, manage your checkbook, and reduce hours of year-end statement preparation to simple clicks of a button. While bookkeeping is a fairly simple job you can do yourself, we recommend that you have a professional accountant help you with your corporate and or personal tax returns. An accountant can be particularly helpful in determining deductions and depreciation.

# 5. FACILITIES MANAGEMENT

## 5.1 Preventative maintenance

It is important that you plan and follow a course of action to keep equipment clean and in proper working condition. Equipment failure is often the result of inadequate cleaning practices. Poorly maintained equipment is often a haven for bacteria, which can be transferred to your products and, ultimately, your customers.

A preventative maintenance program should be set up and then followed in your coffee bar. It is your responsibility not only to direct or carry out the maintenance program but also to instruct staff in the proper use of equipment so they know the danger signs of deterioration and know what corrective action must be taken.

Train staff to become "equipment-conscious" and alert to obvious signs of oncoming breakdowns, such as shaking, noise, or malfunctioning. These signs should be reported immediately to either yourself or your manager so action can be taken.

A preventative maintenance program improves the quality of the products you serve because high quality products cannot be prepared on poorly operating equipment.

If staff notice that you don't care about the condition of the equipment, they won't care either. And this means more expensive repairs or replacements in the long run. Not caring about equipment quality can end up being reflected in not caring about product quality.

If equipment is in poor working condition it affects service. How can you put the product out fast enough if the machine you are operating is working at half speed? How can you put out high quality product if a malfunctioning machine is affecting product quality? Remember that you won't be able to serve at all if the machine breaks down completely. And if this happens, your image is gravely affected. Replacing major pieces of equipment is costly as well.

Most specific preventive maintenance items will vary from manufacturer to manufacturer, so check with your supplier to make sure you have the right information. Also remember to clean the air intake grills on all your refrigeration equipment.

Preventative maintenance should be practiced throughout the coffee bar, including outside. Check outside walkways, entrances, roof, bricks, walls, painted areas, exhaust areas, signage; check inside walls, ceiling, floors, plumbing, heating, air conditioning systems, electrical systems.

Properly maintaining these areas and items will extend their life. For example, a poorly maintained outdoor awning will have a life of three to five years, while a well maintained one will last ten years.

Putting a preventative maintenance system in place will help guarantee a profitable and smoothly running operation.

## 5.2 Security

Good security is the result of common sense precautions and also of a preventative frame of mind. You should be aware (although not paranoid) of potentially dangerous situations in your coffee bar.

### 5.2a General security measures

The following suggestions can be used as deterrents so that there is never a chance for a crime to take place.

- Keep back doors locked at all times from the inside. Too often a robber can open a door and walk in, or knock on a locked door and be let in.

- Install eyeholes or cameras at back doors used by suppliers.

- Reduce the use of back doors to a "must use" basis only. This reduces the chance of someone waiting outside slipping in unnoticed when the door is open.

- Prohibit the use of back doors after dark. Ensure a sign stating this is attached to the door.

- Make sure the area outside the back door is well lit.

- Double-check that all other accesses to your coffee bar are locked at closing time.

- Do not admit any unknown person after hours. If a person is pleading for police or emergency assistance, offer to phone the necessary parties yourself. There is always the possibility that this is just a ploy for you to unlock your doors. If the person requires a telephone personally, direct them to the nearest public phone. Authorities must produce adequate identification before admittance is permitted.

- Do not take garbage outside after dark.

- Leave security lights on during closed hours and install web cameras if you can.

- Move employees' cars to easily accessible areas at night. Whenever possible, have staff leave the coffee bar in pairs.

- Ensure that all staff leaving your coffee bar at night leave from the front of the building, where they are visible and the area is well lit.

- Keep as little cash as possible in the till. A policy of "skimming" your cash register after heavy traffic times is advised.

- Leave the till drawer open during closed hours so that a potential robber will see there is no money in it and, hopefully, be discouraged from breaking in. Keep the float in a safe, secured area (in the safe, if you have one).

- Keep careful track of those staff with keys to the coffee bar. Record total number of keys available and who has how many. Limit key responsibilities to only those staff requiring them. Change locks when a manager has been terminated or transferred, or when keys have been lost and/or stolen.

### 5.2b Robberies

Train your staff to remain calm and listen closely during an armed robbery. They should do exactly as they are told to do, as calmly as possible. Instructions from the robber should be followed exactly, slowly, and carefully.

Train your staff to become observant and to try to remember the eye color, hair color, shape of face and facial features, noticeable features such as scars or tattoos, height, and nationality of robbers.

Avoid being a hero: you could jeopardize the safety of others.

When reporting robberies to police, attempt to diplomatically delay reporting the actual amount of loss until you can determine the exact sum. This will not only make the police record more accurate, but can prevent the press from revealing how much money you had on your premises, since the information will not be available at the time of the media report. Advertising the amount stolen, especially if it's a high amount, only encourages future robberies.

### 5.2c Burglaries

Burglaries often occur at night, when stores are closed. As prevention against burglaries, incorporate a security check into your daily routine. This will not only help to prevent burglaries but will also allow you to recognize a burglary as soon after it has happened as possible. Regularly check doors and window locks for signs of tampering. It may require more than one trip on the criminal's part to complete the break-in. If you can catch a security breach ahead of time, you may deter a future burglary. It is a good idea to have a monitored alarm system installed. Many companies will supply the equipment for free if you buy the monitoring from them.

### 5.2d Con artists

Train your staff to be aware of potential scam situations. Fast change artists thrive on high volume times. Their success is based on confusion — getting the staff to handle more than one transaction at a time. Instruct your staff to keep calm and take things one step at a time.

One common con is to show the staff member on till a large bill, but actually pass him or her a bill of a smaller denomination. This often "tricks" the staff member into thinking he or she actually received the larger amount and to give a large amount of change accordingly.

Con artists also use distractions, sometimes in the form of demanding a staff member's attention with questions, in order to divert his or her attention so a crime can be committed without notice.

Make sure that any containers of money (e.g., tip jars) are well secured.

### 5.2e Employee theft

Employee theft can become a problem if you are not careful in handling money and recording monetary transactions. Fully explain checks and balances to your staff so that they are aware of the importance of accuracy and are less likely to tamper with a system that easily picks up discrepancies.

Open communication with your staff is one of the best deterrents.

Make sure your till system produces no-sales transaction receipts. These can then be placed in the till with the following information:

(a) Name of cashier

(b) Reason for no-sale (e.g., making change)

(c) Initials of cashier

At the end of each day, these are attached to your daily cash sheet.

Count and record no-sale rings on a daily basis. Does one staff member consistently have more no-sales than other staff members? This may be an indication of till tampering. Watch and observe that employee over a period (three or four shifts) before taking any action. If the pattern of excessive no-sales continues, privately and politely confront the employee. Bring up your concern at the inordinately high number of no-sales on his or her shift and ask for an explanation and a solution. If you confront the issue in a polite, nonthreatening way, the behavior will often change. If it doesn't, be prepared to press charges if you have solid evidence that an employee has been stealing. If you don't press charges, you may develop a reputation as an easy employer to steal from, or the employee may go on to another job where the stealing continues.

**Note:** Always assume in your conversation that the employee is not dishonest. However, also assume that if you've noticed a discrepancy, it may in fact be caused by dishonesty.

Here are some additional tips for preventing employee theft:

- If you believe one of your staff is not ringing in sales, check his or her check average against that of another staff member for the same time period; they should be approximately the same. If a staffperson is not ringing up sales, he or she may be building an excess in the cash drawer or may be taking money and then underringing sales.

- Discourage employee theft by doing random till counts. Take a reading of the tape, pull the drawer, and replace the float. Count the remaining cash to make sure it equals the reading.

- Always give receipts to your customers. This means that every transaction is recorded. If an employee wants to steal money, he or she has to ring in a refund, which leaves a paper trail that's easy to spot or cash shortages that are picked up on the daily cash sheet.

### 5.2f Cash theft

There are a number of ways you can minimize cash theft. The first is to keep the cash on hand to a minimum. The previous day's intake should be kept in a secure, locked area — in the safe, if you invested in one — until it can be safely transported to the bank.

The staff member responsible for daily bank deposits should take certain precautions, like taking a different route to the bank each day, going to the bank at a different time each day, walking one day and taking the bus the next, and making the deposit look as inconspicuous as possible (an old, crumpled-up lunch bag can be a safer carrying case than something that looks like it's worth stealing).

Remind the staff member taking the deposit to the bank to be observant, to note descriptions of suspicious individuals and license plate numbers of suspicious vehicles, and to avoid walking past unlit areas or areas that might conceal an attacker.

### 5.2g Information theft

Competitors and suppliers will often attempt to determine your sales figures, customer counts, and other confidential business information. It should be your company policy not to divulge this information to anyone but staff and management. If a customer asks you or one of your staff how the business is doing, respond with general terms (e.g., "great"). If the person persists, ask for his or her name, address, and telephone number, and explain that someone from "head office" will get back to him or her.

Information theft occurs on a regular basis, so be aware. We have received sales information about other coffee bars from dozens of staff members in the past years — it is amazing how talkative some staff are. Make it clear to employees when they leave your employment that they must not discuss any of your confidential business information with anyone.

Divulging information to competitors will only harm your business. On the other hand, don't be so paranoid that you create ill will among fellow business associates.

---

## COMMITMENT BOX

I, _____ , commit to preparing month-end income and expense statements every single month that I am in business. I commit to conducting performance reviews on all my staff every

_____ 3 months

*(check one)*

_____ 6 months

and commit to keeping my equipment and facilities in top, secure condition.

_____
*(your signature)*

_____
*(today's date)*

# 16
# BUILDING SALES

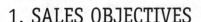

The most important thing about goals is having one.

— GEOFFREY F. ABERT

## 1. SALES OBJECTIVES

Setting sales objectives is critical because these objectives set the entire tone for your marketing plan — and the marketing plan is critical because it outlines exactly how you are going to get those sales. In other words, all your marketing efforts will be designed to meet the sales objectives — from determining the size of the target market and establishing marketing objectives to determining the amount of advertising and promotion dollars to be budgeted, to the number and kinds of distribution channels you use.

Sales objectives must be simultaneously challenging and attainable. If sales objectives are dramatically increased, for example, the cost of doing business will also rise dramatically to accommodate the projected increase in sales. Accordingly, if the sales objectives are set too high and cannot be attained, your resulting expenses-to-sales ratio will be very high, causing profits to fall below expectations.

On the other hand, if you dramatically underestimate your sales objectives and have inadequate capacity to service the business, you will not be able to fulfill demand and you will lose opportunities to your competition. Over the long term, this may translate to the loss of loyal customers and first-time customers.

Also keep in mind your time frame. A five-year sales objective requires that smaller, one-year objectives be set to meet that goal. Similarly, one year objectives will be made up of monthly objectives, and monthly objectives will be made up of daily objectives.

## 2. MARKETING OBJECTIVES AND STRATEGIES

Marketing objectives describe what needs to be achieved to meet the sales objectives. Basically, the marketing objectives for your coffee business will focus on four main areas:

(a) Getting new customers

(b) Keeping your customers

(c) Getting customers to spend more

(d) Getting your customers to come back more often

Marketing strategies describe how the marketing objectives will be accomplished. Below are some of the best strategies we have found for effectively building coffee bar sales.

## 3. GETTING NEW CUSTOMERS

### 3.1 Strategy 1: Cross-promotions

Perhaps one of the fastest ways to build your customer base is through "free coffee" cross-promotions. How do these work? A business in your local area, with a customer profile similar to yours, hands out a coupon for a complimentary coffee (valid at your coffee bar) to each of its customers. The benefit to that business is that it gives a "gift" to each of its customers. The benefit to you is that you gain access to that business's hard-earned customer base, as well as a personal recommendation from that business to visit your coffee bar.

Plan your cross-promotions with these businesses in such a way that you can service them properly. For example, you may want to begin six cross-promotions the first week and six the next week, wait one week, and then do another six.

Proper planning allows your staff to become familiar with the cross-promotion process. Any challenges your staff have can be dealt with before they become major problems.

Accurate record keeping is also important. We have seen hundreds of coupons stuffed in a shoe box by a company with no recording system in place. Failure to keep accurate records defeats the purpose of doing cross-promotions — to find out what works best in your business. If you don't know what is working best, it is very difficult to maintain control over your business and, specifically, to increase sales.

You will also need to plan which product line you want to promote and ensure that it is consistent with the target market of the business with which you are cross-promoting. For example, it would be better to offer 50 percent off freshly squeezed juice than a complimentary coffee to customers at the local health food store.

You will also want to ensure that your promotion is consistent with seasonal patterns. Again, freshly squeezed juice promotions work well in the spring and summer, when the weather is hotter. You will want to run the promotion for as long as it takes to cover the majority of that business's customers. For example, a regular customer at a hair salon visits it every six weeks or so. You would likely want to run a six- to eight-week cross-promotional campaign. While other businesses may have a repeat visit pattern of once a year, you don't necessarily want to run the cross-promotion for a year as staff may get tired of the promotion and the complimentary coffee idea can lose some of its appeal. It is much easier to keep owners and staff motivated and excited for a shorter period.

Here are the seven steps to cross-promoting.

(a) Make a list of businesses near you whose target market is similar to yours.

(b) Meet with the business owner or manager and say something along these lines: "Hi, my name is John from The Coffee Bar next door. As a way to promote both our businesses, we're wondering if you'd like to treat all your customers to a complimentary cup of coffee. Your name goes here on the coupon (show them the sample you've brought with you) and we cover all the costs." Bring along a sample of what you are offering so the owner and staff can enjoy your products. This will increase your response rate, as there is nothing like a first-hand recommendation of a product or service from someone the customer knows and trusts.

(c) Find out how many coupons the business would like to start with, based on its customer counts and customer buying patterns.

(d) Design the coupon. Our template basically has the offer in large, bold letters at the top of the coupon ("FREE COFFEE") and an explanation of the offer below ("Joan's Dresses would like to treat you to a free cup of coffee, compliments of The Coffee Bar.") Be sure to include your address and phone number, as well as a valid-until date. This puts some pressure on the store owner to hand the coupons out on a regular basis.

(e) Have the coupons printed and cut at a quick print shop. Positioning eight coupons per page on your template helps reduce costs.

(f) Deliver the coupons personally to the owner or manager, along with instructions for handing them out. Staff should not hand out multiple coupons or place the coupons on the countertop where customers can pick up handfuls of them. Explain that the coupons are to be handed out one-per-customer. A set of instructions can be posted in the staff room or next to the cash register to explain the promotion and eliminate such problems.

(g) Follow up (this step is very important). Visit that business the second day of the cross-promotion. This will help strengthen the relationship, reinforce the decision to go ahead with the cross-promotion, and will also give the staff there an opportunity to ask any questions that may have arisen over the past day as they have been handing the coupons out. After that, follow up at least once per week. Make sure the business has enough coupons. When it begins to run low, reprint and deliver additional coupons to ensure that there is not a break in the hand-out flow.

Be sure to pass any positive comments you hear from that business's customers back to the business owner, manager, and staff. It is important that the store owner understands that this promotion helps his or her business as well as yours.

## 3.2 Strategy 2: Seek and develop strategic alliances

When Coca-Cola, McDonald's, and Disney get together to promote a movie, the result is often a promotion that kids love. Marketers see a "strategic alliance" — a win/win/win relationship that helps all parties reach their marketing goals.

Strategic alliances can be used by local businesses just as well. The key is to create a win/win scenario for all involved.

Sample alliances include:

- Work with your local kitchenware store — add to its coffee plunger section by displaying your coffee beans and posters.

- Combine a mail-out with your local ice cream store for a spring promotion.

- Donate coffee to the local charity that runs a roadside free coffee stand (remember to supply a sign).

- Offer complimentary coffee to local businesses for their grand openings or special events.

- Offer pounds of coffee (sold at your cost) to the local car dealership for a giveaway with its test drives.

- Offer local automotive repair and service shops free coffee coupons for customers waiting for their cars. Offer to "sell" these to the shops at a nominal cost (e.g., 25 cents each), invoiced once a month — everyone wins.

The opportunities are as large as your imagination. Have fun, be creative, and don't forget to involve your staff.

## 3.3 Strategy 3: Barter

One of the most powerful ways to leverage your cash flow is to barter. Barter is a trading system in which you offer your products in return for credits to purchase other products and services in your barter group.

The largest benefit of barter is the additional business you will get that you otherwise would not have received. Most barter companies also arrange regular networking events that help you make local contacts and help promote your business.

It costs about four to five hundred dollars to join a barter company. You should expect to recoup that investment in the first 60 days if you market your involvement well.

To find a barter company, look under "Barter Exchanges" in the Yellow Pages or go online, or ask other business owners who you know are involved in a barter system.

A good barter system must have the following:

- Lots of other companies with products and services you will want to spend your credits on.

- Lots of companies willing to accept 100 percent barter for each transaction.

- Lots of restaurants (this is important because restaurants all need coffee, so wholesaling your coffee to them is a good way for you to earn credits).

- Full automation (i.e., a computer system that tracks transactions) that doesn't require exact matches for each transaction (it is difficult to sell one person 500 pounds of coffee in one visit, for example).

- Relatively low service charges (5 percent to 6 percent on both sides of a transaction is typical).

As a final point, remember that the barter is considered a sale for tax purposes, so don't forget to budget in the extra revenue.

## 3.4 Strategy 4: Coupon decks

Building business is a process of continually letting people know your business exists and motivating them to come to it. If people know about you but don't come to spend money, you're no better off. Coupon decks, usually made up of a series of coupons delivered by mail in an envelope, allow you to inform and motivate cost-effectively; you can tell potential customers about your product or service while offering some kind of incentive in the form of a coupon.

Coupon decks are cost-effective because you are tying in your mailing with others as a group. They are also cost-effective because of the number of people they are delivered to. You can reach more people at a reasonable cost. Coupon deck distribution is different with each coupon deck company. For example, one Vancouver company divides its mailings by postal-coded regions, with 50,000 to 70,000 residences in each region. There are four mailings in each region per year.

Coupon decks also allow you to measure the result; doing so is vital to your success. Measuring your marketing results allows you to control the amount of income you earn. If you are able to determine how effective an advertisement was, you will be able to make changes to improve effectiveness and, thus, the amount of money you are bringing in.

To measure the results, record each coupon that comes into your store. Also record any add-on sales, and note whether the customer was new to your coffee bar or not.

When the promotion is finished, tally the number of new customers and then divide the amount of money you spent on the promotion by the number of new customers to reach a cost-per-customer figure. Add up the add-on sales, minus your food cost, to determine your profit from the promotion. You can use these figures to compare this effort to your other marketing strategies.

### 3.4a The disadvantage of coupon decks

A certain percentage of customers who use a coupon will be "coupon loyal." They will not — despite all your efforts — be loyal to your coffee bar but, rather, to the coffee bar where they can get the best deal.

However, if you have designed your coupon well, you will still make money, and if the person is coming through your door, you have a better chance of creating a loyal customer than if he or she had never walked into your coffee bar in the first place.

### 3.4b Designing your coupon flier

When designing your flier for the coupon deck, keep in mind the following six keys to increasing the response rate:

- Print full color (or at least two color) and never on white paper.

- Get window positioning if possible. While this will cost more, your promotion will also be more effective because it will have more prominence. A person will grab his or her mail, look at the envelope (view 1), open the envelope and remove the coupons, and then see your coupon on top again (view 2) before flipping through the other coupons. If your coupon is "one of the pack," you rely on the attraction of the window offer to motivate the person to flip through the pack to get to your coupon.

- Use an established coupon deck company (look in the Yellow Pages under "Direct Mail" or "Advertising Companies," and ask for referrals from companies that you see market through coupon decks.

- Use a coupon deck that is consistent with your image and your target market.

- Participate in contests run by the coupon deck company.

- Use the coupon deck regularly for at least one year (response rates always increase over time).

### 3.4c Write a catchy headline

When designing your coupon deck piece — or any other advertisement piece — it is vital that you use an effective headline.

Ninety percent of your advertising success will depend on the effectiveness of your headline. Headlines must catch the attention of your target market so it is interested enough to find out more. Writing a wonderful ad will do you no good if no one ever reads it.

Sample power headline formats include:

- They didn't think I could ___ but I did

- Who else wants ____?

- How ____ made me ____

- Are you ____?

- How I ____

- How to ____

- If you are ____ , you can ____

- Secrets of ____

- Thousands (hundreds, millions) now ____ even though they ____

- Warning: ____

- Give me ____ and I'll ____

- ____ ways to ____

### 3.4d Back up your marketing statements

Backing up your marketing statements is an important key to your success. As consumers become increasingly skeptical, you will need all the proof you can amass to be successful and increase your profits. Here is a list of some of the types of "evidence" you can use:

(a) **Pictorial.** Use pictures, posters, drawings, charts, and graphs.

(b) **Testimonials.** Use testimonials from the following people:

- *Your customers.* Have your customers write their thoughts about your business.

- *Celebrities.* If you can, get a celebrity to autograph a photo or write you a letter. Frame it and hang it on a wall or window so your customers can see it.

(c) **Demonstrations.** Demonstrations are great when selling larger ticket items such as coffee brewing equipment. Set up a table in your coffee bar and do demonstrations for customers.

### 3.4e Make irresistible offers

Your advertising strategies will fail to achieve the results you want unless you stimulate your potential customers to take action now. You will need to make offers so attractive, so tempting, so appealing that your customers are compelled to pick up the phone and call you or drive to your coffee bar.

The offers you make must appeal to your target market. If you are in an upscale part of town, a value-added or free gift promotion works better than a dollar-off promotion, for example.

The following list contains a few of the best methods we've used to get our coffee customers to take action now:

- Limited availability: "We have only 25 in supply so call now" (if it's true).
- Premiums: "Call now and get a free coffee mug with your purchase."
- Deadlines: "A free pound of coffee for those who respond by September 25."
- Multiple premiums: Give multiple incentives for multiple orders (e.g., a free mug with the purchase of five pounds of coffee).
- Discounts for fast response: "Receive 20 percent off a package of coffee this week."

Be sure to give clear directions for what the customer needs to do to respond (call, write, come in person). Make the offer one step so that it is simple and easy for your customers to respond.

Often two or more of these methods can be combined in one marketing vehicle. The key, as in all marketing, is to test and measure what works for you, your area, and your target market.

### 3.4f Offer a guarantee

Guaranteeing your products and services is becoming more and more important as consumers are bombarded daily with hundreds of messages and false claims. Despite this, many companies don't offer guarantees because they fear the worst: "What happens if I have to refund all this money?" they ask themselves. If you have a product or service you think you may have to refund, don't offer it in the first place. You will be successful in business only if you offer something of significant value to your customers. If there is a chance customers won't be happy with what you're offering, improve that product or offer something else.

Your guarantee must be specific, measurable, and, ideally, worth more than the investment the customer is making. A simple "satisfaction guaranteed or your money back" doesn't cut it any more.

For example, we have a home study program called "How to Double Your Sales in Twelve Months or Less" in which we show coffee bar owners in detail exactly what it takes to grow their business. It comes with a guarantee that if you don't grow your sales by 20 percent in the first 60 days and double your sales in the first year, we will gladly refund your money in full. Our company's principles of operations also commit us to deliver more than is expected of us. In this way, we ensure we never have to refund any money because the expectations our customers have of us are so far exceeded that they walk away happy. If you consistently deliver way more to your coffee customers than they expect, where do you think your business will be two years from now? And of course, if you'd like information on this amazing marketing program — recorded live at an International Coffee Expo — email us with "double my sales" in the subject line to info@startandruna profitablecoffeebar.com.

## 3.5 Strategy 5: Banners

Banners are another effective way to gain new customers. They grab the attention of walk-by and drive-by traffic and, if used properly, not only catch peoples' attention but motivate potential customers to come in and purchase what you are offering.

Banners work well if they are large and colorful. Blue and red are colors the eye picks up first, so have lettering in either of these colors. The background must be a contrasting color so that the letters stand out.

Banners are an impulse medium and don't offer customers a chance to sit down and read what you are offering, so you do not have the luxury of using attention-getting headlines. Instead, you must convey your message in a quick and concise way, such as "99¢ cappuccinos!"

You should not need any qualifiers on the banner, but if you do, try to make them generic. For example, "99¢ cappuccinos, December 15 to January 5" limits your use of that banner to one time of the year. Make sure that qualifiers do not limit your use of the banner.

You may want to create a series of banners to run — one week at a time — throughout the year. They should promote items that do well in a particular season (a hot chocolate promotion works best on cold winter days) or the major elements of your business. For example, you might promote gourmet coffees (a 5¢ cup of coffee), specialty coffees (99¢ cappuccino), or bean sales (a complimentary half pound when you buy a pound).

Your banner promotions can also focus on building traffic flow. You can run a "Free coffee from 6 a.m. to 8 a.m." promotion to build early morning traffic, or a $5 latte and cheesecake special from 8 p.m. to 10 p.m. to build late evening traffic.

Your banner offers should be aggressive. There is no point in investing time, energy, and money in a comprehensive banner program if it isn't going to work for you. And the only way banners will work well for you is if they offer items that your customers want.

Banners work best if they are used in conjunction with a complete in-store promotion. This means tying in merchandising displays, the staff's suggestive selling, daily special boards, bottom-of-receipt promotions (see section **6.3**), customer education efforts, and in-store decorations and signage.

Like many other marketing strategies, banners can be used ineffectively. We have seen some businesses leave the same banner up for months on end. This does not create an image of a successful, on-top-of-it business. Not only is your image compromised, but the effectiveness of the promotion declines with time.

## 3.6 Strategy 6: Flier distribution

This strategy involves distributing fliers throughout your area on a regular basis. They can be distributed in one of two ways: inserted into a local magazine or newspaper, or hand delivered by staff or the post office. As with coupon decks, it is imperative that the flier have an attention-getting headline and offer your customer proof, an irresistible offer, and a guarantee.

A flier distribution program must be consistently implemented — distribute fliers once per week for a minimum of six weeks. Flier response rates, as for many forms of print advertising, increase the more people are exposed to them. A poor response rate on an initial flier doesn't necessarily mean that fliers aren't a good marketing strategy.

If you do get a response rate lower than industry average (0.5 percent is typical on any form of direct mail including coupon decks), you will want to examine:

(a) **Your headline:** Was it really an attention-getting headline? Was it consistent with some of the samples we have offered above?

(b) **Your marketing statement backup:** Was it "evidence" your target market would believe?

(c) **Your guarantee:** How did you convey your guarantee message?

(d) **Your offer:** Was it powerful enough? Would it motivate you?

(e) **Your redemption method:** Was it clear? Was it easy to take action on? Was it measurable? (If you can't measure it, how do you know it didn't work?)

(f) **Your layout:** Was it messy and confusing?

(g) **Your colors:** Did you use appropriate colors and enough color?

(h) **Your paper:** Was it good quality or cheap white or tacky fluorescent?

(i) **Your method of delivery:** Was your flier lost among a million other fliers or delivered as a separate item in a postal box?

Fliers usually don't bring in as many customers as a well-established coupon deck and, therefore, are more expensive. Try testing a flier program on an apartment building (make sure you have permission from the landlord first) or subdivision in your area before you invest thousands of dollars on printing and delivery.

## 3.7 Strategy 7: Customer referrals

To make a referral program work, you must first earn the right. To earn the right, you and your staff must do all you can to exceed your customers' expectations each and every visit.

Once you've earned the right, you must then ask for referrals. You can ask through:

- Cards
- Letters and emails
- Phone calls
- In person
- In-store drop boxes

Once you've asked for and received a referral, reward your customer with promotions and incentives. (Rewarding customers who refer people to you by giving them a complimentary package of coffee for each referral means only one thing ... more referrals! Consider thanking those who refer by having a referral thank-you event one night or even a complimentary luncheon.)

## 3.8 Strategy 8: Radio remotes

A radio remote involves having a local radio station come to your business to broadcast.

This is done in conjunction with a major event, such as your grand opening.

Usually the radio station will offer prize giveaways from your business (coffee beans, for example) and, of course, the dj will mention your coffee bar's name repeatedly, and personally encourage people to come visit you.

The best way to get a free radio remote — or at least to get the radio station to off-set your costs — is to offer to do a fundrais-er for a local radio station's favorite charity at your coffee bar in exchange for the free remote.

One promotion that worked extremely well was organized by Pepsi-Cola and a local radio station. Pepsi donated a thou-sand six-packs of Pepsi to be used to pro-mote a local kids' park that the radio station was supporting. A Pepsi pyramid was built around the station's most-listened-to evening dj, and the station's listeners were asked to come buy a six-pack for two dollars to help get the dj out of his "Pepsi Prison."

The Pepsi six-packs were sold out a few hours later, the dj got out of prison, a sub-stantial amount of money was raised for the kids' park, and Pepsi got tremendous cover-age on the air then and for several weeks after from the Pepsi-imprisoned dj.

## 3.9 Strategy 9: Publicity

Publicity is advertising you don't pay for. It could be, for example, a write-up in your local newspaper. Because it seems to be objective (since you didn't pay for it), the impact of such exposure is considered to be ten times greater than any paid advertising you can do. There are two keys to getting publicity:

(a) **Know who your audience is:** What media do they watch, read, or listen to?

(b) **Concentrate on a unique aspect:** Find a unique angle or story that would be of interest to people in your community.

### 3.9a Press releases

Once you've figured out an angle and who your market is, prepare a press release to attract media interest and get some write-ups. Here are some guidelines for writing a press release that will be noticed:

- Type it double-spaced on plain white paper
- Personalize it to the appropriate edi-tor or reporter
- Begin with the city and date
- Include the most important informa-tion in the first paragraph, making sure you include: who, what, where, when, and how
- Follow with the less interesting information, and end with the least important point
- Make your story easy to read and interesting
- Use interesting pictures that help tell the story and that will attract atten-tion

Mail or fax your press release at least nine days before you want it to run in the publication to which you are sending it. Follow up with a phone call to find out if the press release was received. (It is consid-ered impolite to ask the editor if he or she will be running the story; confirming that the press release was received is all you can do.)

Get the most out of articles written about you: merchandise them. Frame printed copies and hang them in your coffee bar. Give copies to your customers and Bean Club members.

### 3.9b Promotions to get media attention

Use unique and creative promotions to draw media attention to your business. For example, you might try to break the *Guinness Book of World Records* mark for the largest bowl of latte.

Tie these events to a local nonprofit or Junior Achievement group, or the charity the local radio/TV station covering the event supports.

### 3.9c Seven ways to create news

(a) Tie in your promotion with the news events of the day.

(b) Stage a special event (e.g., a skills contest with proceeds going to a local charity).

(c) Release information that is useful to the general public.

(d) Announce the formation of a new committee you are a member of.

(e) Give an award (e.g., for the fastest latte drinker).

(f) Be a local expert (be on the lookout for problems to analyze, surveys to report, and predictions to forecast).

(g) Celebrate a birthday or anniversary.

Remember to follow up any article about you or publicity you receive with a thank-you letter. The writer or publisher will appreciate your effort and may be more willing to help you out in the future. Sample 14 is a thank-you letter you can adapt for your own business.

## 4. KEEPING YOUR CUSTOMERS

### 4.1 Strategy 1: Honored guest greeting procedure

The honored guest greeting procedure is simple and cheap, and it's amazing that more people don't use it. Think of the last time you walked into a coffee bar. How were you greeted (or were you greeted at all)? How much of an impact did this greeting (or lack of one) make on your overall impression of the coffee bar, the enjoyment level of your visit, and the purchases you made? Did you tell your friends about this business? Did you ever go back? Did you remember this business a year down the road? Do you think to buy your coffee here when you run out?

The first thing customers should see when they enter your coffee bar is the smiling faces of staff members who are eager to serve and make their visit special. "Good evening," the staff enthusiastically say. "Welcome to The Coffee Bar. How may I be of service to you tonight?"

As consumers, we are all impressed by treatment that makes us feel special. Not only does it make us want to come back and spend more money, but it also makes us want to tell our friends about what a pleasant place it was.

Greeting customers is key to your success. Greeting is important because customers who are greeted will feel appreciated and welcome. Not greeting customers can make them feel unwanted and unimportant. By using a personalized greeting procedure such as the one described in

# MEDIA THANK-YOU LETTER

THE COFFEE BAR
123 JAVA DRIVE
BEANTOWN, CA
(222) 555-6789

September 16, 20--

Larry Jones
City Star
1234 W. 3rd Street
Beantown, CA

Good morning, Larry:

I wanted to say thank you for the great story you wrote about The Coffee Bar. I appreciate the phone calls and the time you took to write it. Thanks! I hope your readers enjoyed it too!

If I can ever help you out in future, please give me a ring.

Best regards,

*Karen Fry*

Karen Fry
Owner

P.S. I've enclosed a certificate for a complimentary package of our delicious coffee. Phone our Call Ahead Bean Roasting Service if you like, and we'll have it all ready for you when you drop by.

Chapter 14, sections **3.1** and **3.2**, you can further enhance the customers' experience of your coffee bar to create the WOW! experience you must offer if you want to be successful.

## 4.2 Strategy 2: Create a WOW! experience

The WOW! experience encompasses everything you do in the coffee bar, from the way you greet your customers to how clean the bathroom mirror is. You want to have each and every one of your customers walking out the door saying "WOW!"

This WOW! experience leads to repeat visits and word-of-mouth marketing. Just think what would happen to your business if every one of your 200 customers a day told just one friend about how great your business was.

### 4.2a Six things you can do to create a WOW! experience in your coffee bar

(a) Use the honored-guest greeting procedure.

(b) Keep your coffee bar sparkling clean (customers don't notice cleanliness unless it's not there).

(c) Deliver only the highest quality products.

(d) Hold the door open for customers when they enter and leave.

(e) Ask customers how they enjoyed their food or beverage.

(f) Tell your customers you appreciate their business.

See Chapter 14 for the 11 WOW! steps to customer service at the counter.

## 4.3 Strategy 3: Make customers feel important

Recently we heard about a man who bought a large business that needed massive sales increases. At the time he took over, the business was making $90 million a year. Eighteen months later, the business was making $1.2 *billion* a year. When asked what he had done to make the business such a success, he attributed the turnaround entirely to making his customers feel genuinely important.

In the coffee business, you can make your customers feel important by —

(a) having honored guest greeting procedures in place and immediately greeting customers when they walk into your coffee bar,

(b) calling regular customers by their first names,

(c) making eye contact with your customers, even if they have to wait to be served, and

(d) using thank-you cards. (To give you an idea of the power of thank-you cards, remember the billion dollar business above? In those 18 months, the new owner sent out 6,000 thank-you cards per week.)

You also make customers feel important by following up after you've taken their money. Ask, "How did you enjoy your cappuccino today?" or "We appreciate your business and look forward to seeing you again soon."

## 4.4 Startegy 4: Pay attention to your online reputation

It pays to know what is being said online about your business. Whether their experience is good or bad, customers can instantly and widely broadcast their opinions of your business over the Internet.

Google your business name periodically and also do a blog search (www.google.com/blogsearch/). For a more current and comprehensive search of what bloggers might be saying about your business, search Technorati (www.technorati.com), a website that indexes millions of blogs in real time. You may find posts about your business published just minutes or hours ago.

Some café and restaurant guide websites are online extensions of popular guidebooks such as Zagat, while others exist only online, such as The Café Guide (www.thecafeguide.com). Pay close attention to websites where anyone can post about their experiences with businesses. Yelp! (www.yelp.com) has quickly become a powerful force in shaping customer opinion of cafés, restaurants, and stores. The site combines social networking with reviews, and some Yelp! members have become very influential. Other popular websites you might check are Craigslist (www.craigslist.org; select your city from the list) and 43 Places (www.43places.com).

When you find out what is being said about your business, positive or negative, don't get overexcited or angry. If the comments are negative, don't retaliate or "flame" reviewers. Look at the pattern of what is being said. Are the comments about your coffee bar's service, atmosphere, menu, or the coffee? Are they generally positive or negative? Do they articulate what went right or wrong, or are they just general opinions? Share the compliments as well as the complaints with your staff, and if necessary, review the principles of WOW!

customer service with them. Your goal is not just to know your online reputation, but to work proactively to build it.

## 4.5 Strategy 5: Telephone etiquette

When answering the phone, you and your staff should have a preplanned script that distinguishes your coffee bar from any other coffee bar ("Good morning, The Coffee Bar. Karen speaking. How may I help you?").

For your answering machine message, consider something like the following:

"Thank you for calling our 24-hour bean ordering line. We are either serving customers or roasting coffee and can't get to the phone right now. We'd be happy to call you back if you leave your name and phone number. If you are calling in a bean order, please leave the following information: your name and a phone number where we can reach you, the bean and roast you want, ground or whole bean, any flavoring, and what time you will be by to pick it up. Unless you hear otherwise, we'll have it all ready for you when you arrive."

## 5. GETTING YOUR CUSTOMERS TO SPEND MORE

### 5.1 Strategy 1: Sample, sample, sample

Sampling is an immediate sales-building tool, although it has long-term benefits as well. As the saying goes, "The proof of the pudding is in the eating." In your case, the proof may be in the muffin or cookie or anything else decadent and delicious you might want your customers to try. Here are some tips for effective sampling:

(a) Sample items that are going to appeal to your customers and be something that they will likely want to buy.

(b) Sample impulse items that don't require a lot of thought on the customers' part to buy (cookies work well for example, espresso machines don't).

(c) Sample items that are consistent with your customers' buying patterns (e.g., muffins in the morning and cheesecake after dinner).

(d) Ensure that your samples are visually appealing — add an edible flower or a sprig of mint to dress up your sample display.

(e) Cut the samples into uniform pieces — this will be more appealing than hand-broken pieces.

(f) Cut the samples into bite-size pieces — samples are to tantalize your customers' taste buds, not fill up their tummies.

(g) Put up clear, professional signage near the sample so your customers know what they are trying and can order it by name if they like it.

## 5.2 Strategy 2: Create a "what's new" section in your coffee bar

Your regular customers often become "robot-ized"; they walk straight to the counter, order their usual cup of coffee, then turn around and walk straight back out again, never noticing what's going on around them.

These regulars represent a huge potential for increasing your cash flow. Creating a "what's new" section in the coffee bar is one way you can catch their attention (as well as the attention of your new customers) and break them out of their "same old routine" pattern.

Here are some tips for creating a what's new section:

(a) Make the section eye-catching — use balloons; posters; something that moves, lights up, or makes a noise; or anything else that will catch the attention of your customers.

(b) Make it attractive and appealing — while catching attention is important, it is equally important to get your customers to walk over to it.

(c) Use professional-looking signage that clearly says what the item is and how much it costs.

(d) Do something different each week — your "what's new" display quickly loses its effectiveness if your customers become used to the display. By changing your merchandising efforts on a regular basis, you train your customers to look forward to finding out what's new.

## 5.3 Strategy 3: Sell through suggestion

Suggestive selling is when you and your staff recommend additional items to your customers, with the goal of increasing your average customer check. A 25¢ increase in your average check doesn't sound like much, but over one year, with 200 customers per day, it adds up to approximately $18,000 in additional gross sales.

Suggestive sell products or services that are suitable to the customer and the order he or she just placed (e.g., suggest a cup of gourmet or specialty coffee if the customer has ordered a piece of cheesecake). Offer a sample for the customer to taste when recommending a daily roast.

Plan your suggestive selling efforts carefully on your marketing calendar (see section **7.2** for more details), and tie it in with seasonal patterns. Remember to involve your staff and to track and reward their suggestive selling results.

Other examples of suggestive selling include:

- A larger size coffee
- A muffin to go with a coffee
- A freshly squeezed juice for a child
- Daily specials or features of the week
- A specialty coffee drink for a gourmet coffee drinker
- Cold drinks, iced coffees, or fresh juices for those who may not want a hot drink
- Hot chocolate or herb tea for those who may not want drinks containing caffeine

Introduce products using phrases such as, "These are our most popular muffins" or "This is our best-seller." If a customer asks "Which is the best?" always answer "They're all great" and then add something such as "The most popular is the Colombian," or "My personal favorite is the Peruvian."

Be careful not to "oversell" your customers (especially regulars) or be pushy in your recommendations. The key to suggestive selling is to suggest an item if it is better for the customer; recommend products that you genuinely think the customer might enjoy.

Many times the best item to suggestive sell is actually a smaller size. This is called downselling. For instance, you might recommend two people with small appetites split a large muffin. Customers will remember you because you cared enough about them (and weren't just thinking about the money). They'll be back, and they'll bring their friends.

Although people may not always take you up on your offer or suggestion the first time, they may remember next time — so never give up.

## 5.4 Strategy 4: Sell through information

One of the characteristics of gourmet coffee drinkers is that they generally are more educated than nongourmet coffee drinkers. Use this to your advantage by encouraging your existing customers to spend more money by informing and educating them about the products and services you offer.

When doing so, ask yourself these questions: What makes your product or service unique? What are some reasons customers might be interested in it? What do they get by purchasing the product or service? (What's in it for them?)

Here are some ideas you can use in your education plan:

- Publish a monthly electronic newsletter.
- Offer informational brochures with specific product purchases.

- Develop a line of brochures designed to answer common questions your customers might have (e.g., How is milk for cappuccinos foamed?), or use the Specialty Coffee Association's brochures.

- Hold an informative workshop.

- Publish a guide to give to your customers.

- Use table talkers (small plastic stands) and in-store signage to promote unique elements of your products or services (e.g., analyze muffins for fat content, calories, etc., and publish the information on a cue card). Table talkers should be used on all tables, counters, and stand-up bars in the coffee bar to educate, inform, and promote products, services, or upcoming promotions.

# 6. GETTING YOUR CUSTOMERS TO COME BACK MORE OFTEN

## 6.1 Strategy 1: Preferred-customer cards (PCCs)

Preferred-customer cards (PCCS) are designed to give customers a complimentary coffee after they have purchased a certain number of coffee drinks. Perhaps you have a preferred-customer card in your own wallet — those coffee cards that are stamped at your favorite coffee bar each time you go in?

Whether you're aware of it or not, these cards exist for a specific sales-building reason: to remind you of that particular business. The theory is that the more you are reminded, the more you will visit. Many places use these cards for one simple reason: they work. Over the years, our coffee bars have given away literally tens of thousands of PCCS and it is our belief that this is one of the elements that has made many of our coffee bars very successful.

Encourage all your customers to use your coffee bar's PCCS regularly. Why? Because PCCS are important tools to reward customers for visiting your coffee bar, create customer loyalty, and encourage repeat visits.

How? By offering a complimentary item after a number of purchases, you are rewarding customers for spending money with you. By recognizing them as preferred customers, you are helping to create customer loyalty. (We've found that offering one free after five purchases is the most effective.)

PCCS also remind customers of your coffee bar when they open their wallets and see your card. It reminds them about your great coffee and the wonderful service they received last time they were in. It may even trigger a customer to mention it to the friend they are with at the time, thereby creating word-of-mouth marketing.

An added benefit is that you can put your phone number on a PCC so your customers can easily call your coffee bar's Call Ahead Bean Roasting Service.

On the other hand, it is also a customer convenience to keep the PCCS filed in the coffee bar. Our PCCS are designed so there is room at the top of the card for the customer to write his or her name. The card can then be filed in a Rolodex or other indexing system so that regular customers don't need to remember to bring their card every time they come for coffee. (How many times have you ordered a cappuccino and then realized you didn't have your card handy to get stamped? This frustration can turn customers off.) Keeping the card on file also helps build customer loyalty because many customers feel compelled to come back just to make sure their card is still there.

Both systems — customers keeping their PCCS or the coffee bar keeping them — have pros and cons. Use whichever system suits your customers best, or you can use both systems at the same time in your coffee bar.

### 6.1a The "free" time

When your customer has bought the required number of beverages, use the complimentary time to reward and thank him or her for coming to your coffee bar frequently. There are two ways to reward customers. One is to offer customers what they usually order, the second is to offer customers any coffee drink.

The disadvantage of the first system is that you are not encouraging customers to try other specialty coffee drinks or larger sizes of what they usually order, which, if they enjoyed them and ordered them again, would help increase average customers' checks.

If you use the second system, you will undoubtedly get customers who take advantage of the complimentary offer by ordering your most expensive item, thus negatively affecting your food cost. However, you are encouraging customers to experiment with more expensive items.

Whichever system you decide to use, make sure that you stick with it. Also, be sure to record any items that you are giving away, for two important reasons:

(a) To maintain control over your food costs.

(b) To record your add-on sales and record the profits made on the PCC "free" times. If your staff is doing a good job, you will find that the sales you make from suggestively sold items will offset the costs of the products you are giving away.

### 6.1b Card tips

- Do not ask customers if they want a PCC, simply give it to them. If you ask, "Do you want one?" they may say no.

- Make sure you say, "We treat you," to help drive home the fact that the coffee isn't magically appearing from nowhere. Don't say, "And your sixth one is free." Coffee is not free, it is a valuable product you provide, and you don't want to say anything that will cheapen its value.

- If the customer has been in the coffee bar before, ask, "Do you have your preferred-customer card with you today?" If the customer has not been in before, hand him or her a card while saying, "Here is one of our preferred-customer cards — after five more coffee beverages, we treat you to one."

- If you are storing cards in your store, date stamp new PCCS as they are filed so that you can discard cards after two or three months if they are not being used on a regular basis.

- If storing in-store, alphabetize by first name and last initial.

- If cards are kept in-store, have customers look up their own cards when they come in. If your staff look for customers' cards but are unable to find them, other customers in line may become upset because they have to wait for your attention. Customers will have time to look up their card while you are ringing their sale in or making change.

- Do not give stamps for cold drinks such as pops and juices, as these tend to be higher cost items.

- Once cards are full, have customers write their phone numbers on the front and drop the cards into a weekly draw box to win a thermal mug or pound of coffee as an extra reward for completing a card.

## 6.2 Strategy 2: Offer your customers free Wi-Fi Internet access

As discussed in Chapter 6, setting up a Wi-Fi access point can be a way to draw customers to your café and get them to stay longer. If your business is near a college or university or in an area where there are lots of people whose work depends on a laptop and an Internet connection, this strategy will entice them to do their work in your coffee bar and spend money while they do so.

The downside is that you may bring many customers who spend a lot of time in your business but perhaps not a lot of money. Depending on the sophistication of your network setup, you can set limits on the amount of time a customer spends on your network and send "reminders" to them that they should buy something (and get another access code) in order to receive more network time. Providing great customer service is the best strategy: train staff to inquire after laptop users' needs. For example, while staff are making the rounds to clean tables and refresh supplies, they might ask laptop users: "Can I get you another coffee?"

Whether you choose to offer Wi-Fi and how you manage it depends on the atmosphere you are trying to create in your coffee bar. For some café owners, laptop users "cocooned" behind their screens dampen the lively social atmosphere they want in their business. A café in Seattle made national headlines in 2005 after they decided to turn off the Wi-Fi on weekends. The café owners saw too many groups of customers walk out the door while solo Internet users took up tables. Other cafés have decided to cater to laptop users, recognizing that such customers do generate a higher per-check average than other customers. Still other cafés try to accommodate both Wi-Fi and "unplugged" customers by creating "laptop zones" with electrical outlets and printing facilities alongside tables with the usual niceties of a coffee bar such as comfy seats, newspapers, and magazines.

Most customers who are attracted to your coffee bar for free Wi-Fi and great coffee will probably follow the basic etiquette of patronizing service-oriented business: buy things, be nice, and maybe even tip well. There will always be, however, some who take advantage of the free Internet, buy little, and treat staff badly. In the latter case, your staff should not be thrust into the role of enforcer. Remind your staff to solve problems through great customer service.

## 6.3 Strategy 3: Use bottom-of-receipt specials

Whether you use a cash register or a computer system in your coffee bar, make sure you can program it to print out specials on the bottom of the receipts you give to your customers. Most businesses give receipts with every purchase anyway, so why not turn this into a money-making tool? Use bottoms of receipts (BORS) to —

- promote evening traffic by offering evening discounts to your morning customers (e.g., offer all your morning regulars a 2-for-1 cheesecake special valid from 7 p.m. to 10 p.m.),

- promote your morning business by offering morning discounts to your evening customers (e.g., hand out a coupon for a complimentary coffee from 6 a.m. to 8 a.m. to people visiting your business at night),

- promote a product (e.g., offer 20 percent off a new line of grinders),

- promote bean buying (e.g., offer a complimentary half-pound of beans with the purchase of any pound).

Always put a "valid until" date on your BORS, and make sure your staff hand them out with each order. Change the promotion regularly.

## 6.4 Strategy 4: Run in-store contests

In-store contests are a fun way to get your customers to come back more often. Here are some tips for planning, promoting, and holding an in-store contest:

- Make your contest easy. You don't want to have to stop and explain your contest to each customer.

- Make your contest time-friendly. You don't want to take up a lot of your customers' time. This can create bottle-necks and traffic jams in your coffee bar and will upset and frustrate customers.

- Use clear signage to get your message across. Make your instructions simple and understandable.

- Abide by contest rules and regulations in your area (people may not need to make a purchase to enter).

- Keep in mind your target market when designing the contest (remember that 70 percent of gourmet coffee beans are purchased by women).

- Stick to your contest timelines — if the contest is over on May 20, make sure you complete it on that date. If the contest involves a draw, ensure that the draw is done on the specified day in the presence of a customer (or two) as a witness.

- Promote the contest after it is over by announcing the winner through your coffee bar's regular newsletter or by posting a photograph of the winner in your coffee bar (this has the added benefit of proving that you follow through on what you promote).

# 7. MARKETING PLAN
## 7.1 Marketing time

Now that you are familiar with some of the things you can do to build your business, how do you get it all organized? The first step is to decide how you want to invest your time in building your business. Obviously, the more you invest, the higher your returns.

The key here is that you set aside time each day or each week and devote it entirely to marketing your business. This means you don't return phone calls or go to the dentist; this is sales building time. Invest in your future.

How do you decide how much time to spend marketing your business? Determine how much money you want to make! One word of caution: you must have the foundation of a great business laid so that as you go out and generate new customers, those customers are treated well in the coffee bar. We know of one business that got about 1,500 new customers from one mailout. There was one problem. When the new customers came into the coffee bar, they were treated like any other customer. There was no WOW! As a result, the mailout, while a success from the outside, was really a failure.

Don't let this happen to you. Make sure that your sales-building efforts aren't wasted. Plan your time outside the coffee bar carefully. Make sure you have support staff who can uphold the high levels of customer service in your coffee bar while you aren't there. In other words, don't let customer service suffer as a result of the time you spend building sales.

Assuming you can maintain the balance, we recommend a minimum of one day per week be dedicated entirely to building sales. Alternatively, you may want to devote a part of each afternoon (during a quieter period in your coffee bar) to building sales. If you choose the latter, be sure that you aren't distracted by impromptu meetings or receiving supplies at these times.

## 7.2 Marketing calendar

You will get the best return on your time investment if you know exactly what you should be doing with your time. Planning for a few hours now will save you many hours of confusion later on. Planning now will also keep you focused. It will help you make the decisions you must make on a daily basis as a coffee bar owner.

Use a large calendar or your time management system. Write in your sales objective at the beginning of each month. Then write in what action you must take each day of the year to carry out your marketing strategies. Start with major events and work backward to determine exactly what has to be done, when, and by whom. Sample 15 shows a sample marketing calendar for a Valentine's Day promotion.

## 7.3 Marketing budget

Commit to setting aside a fixed percentage of gross revenue for your marketing efforts (ideally, you should put it into a separate bank account). By setting aside a predetermined percentage — or at least a fixed dollar amount — every day, you will have the budget necessary to build your business.

Remember: when it comes to marketing, you must invest money in your business to make money in your business. The key is to invest your funds, measure your results, make adjustments, stop what doesn't work, and continue with what does work. By using this method you will ultimately have complete control over your income,

# MARKETING CALENDAR (VALENTINE'S DAY)

| Sunday | Monday | Tuesday | Wednesday | Thursday | Friday | Saturday |
|---|---|---|---|---|---|---|
| **1** | **2** | **3** | **4** | **5** | **6** | **7** |
| • Hold staff meeting re this month's promos; set goals with staff; go over timeline implementation | • Order red flowers for pickup on Feb. 13<br>• Order red balloons<br>• Start BOR promo for Lovers' Blend<br>• Pick up envelopes and letters at printer for mailout<br>• Stuff and mail | • Place order for Valentine cheesecake and cookies to arrive Feb. 9<br>• Pick up small bags, chocolate, red mints, red sprinkles, red ribbon, red balloons, red ties for staff | • Do all store signage, including table talkers, impulse buys, pricing, and Valentine food items<br>• Prepare impulse bags of chocolate and red mints; tie with ribbon | | | |
| **8** | **9** | **10** | **11** | **12** | **13** | **14** |
| • Start roasting Lovers' Blend; decorate bags with ribbon<br>• Blow up balloons | • Decorate store inside<br>• Display Valentine cheesecake and cookies<br>• Call or send press release to local media about free latte for lovers promo<br>• Start red sprinkles<br>• Start red ties on staff | • Continue to promote Saturday's specials<br>• Take fliers and invites to printer | • Continue to promote Saturday's specials<br>• Pick up fliers and invites at printer | • Continue to promote Saturday's specials | • Continue to promote Saturday's specials<br>• Pick up red flowers<br>• Pick up helium balloons<br>• Decorate store outside<br>• Deliver fliers/invites to local businesses | • Have fun, sell lots of beans! |

**Budget for promo:**
$50 (excluding product)

**Sales goal:**
Additional $500

**Marketing strategies:**
1. Get new customers with creative window display (walk-by), cross-promotion with local businesses' customers, local newspaper ads/write-ups
2. Get existing customers to spend more through impulse gift items and Lovers' Blend promotion
3. Get customers to come back through —

(a) in-store BOR promo and staff promotion of Saturday's specials, and
(b) mailout to existing Bean Club members.

**The focus:**
1. Latte sales
2. Cheesecake sales
3. Bean sales

**The promo:**
• Free latte for your lover (2 for 1)
• Free piece of cheesecake for your lover (2 for 1)
• Lovers' Blend coffee 20% off all week

• Free half-pound of Lovers' Blend for customers with BOR
• Free half-pound of Lovers' Blend for Bean Club members with presentation of coupon mailed to them

**Store decorations:**
• Lattes decorated with red sprinkles
• Coffee bags decorated with red ribbon
• Red helium balloons outside storefront
• Red balloons inside
• Free latte poster at storefront
• Other decorations, budget permitting

and isn't this one of the main reasons you got into business for yourself?

By setting money aside, you will also have access to cash when you come up with that great idea, or when that genuine once-in-a-lifetime marketing opportunity appears.

We recommend a total marketing budget of no less than 5 percent of gross sales for an established coffee operation and 10 percent minimum for a new operation. Pledge to set aside this amount to implement your marketing plan.

## COMMITMENT BOX

I, _____ , commit to taking action on each of the marketing strategies listed in this chapter. I also commit to setting aside at least one hour per day (or one day per week), as well as enough funds, to carry out my marketing plans, as outlined in my marketing calendar.

_____
(your signature)

_____
(today's date)

# 17

# SEVEN CHARACTERISTICS OF A SUCCESSFUL COFFEE BAR OWNER

Achieving goals by themselves will never make us happy in the long term; it's who you become, as you overcome the obstacles necessary to achieve your goals, that can give you the deepest and most long-lasting sense of fulfillment.

— TONY ROBBINS

So now that you know how to open and run a coffee bar, you're probably wondering what kind of superperson it takes to run one and make it successful. We have discovered that there are seven basic skills common to all highly successful business owners:

(a) Leadership skills

(b) Management skills

(c) Communication skills

(d) Goal-setting skills

(e) Problem-solving skills

(f) Sales-building skills

(g) Customer service skills

This chapter gives you the chance to learn more about these characteristics and to compare them with your own skills.

## 1. YOU AS A GREAT LEADER

Becoming involved in the coffee industry gives you the opportunity to strengthen and develop your leadership skills. Nowhere will they be more valuable to you than in owning and operating your own business.

Great leaders have visions which give their lives purpose. They are able to communicate their visions to others and inspire purpose in the lives of others. Great leaders are also willing to accept responsibility for their actions and the actions of their followers. They are willing to be accountable for achieving goals that support their vision.

How can you become a great leader? Here are some points to follow:

(a) Become an expert in human behavior; ask questions in order to understand the reasons why people act the way they do and what sort of behavior they are likely to show in different situations.

(b) Attempt to see issues from the point of view of others.

(c) Learn to plan and organize; know what has to be done, when it has to be accomplished, and who is going to do the job.

(d) Set and prioritize goals, and help others set and prioritize goals in their own lives.

(e) Communicate effectively with others through sight, sound, and touch.

(f) Take control of your state of mind by asking positive questions that help you focus on the possibilities.

(g) Become a motivator and help others unlock the potential within them.

(h) Earn the respect of others by becoming an example that others strive for — respect comes only from exercising and displaying leadership skills and abilities on a daily basis.

## 2. YOU AS A GREAT MANAGER

People are your most valuable asset, and learning how to manage them can help make your coffee business that much more profitable. Great managers motivate people. They create a sense of teamwork within their organizations and they help make each team member a productive part of the team.

How do you become a great manager? Follow the tips below:

(a) Create a sense of teamwork by involving your staff and management in reaching common goals.

(b) When setting goals, focus on those that will produce the most (80 percent of your most important results will come from only 20 percent of your goals).

(c) Focus your attention on the results to be achieved rather than the things to be done. Building a "result-getting" attitude in your business helps foster self-reliance and confidence in staff and managers.

(d) Make sure your staff know what is expected of them by making performance standards clear and expressing them in observable, measurable terms.

(e) Catch staff members doing something right — compliment them immediately and specify exactly what was done right.

(f) Focus on improvements rather than shortfalls.

(g) Recognize achievements with praise, compliments, and congratulations.

(h) Be creative and help others develop their creative potential.

(i) Be an environmentally and socially responsible citizen of the planet, and help others to be so as well through education and setting an example.

## 3. YOU AS A GREAT COMMUNICATOR

The coffee business is a people business and the people business is a communication business. You will need to develop communication skills to deal with your customers, staff, suppliers, and other business owners in the community.

Your thoughts, ideas, and feelings are conveyed to others through —

- your attitude,
- the words you say,
- the things you talk about and the way you talk about them,
- the questions you ask,
- the way you listen and care about the responses,
- the way you use your body to convey your words, and
- the way you dress.

Here are 12 ways to become a great communicator:

(a) **Have a positive mental attitude.** Foster a positive mental attitude by seeing the potential in a situation, by seeing not "problems" but only "challenges" to overcome, and by asking yourself questions that produce helpful answers such as, "What is good about this situation?"

(b) **Be flexible in your communication style.** Realize that not all people process information the same way. Some people need to experience an idea before it is understood — encourage these people to experience and "feel it for themselves." Other people are more visually oriented and prefer to use their eyes to help them understand — use visual aids to improve your communication with these people. And still others learn best from what they hear — use your voice and words to communicate your ideas.

(c) **Use positive power words.** Negative words such as "rotten" or "bad," do nothing to make a good impression on customers or your staff (and they certainly don't help you foster a positive mental attitude). Instead, use positive power words that help you focus on accomplishment and possibility.

| NEGATIVE WORD | TRANSFORMS INTO |
| --- | --- |
| angry | challenged |
| frustrated | fascinated |
| nervous | energized |
| overwhelmed | in demand |
| stressed | busy |
| stupid | discovering |

(d) **Make positive conversation.** Positive conversation helps direct your customers' and staff members' focus to something good. When people focus on something that's good, they automatically feel good too.

(e) **Use a tone of voice that energizes.** Change the tone of your voice so that it is upbeat and exciting. You'll find that your energetic tone of voice will actually give you, your staff, and your customers more energy.

(f) **Ask genuine questions about people.** People like to talk about themselves. Ask genuine questions about people. Be curious — you may learn something.

(g) **Listen to show you care.** Answers don't count unless you hear them. Use your ears to hear what the customer is saying to you. Repeat back to customers what you have heard so they know you are listening. Asking a question shows you care, listening to the answer proves it.

(h) **Hear a compliment, pass it on.** When you hear a compliment about a product you are carrying, pass it on to the supplier. When you hear a compliment from a customer about the great service he or she received, pass it on to the staff member who served that customer.

(i) **Smile, smile, smile.** Smiling not only affects muscles that tell your brain you're happy, but it also lets the people you come into contact with know that you are happy. You can make others feel good by smiling.

(j) **Use your body to energize.** Sixty percent of what you communicate is received through body language, so learn to move your body quickly and confidently. This will help you stay energized and focused and will give you more confidence to be the best you can be.

(k) **Dress for success.** Make sure you dress for great performance — consistently. Conveying a professional image will instill confidence in your customers, your staff, and other people you do business with.

(l) **Be a contributing team member.** Think of yourself as part of a winning team. Never ask someone to do something you wouldn't do yourself.

## 4. YOU AS A GREAT GOAL SETTER

Goals are destination points along your path to success. Goals are tools that concentrate your focus, move you in a positive direction, and ultimately give you control over your destiny. In your coffee business, you will find goal setting especially helpful as you build your sales. You may set a goal with your staff to double take-home coffee volume or to increase flavored coffee sales by 20 percent. Unless you know where you are going, it is difficult to get there.

Here is how to set goals for yourself and others:

(a) **Identify the goal.** Make sure you can measure your goal. For example, if one of your goals is to build sales of take-home coffee, write down exactly what it will take to build this volume.

(b) **Set a timeline for achievement.** If your goal is to accomplish a task "in the fall," commit to a specific date.

(c) **List any obstacles necessary to overcome to achieve your goal.** Obstacles may be people related, money related, time related, or skill related.

(d) **Identify the people and groups you need to work with in order to reach your goals.** This may involve friends, family, or business acquaintances, or it may involve a charity or business association.

(e) **List the skills and knowledge necessary to reach your goal.** What will you need to know in order to reach your goal? What skills will you need to develop? What knowledge will you need to acquire?

(f) **Develop a plan of action.** Your action plan must spell out what, how, when, where, and by whom the work will be done.

(g) **List the benefits and disadvantages.** Ask yourself these two key questions: "What will happen if I don't reach the goal?" and "What's in it for me when I do?" Identifying the answers will help motivate and inspire you to take action.

(h) **Take action.** Doing all the above steps doesn't do any good if you don't take action. If your goals include others, always make it clear what their responsibilities are and what they are being held accountable for. Know what a good performance is. It is difficult for a staff member, for example, to take action if he or she doesn't know what action to take.

(i) **Evaluate your progress.** Take time to stop and look at where you are — recognize your accomplishments and the accomplishments of others. Reevaluate your plan and maybe even reevaluate your goals. If something's not working, stop doing it.

# 5. YOU AS A GREAT PROBLEM SOLVER

The word "problem" in the Chinese language is depicted by two characters: one symbolizes crisis, the other, opportunity. Use problems as an opportunity to learn. Think of them as "challenges" instead of problems.

You'll be amazed at how effective this is in changing a negative situation into a positive one. Take the challenge of a customer complaint and turn it into a success. Here's how:

(a) **Have a positive mental attitude.** Be 100 percent committed to having a positive mental attitude, despite any negative feedback you may be receiving. (Be careful, however, not to negate a serious complaint from a customer.)

(b) **Ask yourself, "What can I learn from this complaint?"** Complaints are an opportunity for you to discover a way to improve.

(c) **Deal with complaints as soon as possible.** Customers will be impressed if their complaint is dealt with in a timely manner.

---

**PROBLEM SOLVING**

"This coffee is cold!" cries the customer.

Your staff member immediately approaches the customer and politely asks, to ensure she has understood the customer, "Your coffee isn't hot?"

"That's right," the customer replies.

"I'll happily give you a new cup — and would a complimentary coffee card make up for it?"

"Yes, I suppose," states the customer, less upset now.

"Thank you very much for bringing this to our attention. Here is another cup for you, as well as a coffee on us. I will double-check our brewing schedules to make sure it doesn't happen again. Have a great day!"

---

(d) **Be professional.** You'll impress not only the customer with the complaint but also any staff members or other customers who may be listening.

(e) **Be a good listener.** Listen carefully to what the customer is saying (and maybe even to what they aren't saying). Listening proves you care.

(f) **Empathize, don't criticize.** How would you feel if the same thing happened to you? Try to understand where the customer is coming from.

(g) **Thank the customer.** Thank the customer for bringing the complaint to your attention. They have just given you an opportunity to learn, grow, and improve.

(h) **Ask the customer what you can do.** Ask the customer what you can do to turn the situation into a positive, WOW! experience for him or her.

You may, from time to time, wish to respond to a formal complaint in written form. Sample 16 shows the kind of letter you might write to a customer who has brought a complaint to your attention. As with any complaint, respond in a timely, professional manner. Keep your letter short, simple, and to the point. Focus on what is good about the situation, and include a gift certificate as a way to make it up to the customer.

(i) **Make sure it doesn't happen again.** Make sure you and your staff don't become complacent and start providing shoddy service, knowing you can placate customers with a free coffee. Although you should see complaints as opportunities, you should also try to avoid this kind of opportunity!

## 6. YOU AS A GREAT SALES BUILDER

Many people get into the coffee business with the idea that as soon as they open their doors, people will flood in. It doesn't work that way. Any business we've seen open and be successful is the result of good planning, smart decision making, and plain old hard work. Being a great sales builder is perhaps the most important habit you can develop — the other habits above aren't worth much if you don't have anyone to lead, communicate with, or manage. Here are four secrets to sales building success:

(a) **Set aside time to build sales every day or every week.** By working sales building into your schedule, you will ensure that building sales doesn't get pushed to the bottom of your to-do pile but becomes a daily part of owning your own business.

(b) **Set aside enough funds to build those sales.** Ideally, set aside money every day and place it in a separate bank account. Having these marketing funds means you will have control over your financial destiny.

(c) **Take time to keep a marketing calendar and then stick to it.** A marketing calendar will help you identify what you need to do throughout the year to reach your sales goals. By being forced to plan well ahead of time, you will find that you are able to get promotions and campaigns in place in enough

# SAMPLE 16
## COMPLAINT RESPONSE LETTER

THE COFFEE BAR
123 JAVA DRIVE
BEANTOWN, CA
(222) 555-6789

November 2, 20--

Sue Low
456 1st Avenue
Beantown, CA

Dear Sue,

Thank you for your recent letter. I appreciated your taking the time to bring your experience to our attention. By doing so, you have given us an opportunity to learn and improve.

I have taken steps to ensure that this doesn't happen again, including holding a staff meeting where we discussed your complaint in detail.

I apologize for the mix-up on your coffee order and would like to make it up to you by offering you a complimentary half-pound of coffee next time you are in. I have also enclosed a certificate for a complimentary latte while you are waiting for your coffee to roast. (If you are unable to wait, please call us ahead of time so we can have it ready for you.)

At The Coffee Bar we are committed to providing our customers with ten times more than we promise to deliver, and we greatly appreciate feedback when we fall short on our commitment.

We sincerely hope that you will give us another chance and will continue to patronize our store.

Best regards,

*Karen Fry*

Karen Fry
Owner

time for them to be effective. (See Chapter 16 for information on sales building and how to create a marketing calendar.)

(d) **Take action!**

# 7. COMMITMENT TO CUSTOMER SERVICE

The key to great service is to deliver ten times more! Giving ten times more means giving service to your customers that is so incredible, so memorable, so positive that they walk away saying "WOW!" You can create a WOW! experience for your customers by being a little bit better in everything you do, from greeting to thanking your customers, from the way you answer the phone to the way you follow up with customers when they leave.

Strive always to exceed your customers' expectations, whether it be in the service they receive, the cleanliness of your coffee bar, or the products you serve.

By following the tips that we have given in this book, such as greeting your customers within seconds of their arrival in your coffee bar and keeping your coffee bar

and all equipment in top-notch condition, you will deliver ten times more than what your customers expect.

Remember to always make the customer the highest priority in the coffee bar. You are in the business of serving your customers, and to serve them well you must be totally focused on their needs. This means that there is no other task that is as important as serving the customer. If you are grinding coffee and a customer walks in, immediately stop what you are doing and focus your attention on the customer. Focusing means explaining where the cream and sugar station is so that customers are not wandering aimlessly in search of a coffee lid. It also means asking questions to discover exactly what their needs are.

Be "customer aware" — no matter what you are doing or who you are serving. Always be aware of other customers around you and waiting in line. Focus completely on the customers — on what they are doing, what they are saying, and what they aren't saying.

Always serve products you feel good about serving. If it's not quite right, don't serve it.

---

# COMMITMENT BOX

I, _____ , commit to developing the seven skills necessary to become a successful coffee bar owner.

_____          _____
(your signature)                                      (today's date)

---

# 18
# EXPANDING AND FRANCHISING

Life shrinks or expands in proportion to one's courage.

— ANAÏS NIN

## 1. EXPANDING: WHEN AND WHY

It's a year (or two) down the road and there you are — the owner of a successful coffee bar. You are making a good profit, have a terrific manager in place who is running the business for you, and you are beginning to realize that there would be some advantages to having a second spot.

For one, you would have better negotiating power with your suppliers. This would help reduce your food cost in both locations and push your bottom line profit figures up.

You would also be able to combine your marketing efforts for the two locations and create a stronger presence in the community, thus helping increase top-end sales numbers.

A second location would help diversify and protect your investment. If your first location ever failed, you would have another location to fall back on. It's like putting your eggs in two baskets, so they don't all break if you drop one!

As well, running two locations is much easier than running one location. Why? Because with two locations, you must delegate authority, not just tasks. You learn to rely heavily on your staff. And you can then focus on what you love to do (not just what you need to do to survive — as in your early days).

Opening another coffee bar will be far easier the second time around. While you'll still have to research a site, you'll know how to go about doing it. You'll have the name, design, and staff uniforms already created. You'll know who to call in for building the coffee bar and how to choose the right bid. You'll know how to get the coffee bar constructed on time and on budget. You'll know how to hire and train your staff, place your first order, and get your doors open.

You'll know how to plan and host a grand opening and how to kick start your marketing plan. It will still take a lot of hard work and effort, but at least you will have done it all (or at least most of it) before.

Duplicate or perish. Your competition will always seek ways to capture your customers. If you sit and wait, you will not survive in the long term. Whether it is a second location for yourself or even franchising, plan for your growth. You owe it to yourself, and your business, to duplicate.

# 2. FRANCHISING

Franchising any business is a big undertaking and a big responsibility. You go from being responsible for your coffee bar, your staff, and your customers to being responsible for the success of someone else's coffee bar, staff, and customers. For this reason, it is important that you do serious research and extensive planning before deciding to undertake the task of franchising.

Franchising takes you out of the world of serving customers and into the world of serving coffee bar owners. It requires that you set up a head office and develop the people systems and operational networks to support franchisees in all areas of their business, from financial to operational.

## 2.1 Do you really want to become a franchisor?

The first step in deciding whether or not to franchise is to examine yourself. Becoming a franchisor means that you will no longer work behind the counter of your coffee bar. If this is the part you enjoy most, are you willing to give it up?

Becoming a franchisor means that you lease an office, buy office furniture and equipment, hire and train office staff, and develop a management team — are you prepared to make this financial investment? This time investment?

Building and developing a successful franchise company takes time — are you prepared to make a long-term commitment to yourself, your staff, and your franchisees?

As a franchisor, your individual location owners become, in a sense, your boss. You can't tell them what to do as if they were staff. We know a fast-growing franchisor who could never adjust to this reality. In the end the business self-destructed; individual owners felt they were not part of the team.

On the other hand, if you seek new input and love change, the constant feedback will inspire you. You will grow better and faster because a team is seeking improvement. Ultimately, you will be in the business of nurturing and supporting entrepreneurs, not in the coffee business.

## 2.2 Do you have a franchisable concept?

Successful franchises all have two things in common: they are unique and they are "on-trend." Your concept must offer potential franchisees the opportunity to attract customers and to still be in business in ten years.

If you feel that franchising is the right path for you, your next step will be to investigate the pros and the cons.

Seek professional advice from experts. You will want to choose a company that focuses on helping people evaluate how "franchisable" their concept is and how suitable they are to running a head office and supporting franchisees, and that then puts all the systems in place to market a successful franchise.

# AFTERWORD

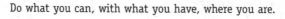

*Do what you can, with what you have, where you are.*

— THEODORE ROOSEVELT

"I live, eat, sleep, and breathe coffee!" "Coffee is my life." "If I could make a living helping people learn about great coffee, I'd be in paradise." "Nothing personal, Tom, but I don't think there is anyone more into coffee than I am."

These are the types of comments we hear every month from people interested in opening a coffee business. They want to be in a business that aligns with their passion, and enjoy what they're doing day in and day out. We hope that we have been able to shed some light on the advantages and disadvantages of owning your own coffee bar so that you will be able to make well-informed decisions that will contribute to your success.

As a final point, we would like to stress that your business will be successful only if you are successful in taking action on the many items we have covered in this book. No one thing will make you a millionaire in the coffee business, but lots of little things all done well do add up.

Think of a horse that has been trained for many months and has developed a small edge over its competitors. That horse may win by only a fraction of an inch, but a fraction is all it takes to be a winner. This book has outlined many advantages that will give you an edge over your competitors and hopefully place you in the winner's circle!

If you find you have questions or would like to make any comments, please give us a call at the Entrepreneur Coach Inc. at 1-800-663-2331 or email us at info@start andrunaprofitablecoffeebar.com. We will be happy to be of any assistance that we can.

We hope we can help make your dream of owning and operating your own coffee bar a reality. Good luck, and we look forward to tasting your just-roasted organic coffee at some point in the future!

*Tom and Marybeth*

P.S. Let us know what happens with your journey into the coffee world, especially if you found this book helpful! We hope to include your story in the next edition of this book.

# APPENDIX

# COFFEE ORGANIZATIONS AND SUPPLIERS

These suppliers are available for coffee bars in both the United States and Canada. If an owner in Canada, for example, wishes to purchase a US product, he or she just has to call the company to determine the Canadian supplier or representative. If the company does not have one, the owner will place the order directly. Call or check the websites of the companies for information; they'll be happy to fax or mail it to you.

## ASSOCIATIONS

Coffee Association of Canada
Phone: 416-510-8032
Website: www.coffeeassoc.com

Coffee Kids
Phone: 800-334-9099
Website: www.coffeekids.org

National Coffee Association of USA
Phone: 212-766-4007
Website: www.ncausa.org

Specialty Coffee Association of America
 (SCAA)
(The major gourmet coffee association)
Phone: 562-624-4100
Website: www.scaa.org

Organic Crop Improvement Association
 (OCIA)
Phone: 402-477-2323
Website: www.ocia.org

## COFFEE EQUIPMENT

### 1. Coffee brewing systems

Newco Enterprises
Phone: 800-325-7867

### 2. Coffee grinders

Bunn-O-Matic
Phone: 800-637-8606 (USA)
Phone: 800-263-2256 (Canada)
Website: www.bunnomatic.com

Grindmaster
Phone: 800-695-4500
Website: www.grindmaster.com

250

### 3. Espresso machines

Crossroads Espresso
Phone: 800-552-4424
Website: www.coffeestuff.com

### 4. Packaging (bags)

Ampac Packaging LLC
Phone: 800-543-7030
Website: www.ampaconline.com

### 5. Packaging (cups)

Solo Cup Company
Phone: 800-FOR-CUPS
Website: www.solocup.com

### 6. Packaging (thermal mugs)

Thermoserv
Phone: 800-635-5559
Website: www.thermoserv.com

### 7. Roasters (batch)

Diedrich Manufacturing
Phone: 877-263-1276
Website: www.diedrichroasters.com

Probat Burns
Phone: 901-363-5331
Website: www.probatburns.com

### 8. Roasters (hot air)

San Franciscan Roasters
Coffee/PER
Phone: 775-423-8857
www.coffeeper.com

## COFFEE PRODUCTS

### 1. Decaf, Swiss Water

Nabob Coffee Company
Phone: 800-661-4063

### 2. Flavor concentrates

Danisco
Phone: 800-255-6837

Sensient Flavors
Phone: 800-558-9892
Website: www.sensient-tech.com

### 3. Flavor syrups

Torani
Phone: 800-775-1925
Website: www.torani.com

### 4. Green bean importers

MP Mountanos
Phone: 800-394-2525
Website: www.mpmountanosofsocal.com

Organic Products Trading Co.
Phone: 360-573-4433
Website: www.optco.com

Royal Coffee
Phone: 800-843-0482
Website: www.royalcoffee.com

Sustainable Harvest Coffee Importers
Phone: 503-235-1119
Website: www.sustainableharvest.com

### 5. Organic coffee developers

Equal Exchange
Phone: 774-776-7333
Website: www.equalexchange.com

TransFair USA
Phone: 510-663-5260
Website: www.transfairusa.org

TransFair Canada
Phone: 888-663-FAIR
Wesite: www.transfair.ca

### 6. Tea

Royal Gardens Tea
Thanksgiving Coffee Company
Phone: 800-462-1999, ext. 34
Website: www.thanksgivingcoffee.com

Tazo
Phone: 800-299-9445
Website: www.tazo.com

Stash Tea Co.
Phone: 800-547-1514
Website: www.stashtea.com

## CONSULTANTS

Cafemakers
Phone: 877-686-8287
Website: www.cafemakers.com

Entrepreneur Coach Inc. (Us!)
Phone: 800-663-2331
Email: info@startandrunaprofitablecoffee
bar.com

## PUBLICATIONS

*Tea & Coffee Trade Journal*
Phone: 800-766-2633
Website: www.teaandcoffee.net

*Coffee Talk*
Phone: 206-686-SERV
Website: www.coffeetalk.com

*Fresh Cup Magazine*
Phone: 503-236-2587
Website: www.freshcup.com

*Specialty Coffee Retailer*
Phone: 847-550-0207
Website: www.specialty-coffee.com

*Ukers' International Tea & Coffee Directory and Buyers' Guide*
(The major directory of coffee)
Phone: 800-766-2633
Website: www.teaandcoffee.net/ukers/

# ENTREPRENEUR COACH INC.

Do you love coffee? Do you want to make it your business? Feel free to give us a call to help you reach your goals.

We specialize in five areas of business support and entrepreneurial coaching:

1. **Start-up consulting.** Are you thinking about starting your own business? Eighty percent of businesses fail in the first five years of operation. We save you from becoming another statistic with our Start-Up Consulting program. Services range from helping you evaluate what type of business is right for you personally to prototype setup and long-term marketing planning.

2. **Start-up tools.** Want to save time and money getting your coffee bar open? Consider investing in business plan templates, operations manuals, hiring seminars, and other documents designed to save you time and money.

3. **Turn-key coaching.** Only available to a few clients a year, this program involves coaching in every aspect of opening your business, including site selection, lease negotiation, site design, marketing, training, and more.

4. **Public speaking.** "One of the most popular of all the sessions at the conference." "Tom's presentation made a definite, positive impact on our conference attendees. Many participants said that Tom's presentation was the most useful and inspirational part of their [seminar] experience." "A powerful presentation!" These are just some of the rave reviews of Tom Matzen's educating, entertaining, and inspiring seminars on topics such as marketing, turn-keying your business, and how to earn twice as much with half the stress.

5. **Online forum for support.** Do you know what you want to do, but think a little bit of support along the way would help? Consider joining our online forum and get access to great information for a fraction of the price of private coaching.

For more information, write to —

1500 West Georgia Street
Suite 1400
Vancouver, BC, Canada  V6G 2Z6
Phone:  800-663-2331
Fax:  800-416-6325
Skype: parmasters007
E-mail: info@StartAndRunAProfitableCoffeeBar.com

The following is included on the enclosed CD-ROM for use on a Windows-based PC. The worksheets are in PDF, MS Word, and MS Excel formats.

## Before opening a coffee bar
- Site selection criteria
- Coffee bar design and layout checklist
- Pre-opening checklist
- Start-up budget

## Financial spreadsheets
- Pro forma — projected
- Month-end income and expense statement

## Staff
- Staff application form
- Interviewer's form
- Training completion certificate

## Day-to-day logistics
- Opening checklist
- Closing checklist
- Brew record
- Inventory order sheet
- Daily prep sheet
- Daily cash sheet

## Management & marketing
- Weekly summary
- Manager's meeting form
- Marketing calendar